SPECIAL EDUCATION

By

M.Alice Raj Kumari
M.A., M.Ed., (Ph.D.)
Principal
Tarlupadu College of Education
Tarlupadu, Prakasam Distt., A.P.

D.Rita Suguna Sundari
M.Sc., M.Ed.
Principal
St. Paul's College of Education
Giddalur, Prakasam Distt., A.P.

General Editor
Dr. Digumarti Bhaskara Rao
M.Sc., M.A., M.A., M.Ed., Ph.D.
Reader
R.V.R. College of Education
Srinivasa Nagar Colony
Guntur–522 006
Andhra Pradesh
India

DISCOVERY PUBLISHING HOUSE
NEW DELHI-110002

First Published - 2004
Reprinted - 2017

ISBN: 978-81-7141-846-6

Special Education

Published by:
DISCOVERY PUBLISHING HOUSE PVT. LTD.
4383/4B, Ansari Road, Darya Ganj
New Delhi-110 002 (India)
Phone: +91-11-23279245, 43596064-65
Fax: +91-11-23253475
E-mail: discoverypublishinghouse@gmail.com
sales@discoverypublishinggroup.com
web: www.discoverypublishinggroup.com

Printed at:
Infinity Imaging Systems
Delhi

PREFACE

In India, Special Education is an emerging discipline and an essential part of the modern education system. It includes all aspects of education, which are necessary to successfully run the courses and training programmes for abnormal students.

The stream of Special Education requires specially designed courses and a particular type of instructions to be used for teaching the students, who are uncommon. In fact, Special Education demands special techniques, tacts and strategies to be adopted for a successful exercise.

Special Education needs those teachers, who love to take up challenging tasks and common people cannot be able to deliver goods in this area. In fact, Special Education is not a separate system, it is an integral part of the total programme of Education only. The teachers and trainees in the field of Special Education are supposed to be apt in normal teaching first and further require special acumen in this discipline, for imparting education to those children and students, who are not ordinary. They lack some capabilities and have a special knack for some other things. Hence, a comprehensive course is required to fill the bill.

This book covers all aspects of Special Education and may prove to be a perfect guide for teachers, educators and of course a rich source of knowledge for the B.Ed students.

Author

CONTENTS

1

INTRODUCTION

SPECIAL EDUCATION

The very term 'Special Education' includes all aspects of education which are applied to exceptional children – Physical, Mental, Disadvantaged and Gifted children. But these methods are not usually adopted for average children. Special education has a long history. The basis of caste system is connected with the concept of Special Education. In the primitive era, the Brahmins were supposed to be academically talented, the Kshatriyas talented in warfare. Similarly, the training of Vaisyas were also different. This was done primarily to bring out the different categories of people with various talents.

Student have been individually tutored by their parents or teachers who recognised their talents. Modern educational techniques also follow the same procedures for educating gifted children. Our educationists pay little attention to gifted children due to preoccupation with the normal and backward children. The different views taken on Special Education have sparked off controversies of segregating some children from the mainstream and providing them with extra opportunities.

As generally considered, special education is not a total programme which is entirely different from the education of ordinary children. Rather it includes those aspects of education which are specific in addition to the regular programme for all children. In some developed countries like USA and UK, these type of schools are mostly residential. But in a developing country like India, residential schools are very rare and now care is being taken to provide certain facilities to these types of children in some metropolitan cities.

Meaning of Special Education

Special education means specially designed instruction which meets the special education and related needs of an exceptional child. It is distinguished from regular educational programme for non-exceptional children by some unusual quality, something uncommon, noteworthy. It is something special – special materials, special training techniques, special equipment and special help and for special facilities may be required for special categories of children having special needs. For example,

1. Visually impaired children may require reading materials in large print or braille.
2. Hearing impaired children may require hearing aid, auditory training, lip reading etc.
3. Orthopaedically handicapped children may require wheel chairs, and removal of architectural barriers.
4. Mentally retarded children may need skill training. Related service, such as special transportation, medical and psychological assessment, physical and occupational therapy and counselling may be required if special education is to be effective.

Special Education as Teaching

We may look at special education in terms of who, what, where, and who ? Special education meant for exceptional children whose special needs or abilities necessitate an individualized programme of education.

An inter-disciplinary team of professionals – special educators, regular classroom teachers, psychologists, speech therapists, physiotherapists, specialist doctors bear the primary responsibility for helping exceptional children maximize their capabilities.

What ? Special education is sometimes differentiated from regular education by its curriculum, that is, by what is taught. For example, teaching self-help skills or training in reading and writing braille is an important part of curriculum for severely handicapped children (the blind) in special education institutions which is not found in regular education the school system dictates the curriculum, but in special education the child's individual needs dictate the curriculum.

Where ? Special education can sometimes be identified by where it takes place. Whereas regular education is provided in the regular classroom special education may be provided in special class, resource room, special school or in residential school.

How ? Special education can be differentiated from regular education by the method used by teachers. One special educator may use sign language to communicate with his students. Another special educator may use task analysis and skill training for mentally retarded children. Still another special educator may use multisensory approach and process training while teaching a learning disabled child.

Preventive Efforts: Keeping possible problems from becoming a serious handicap.

Remedial Programme: Overcoming disability through training or education.

Compensatory Efforts: Giving the child new ways to deal with the disability.

Special education is a profession, a service with tools and techniques to meet the special needs of exceptional children. It is individually planned, systematically implemented, and carefully evaluated instruction to help exceptional learners achieve the greatest possible personal self-sufficiency and success in present and future environments.

Objectives of Special Education

Special education has the same objectives as those of regular education-human resource development through providing appropriate education to children, national development, social reconstruction, civic development, vocational efficiency, etc. In addition to these objectives special education has certain special objectives such as the following :

(1) Early identification and assessment of special needs of handicapped children.

(2) Early intervention to prevent a handicapping condition from becoming a serious one for remediation of learning

problems and compensation by teaching the child new ways of doing things.

(3) Parent counselling about prevention and remediation of defects, care, and training of handicapped children in daily living skills, self-help skills, pre-academic skills and communication skills.

(4) Community mobilization and awareness of problems of handicapped children and their education.

(5) Rehabilitation of the handicapped. The National Policy of Education (1986/1992) clearly stipulates that.

(6) By means of this, the realistic self-concept of that strategically determine for effective living.

Principles of Special Education

Special education is based on the following principles:

Individual Differences: There are inter-individual differences and intra-individual differences. In other words, some students are very different from most in ways that are specific regarding education, and special education is required to meet their educational needs.

Zero Rejection : All children with disabilities must be provided a free and appropriate education. The school system do not have the option to accept or reject a child for education in a regular school.

Non-discriminatory Evaluation : Students who need special education must be clearly identified to ensure that they receive appropriate services. Each student must receive a full individual examination before being placed in a special education programme with tests required at intervals to assess his progress and difficulties in learning.

Individualized Education Programme : Student with special needs require individualized education programme either in a resource room or a special class in the regular school for some part of the day. Such education must match with their current level of functioning and their special needs.

Least Restrictive Environment: As much as possible, children with handicaps must be educated with children who are not handicapped in the regular classroom. The regular classroom provides the least restrictive environment for handicapped children.

Special Process : The process implies that the parents of handicapped children have the right to evaluate the efforts of the school system to identify and assess the handicapped children, to modify the programme of the school to meet the special needs of these children and, if they are not satisfied with the programme of the school, they have the right to withdraw their children from that school for a better programme in any other educational institution.

Parental Participation : Parental participation: Special education can be made effective if parents participate actively in the educational programme designed for handicapped children.

Needs of Special Education

It is true that the backward children and the talented children need specific facilities for their development. So educationists feel the importance of special education for them.

(1) Special classes necessary for backward children because they require specific teaching methods and techniques.

(2) Talented children face difficulties in adjusting themselves with average children because they belong to a higher I.Q. group. In general, it is found that the teaching expert moves at his speed, it is found that the teaching expert moves at this speed which suits average children. But a child with superior intelligence finishes the task much earlier. Here the problem is how a talented child will spend the rest of his time while the teacher continues the same task for the average children. Very often, the talented child is up to mischievous pranks. Also the curriculum meant for the average child is too simple and gets monotonous for the gifted one. Here the talented children do not get any kind of stimulation and lose interest in their studies.

(3) Special teaching facilities are required to meet the personal and social needs of exceptional children. So additional facilities enable the children to realise. So additional facilities enable the children to realise their

potentialities and to minimise the handicaps arising from their anomalies. Here superior children are provide with the opportunity to work according to their talent. In an average class, a bright child feels the handicap. With little endeavour he comes out exceptional. He can stand and keep a position in the class with minimum effort. Of course, accelerated promotions call for many drawbacks.

(4) Experimental data reveal that social mal-adjustment is found to be rampant with bright children in regular schools. The talented children stay idle in the class due to the light load of work. So they engage themselves in mischievous pranks and unapproved behaviours.

(5) In the special classes, the bright children get a chance for proper stimulation, but it becomes a problem for teaching experts to provide proper stimulation to both the talented and average students in an average class. Generally gifted children are more sensitive in comparison with the average children. They are quick and alert in thinking. So they require special techniques for being handled.

(6) In a special class of gifted children, every student feels that he is not superior alone, but there are some other brighter ones. This thought helps a great deal in developing confidence. Again, special classes also provide opportunities for developing leadership in special branches. Among the group, there may be some children with special interest in poetry, drama, games and in other branches of knowledge. Proper encouragement and training under special programme of education may help them in the long run.

(7) Selective placement is entailed through special education. It involves the complete assessment of children as well as their social environment by professionally qualified experts from different fields. Physical examinations and evaluations by specialists and experts like ophthalmologists, audiologists,

pathologists, psychiatrists, paediatricians, neurologists, psychologists and educational personnel are necessary for proper selective placement of many types of exceptional children.

(8) Special education requires many auxiliary services. For example, the orthopaedically handicapped require physical therapy, occupational therapy and periodic physical examination. Some exceptional children need to be kept under constant medical supervision. Periodic examination may be necessary for blind children and the children who are practically blind and hard-of-hearing. Occupational and physical therapy with psychiatric and psychological services are also necessary for some exceptional children.

Of course, some special equipments and additional training are necessary for teaching experts and sometimes these are very expensive. As a matter of fact, neglect of exceptional children as well as the handicapped is more expensive than adequate training.

(9) The importance of special education can be associated with the problem faced by a teacher in the average class. An average class, generally, consists of children of many categories such as handicapped (both physically and normal), gifted (bright and superior) and some average or normal. The teacher has to devise a method of instruction which is suitable for all. But in putting this into practice, it is difficult for the teacher, for the students also face problems to understand the instructions. Some students also underestimate the instructions. Here the need for a special class is seriously felt. In a way, special education is not only meant to help the exceptional children but is also conducive for the regular class teachers.

(10) Very often, it is said that education begins where medicine ends. Providing a hearing aid to a hard-of-hearing child is, of course, of medical concern. But teaching the child to use his vision or hearing capacities

effectively is certainly an educational function.. If the hearing anomaly is corrected, then it is also a medical concern. But if it is not corrected, then it becomes and educational concern. For totally blind children, instruction in Braille, provision of special Braille materials, travel training and counselling are advised by educationists through special education.

Unfortunately only 5 percent of the physically handicapped children (i.e., blind and deaf) are estimated to be in special schools and special care is being taken to educate them by experts in different disciplines. But most of these special schools are located in the metropolitan cities, or in urban areas. But children by having rural background remain practically unserved by these educational schools. This accentuates the fact that a large number of special schools are needed to accommodate these children.

First, special education needs the identification exceptional children and some provision made for experts to take them into account. This special education may be imparted in the regular classroom, special or in combination of both. Previously it was primarily confined to special classes. But now, a special education programme development for exceptional children is a part of total general education.

However, exceptional children require special education which include three elements, and these are as follows :

(i) Trained professionals including teachers, educationists, psychologists, physiotherapists and others are required.

(ii) Special curriculum is made for the children which suit different areas of exceptionality such as mental retardation, giftedness, deafness, blindness, orthopaedic handicap, cerebral palsy and social and emotional problems, and

(iii) Some facilities including special building features, study materials and equipment are also collected for this purpose.

2

Training of Teachers

The development of special education depends on the quality of teachers. The teacher can be prepared through special training for teacher disabled children in mainstreaming. The irony of fate, however, is that teaching is the most unattractive profession and teacher no longer occupies an honourable position in the society. Teaching can regain its earlier noble status in case the quality of teacher-education in our country is improved. It is probably for this reason that the education commission recommends the introduction of "a sound programme of professional education of teachers ." The commission further remarks that investment in teacher education can yield rich dividends because the financial resources required are small when measured against the resulting improvements in the education of millions. In the absence of other influences, a teacher tries to teach in the way in which he himself was taught by his favourite teacher and this tends to perpetuate the traditional methods of teaching in a situation like the present when new and dynamic methods of instruction are needed, such an attitude becomes an obstacle in progress. He can be modified only by effective professional education which will initiate the teacher to the needed revolution in teaching and lay the foundations for their future professional growth.

NCERT: Role in Teacher Training

The National Council of Education Research and Training (NCERT) was established on 1st September, 1961 with its headquarters at New Delhi with a view to improving school education. It is an autonomous organisation registered under the Societies Registration Act, 1860 and functions as the academic adviser to the Ministry of Education and Social Welfare. In formulating and implementing its policies and programmes in the field of school education the Ministry of Education draws upon the expertise of the NCERT.

With reference to special education, NCERT has earlier a department of special education within teacher education and special education cells in all its four Regional Colleges of Education. It is pioneer in running six months key/ resources Teacher Training at is its headquarter and multi-category training of teachers in the four Regional Institutes of Education. Besides, It has assisted in running one week course for teachers training of primary teachers, six week's intensive course for selected teachers of PIED.

NCERT has introduced MCT programme to prepare manpower for meeting the needs of integrated education in schools. The course is run in its four Regional Institutes of Education and in a few centres e.g., Amarjyoti Trust, New Delhi, and JSS Teacher Training Institute in Bangalore. The course is of one year duration and is not disability specific. About 100 teachers are trained every year. The course structure includes comprehensive coverage for enabling the teachers to develop competency to handle major debilities.

Regional Institutes

The Regional Institutes of Education also run B.Ed. and M.Ed. courses with specialisation in one area of special education until recently. Teacher courses are on the process of being phased out. The special education unit is now with the new department on disadvantaged groups.

At the centre, several in-service programmes also being run for Principals of DIET, special education faculty of SCERT/SIE, PIED Block supervision at various times. The main contribution has been among others implementing of PIED project, development of instructional manuals. Promotion of research and documentation, preparation of Handbooks, Hearing impairment, visual impairment, PIED, etc. It has been also responsible for feéding information to data base for POA 1992 and Policy Guidelines NPE 1986 and NCTE Committee of Special Education as well as to RCI.

The Objectives

The following are the main objectives for preparing teacher for' special education.

1. To develop an awareness that all school teachers whatever the age group of their pupils or level of their work are likely to be concerned with helping some children who have special education needs.
2. To enable teachers to recognise early signs of variable special educational needs.
3. To give the knowledge of the part which they can play in the amount of child's educational needs and in the execution of any special measures prescribed.
4. To give teachers what special education is like together with the knowledge or range of various forms of special educational provision and of specialist advisory services.
5. To provide some acquaintance with the school classes and units.
6. To give teachers understanding of how to communicate effectively with parent's anxieties and encouraging their continued involvement in their child's progress.
7. To give teachers in service training of when and where to refer for special help and knowledge in general terms of teaching to handicapped.

The following skills are to be developed:

1. Practical skills in observation of children both individually and in groups to help teachers sharpen their perception of variations in children's learning and behaviour and develop their awareness of variation in children's circumstances (home-school difficulties).
2. Appreciation of the educational needs of children with developed difficulties-physical, sensory, emotional behavioural or learning the needs of their parents, and

the value of the contribution which parents can make to their children's development.

3. Understanding of the practical steps necessary for meeting a child's special needs and an ability to adopt the attitude must suit to dealing with particular difficulties and to appreciate the need for modification of the school or classroom organisation the curriculum or teaching techniques.
4. Appreciation of the special services available to children with special needs of their familiar and of the advisory services available to teachers. This might be developed by inviting professionals for the various services to visit the college so that through discussion, the students can learn about the work of teachers in relation to other professionals the contributions which different specialist can make, the services to expect from them, and the kind of question to put to them.
5. Awareness of the range of career and professional opportunities in special education and the availability of further qualification in special education and the fact the special education offer the teachers engaged in it an intellectual challenge.

Teacher Competencies

Based on the roles and responsibilities mentioned above, the regular educators should inculcate the following skills and competencies in them:

Teaching Basic Skills : These include : (a) Literacy skills (reading, arithmetic, writing, spelling, study skills, speaking). (b) Life maintenance skills (health, safety), (c) Personal development skills (moral behaviour, basic life issues).

Class Management : This includes developing skills in selecting appropriate techniques to manage individuals and group behaviour. It requires proficiency in techniques of behavioural analysis, group altering, guiding transitions, material arrangement and crisis intervention.

Professional Consultation and Communication: Mainstreaming makes in imperative that regular classroom teacher develops competence in ways to consult and communicate with these professionals. Teachers should known how to collect and report the type of information that will be most useful to the specialists.

Referral : Teacher should know how to collect useful data for diagnosis and how to refer the child.

Individualised Teaching: Teacher needs to be adept at assessing a student's individual needs and in designing instruction to meet these needs. This does not mean that each child should be taught individually. It means permitting child to pursue a preferred mode of learning.

Inter-actional Skills : Teacher should be able to interact successfully with the parents, siblings, children. He/he should be able to interact and collaborate with others in the school.

Orientation Strategies for Entry into Mainstreaming: Teachers should be bale to prepare special students as well as regular class for mainstrearning. This also includes preparing parents of all children for normalisation. He/she should be able to develop positive attitudes towards mainstreaming.

Identification and Assessment of Children : Teacher should be to observe children in various settings without affecting their behaviour. Teacher should be able to identify children with special needs and assess their needs, use and interpret individual assessment measures.

Coal Setting : Teacher should be able to establish appropriate goals for the exceptional child. The goals should be realistic, measurable and also give opportunity for optimum development of potentials of such children.

Adjusting Curricula : Teacher should be able to adjust curricula to suit the ability, needs and interests of disabled children.

Use of Teaching Strategies : Teacher should be able to plan and implement a variety of instructional techniques.

Promoting Classroom Climate: Teacher should be able to promote acceptance of individual differences among all children. Teacher should be able to conduct class activities to encourage interaction among students.

Resources Managing : Teacher should be able to manage resources which can be used for instruction of disabled children.

Evaluation and Monitoring : Teacher should be able to assess the extent to which the needs of disabled children are met in the classroom evaluate the appropriateness of the resources for these children, modify his methods, materials to meet these needs.

As the regular educator has to work as a member of the team, it is important that he appreciates the role of special educator also. Based on the tasks that the special educator is required to perform following skills should be inculcated by special educators.

Special educators should posses ability to

1. Observe child's behaviour systematically.
2. Assess present status and needs of special child.
3. Develop individualised education programmes.
4. Write reports on basis, of data gathered.
5. Interact with others to build up relationship and collaborate.
6. Communicate results to other staff members and parents,
7. Change attitudes and advocate for them.
8. Carry out remedial work.
9. Evaluate and monitor methods, materials and progress.
10. Develop and administer therapeutic programmes.
11. Solve problems and deal with different situations that may arise due to unique needs of special children.

Classroom Teaching Skills

Micro-teaching is used for developing certain teaching skills. A teaching skill is defined as a set of teacher behaviours which are especially effective in bringing about desired changes in pupil-teachers. There are various teaching skills which can be developed among pupil-teachers. Allen and Ryans, have suggested, the following fourteen teaching skills :

1. Stimulus variation, 2. Set induction, 3.Closure, 4. Silence and non-verbal cues, 5. Reinforcement, 6. Asking questions, 7. Probing questions, 8. Divergent questions, 9. Attending behaviour, 10. Illustrating, 11. Lecturing, 12. Higher order questions, 13. Planned repitition, and 14. Communication completeness

B. K. Passi (1976) has described the following thirteen skills in his book 'Becoming Better Teacher': 'A Micro-teaching Approach':

1. Writing instructional objectives.
2. Introduction of a lesson.
3. Fluency and questioning.
4. Probing questioning.
5. Explaining.
6. Illustrating with examples.
7. Stimulus variation.
8. Silences and non-verbal cues.
9. Reinforcement to student's participation.
10. Increasing pupil's participation,
11. Using Black Board.
12. Achieving closure, and
13. Recognising attending behaviour.

The Importance

The meaning of importance teaching skills have been discussed here:

Stimulus Variation : This skill involves deliberate changing of various attention producing behaviour by the teacher in order to keep pupils attentive at high level.

Set Induction : It refers to the development of cognitive rapport between pupils and teacher to obtain immediate involvement in the lesson.

Closure: This skill is complementary to set induction. It is more than a quick summary of the portions taught and the pupils are able to relate new knowledge with the previous one.

Silence and Non-verbal Cues: The use of silence and non-verbal cues in powerful device in order to encourage pupil's participation in classroom teaching.

Skill of Reinforcement: It involves teacher encouraging pupils response using verbal praise, accepting their responses or non-verbal causes like a smile.

Fluency in Questioning : This is a skill in asking questions. By fluency means the use of as many question as possible in a given period of teaching.

Probing Questions : Probing requires that teacher asks questions that need pupils to go beyond superficial first answers of question.

Recognition and Attention Behaviour: The successful teacher is more sensitive to note the interest of boredom of pupils through visual cues.

Recognising and Attention Behaviour: The successful teacher is more sensitive to note the interest of boredom of pupils through visual cues.

Skill of Explaining : An explanation is a set of inter-related statements made by teacher in order to increase the under standing in the pupils about ideas and concepts.

Skill of Increasing Pupil's Participation : This skill involves the four components creating set questioning, encouraging pupil activities and pausing in such a way that pupil participation is maximised.

Skill of Writing Objectives : It involves the following activities identifying objectives, analysing the task and writing objectives in behavioural terms with regard to adequate learning.

Skill of Using Blackboard: This skill requires legibility, neatness, appropriateness continuity, simplicity of blackboard work. It is very essential skill for a successful teacher. The effectiveness of presentation depends upon the proper use of blackboard.

Skill for Classroom Management: This skill involves a number of activities that a teacher performs for creating and maintaining conducive environment for learning in the classroom.

Skill of Using Audio-visual Aids : It implies the effective use of appropriate teaching aids to make teaching interesting and desired objectives can be achieved. The effective use of audio-visual aids makes the pupil active and attentive in classroom.

Skill for Giving Assignment: This skill consists of the pupils to organize and assimilate the learnt material.

Skill of Pacing Lesson: The pacing of a lesson means the variation in the teaching speed. This skill involves adjustive devices for satisfying the needs of the pupils or student-variation.

The Use of Higher Order Questions : This skill involves the questions which can be answered by memory or sensory description. The question consist of rules, principles and generalization.

Divergent Questions : It requires the respondent to organize elements into new pattern, predict, and infer from the situation. This skill involves higher order of thinking creativity. .

Lecturing **:** It requires the effective presentation of content by using appropriate techniques and devices of teaching aids. This is known as communication competency.

Planned Repetition : It is a powerful skill in focusing and highlighting important points of teaching:

Competencies of Communication : It is a skill which is developed by sensitivity training for a clear communication of ideas and concepts in teaching. The teachers are more responsive to possible miscommunication.

Classroom Teaching Skills and their Components

	Skill	*Components*
1.	Writing instructional objectives	Clarity, relevance to the content, adequacy with objectives reference to the domains and level of objectives, attainability in terms of pupil outcomes.
2.	Organising the content	Logical organisation according to content and psychological organisation as per need of the pupil
3.	Creating set for introducing the lesson	Greeting, accepting creating, securing attention and introducing the giving instructions, establishing rapport, ensuring facilities like chalk, duster, aids, apparatus etc.
4.	Introducing the lesson	Linking with past experiences, link between introduction with main parts, use of appropriate devices/techniques like questioning, examples, exhibits arousal.
5.	Structuring class room questions	Structuring questions at different levels which are grammatically correct, precise and relevant to content.
6.	Question delivery and distribution	Questions delivered with appropriate speed with proper intonation and pitch, allowing pause for thinking, and questions well distributed covering even non-volunteers.

Contd.

	Skill	*Components*
7.	Response management	Management of pupil responses using techniques like prompting, eliciting further information, refocusing and asking critical awareness questions, accepting-rejecting, redirection.
8.	Explaining	Clarity, continuity, relevance to the content, using beginning and concluding statements, covering essential points.
9.	Illustrating with examples	Simple, interesting and relevant to the point being explained.
10.	Using teaching aids	Relevant to content, appropriate to the pupil's level, proper display and appropriate use.
11.	Stimulus Variation	Body movements, gestures, change in intonation and pitch, change in interaction pattern and pausing.
12.	Reinforcement	Use of praise words and statements, accepting and using pupil ideas, repeating and rephrasing pupil ideas. Use of pleasant and approving gestures and expressions, writing pupil answers on blackboard.
13.	Pacing of the lesson	Adjusting the speed of the lesson to the level of the pupils and difficulty level of the content
14.	Prompting pupil's participation	Providing, opportunity to pupils to increase participation through, asking questions, creating climate of participation, use of silence and non-verbal cues, calling upon pupils' physical participation.
15.	Use of Black Board	Legible, neat, adequate with reference to the content covered.

Contd.

	Skill	*Components*
16.	Achieving Closure of the Lesson	Summarization, establishing link between the present learning with earlier as well as future learning, creating a sense of achievement in pupils.
17.	Giving assignments	Relevant to the content covered and level of pupils. Relevant to the instructional objectives. Use appropriate questions and observations.
18.	Evaluating the pupil's progress	Identifying learning difficulties along with causes, remedial measures suited to the type of the learning difficulties and the level of pupils.
19.	Diagnosing pupil learning	The student's difficulties are assessed by putting questions. The remediation is provided accordingly
20.	Management of the class	Attention behaviour reinforced and directions given to eliminate non-attending behaviour, clarity of directions, appropriate handling of pupils disruptive behaviour.

Instructional Procedure

The concept of managing teaching-learning of I.K. Davies involves four steps of teaching-planning, organizing, leading and controlling. In these steps the main emphasis has been given on objectives, strategies of teaching, and evaluation techniques. But a teacher concerns with teaching concepts, principles, skills and problem solving his subject. These are the means to achieve objectives and to evaluate the student's performance. The knowledge of above concepts and understanding are very essential to a teacher for developing effective instruction.

Robert Glaser has developed basic teaching model. This model divides teaching process into four parts : 1. Instructional objectives.

2. Entering behaviour, 3. Instructional procedures, and 4. Performances assessment. The instructional procedures provide the awareness of dealing with teaching of skills, language, concepts, principles and problem solving of a content.

Meaning and Definition

Instructional procedures describe the teaching process, most of the decisions a teacher takes on the basis of these procedures. The management of teaching of skills, language, concepts, principles and problem solving bring these changes in student-behaviours which we call learning outcomes or level of performance.

"The instructional procedures imply the components of skill and knowledge. They are clearly analysed and defined and instructions are arranged to the component not already possessed by the students and instructions are revised until objectives are attained."

Glaser Tiedimann and Anderson have defined the instructional procedure "A process that includes specifying objectives, managing of teaching of skills, language, concepts, principles and problem solving, then trying and revising material and techniques, usually result in effective instruction."

The Essentials

An effective instruction strategy is required to develop the following components :

Preparation of Objectives : The first requirement of at effective instructional procedure is to identify objectives and write them in behavioural terms. The instructional decisions are based upon these objectives-cognitive, affective and psychomotor.

Task Analysis : The second requirement is to analyse the skills and knowledge, that a student requires to achieve the objectives.

Entering Behaviour: This step is to determine the prerequisites in terms of skills and knowledge of students.

Content of Teaching : This is crucial aspect in instructional procedure. In this step instructional materials and technique for teaching the concepts, principles, problems solving, skills and language are identified in the task analysis.

Procedure for Teaching: Concept, principles, problem solving, skills and language are the components of teaching. The different activities are required for teaching these components.

Evaluation of Student's Performance: After teaching, student's performance is evaluated to determine that all students have attained each objectives.

Diagnosis and Remedial Teaching : The purpose of evaluation is not only to determine the level of performance but also to diagnose the cause of student's poor performance. This provides the basis for preparing remedial instruction to reteach the students.

The Purpose

The instructional procedure appears to occupy a position somewhere between the teacher and students. The major purpose of instructional procedure is to implement the desirable changes of instructional procedure is to implement the desirable changes in learner's behaviour. Three types of learner behaviours are considered in the teaching process, but instructional procedures developed two types of changes in the behaviour: 1. Cognitive behaviour, and 2. Psychomotor skills.

Cognitive Behaviour or Objectives: The cognitive objectives are achieved by teaching the following phenomenon:

(a) Teaching concepts.
(b) Teaching of principles.
(c) Teaching of problem-solving.
(d) Instruction for creativity or discovering learning and expository teaching

Psychomotor Skills or Objectives: The psychomotor objectives are achieved by emphasizing the following abilities

(a) Abilities in physical proficiency, and
(b) Abilities in manipulative proficiency.

Development of Verbal Learning : The language objectives are attained by:

(a) Teaching of Language.
(b) Teaching of Transformation.
(c) Teaching of Grammar, and
(d) Instruction in Raiding.

An effective instructional procedure considers both the processes of teaching and learning. The above objectives are related to both teaching and learning. The concept learning may be facilitated by teaching activities. The problem solving is learning as well as teaching. Thus, the main focus of instructional procedure is to relate teaching to learning so that objectives may be attained.

Basic Conditions of Learning

Learning is a permanent change in behaviour and is the result of reinforced practice. The reinforced practice is the cause of learning.

Gates has defined this team learning as the modification of behaviour through experiences, and training but not through motivation, fatigue and maturation.

Learning is an inferred state of an organism which should be distinguished from performance and observed state of an organism. These statements indicate the some external conditions are essential for learning. These external conditions may be generated by teaching, activities. The external situations are termed as basic conditions which are essential for both learning and teaching or instruction. The important basic conditions are: contiguity, practice, reinforcement, discrimination and generalization. These conditions are important in various learning types. Robert Gagne has also advocated eight learning conditions which have been discussed in the 'Relationship of Teaching and Learning' chapter. A brief description has been given about these basic conditions of learning.

Contiguity as Condition of Learning : One of the basic learning condition is contiguity. It means two stimuli are presented side by side for one response. This has been emphasized by Pavlov and Guthrie in their experiments of learning.

Classical conditioning involves condition of contiguity of the natural and the unnatural stimulus. Operant conditioning involves contiguity of the response and the reinforcing stimulus.

In planning teaching and instruction, we involve such conditions of teaching. The language teaching at elementary stage is based upon the basic condition of contiguity, e.g., A for Apple (by showing figure or apple), D for Dog (by showing picture or model)., i.e., simultaneous presentation of two stimuli. The skills learning, concept learning, and principle involve contiguity.

Practice as Condition of Learning : Another basic external condition of learning is practice. The practice may be defined that it is the repetition of a response in the presence of the same stimulus.

Thorndike's connectionism involves the condition of practice, i.e., law of exercise. The S-R connection can be strengthened by practicing or repeating and can be retained for a longer period.

In organizing teaching and instruction teaching provide an opportunity to practice the learning conditions. The practice is very important in skill learning and verbal learning but it is more important for concepts, principles and problem-solving learning.

Reinforcement as Condition of Learning : Reinforcement is an important condition for learning. Learning is not possible without motivation or reinforcement. Reinforcement is a condition which increases the probability of desirable response. Reinforcement is of two types : Positive reinforcement increases the probability of desirable responses whereas negative reinforcement decreases the probability of undesirable behaviour or response. Hull's theory of learning involves the condition of reinforcement. B.F. Skinner operant conditioning is based upon the condition of reinforcement. There are various schedules reinforcement but continuous schedule of reinforcement is used in most of the instructional strategies. Linear programme of Skinner is a good example of continuous reinforcement. In leading the teaching, the student's behaviour should be reinforced. In leading the teaching, the student's behaviour is reinforced by confirming their correct responses or verbal praise. As a basic learning condition, reinforcement is important in most of the learning.

Discrimination as Condition of Learning : Discrimination and generalization are better defined as phenomena than as conditions of learning. The word discrimination refers to a behaviour which occurs specific learning situations. In discrimination behaviour, the individual makes different responses for two or more stimuli,

$S_1 \rightarrow R_1$ $H_2O \rightarrow$ Water
$S_2 \rightarrow R_2$ Cu $\rightarrow$ Copper
$S_3 \rightarrow R_3$ Zn $\rightarrow$ Zinc

The discrimination condition of learning is most important for concept, principle find problem-solving learning but it is least important for skill learning and verbal learning. This condition is essential for developing understanding among learners. It is the general tendency in the classroom to stress discrimination and to suppress generalization. The discrimination explains both types learning—simple as well as complex.

Generalization Condition of Learning : Generalization is more a phenomena and less a condition of learning. Generalization is a behaviour which takes place under a particular learning situation. It refers to a behaviour which an individual responds for one or two more stimuli-

S_1 –		Red		Apple	
S_2 –	$\rightarrow$ R	Yellow	$\rightarrow$ Colour	Mango	Fruits
S_2 –		Green		Banana	

Generalization is more complex type of learning condition. In this type of learning, external and internal conditions are equally important. Generalization is an important aspect of human behaviour.

The generalization condition of learning is most important for concept, principle and problem-solving, creativity and discovering learning. This condition of learning is not required for skill learning and verbal learning.

The basic conditions of learning are essential for developing effective instructional procedure for teaching concepts, principles, problem-solving, skill and verbal learning.

Achieving Cognitive Objectives

An instructional procedure is followed to achieve certain objectives of learning. Teaching and instruction processes have the focus to achieve the cognitive objectives. According to B.S. Bloom these objectives range from knowledge to evaluation. The various type of concepts and principles operate from recall or recognition to judgement level. Hence teaching and learning of concepts and principles are basic for developing an instructional procedure:

The teaching and learning related to cognitive domain have been discussed in the following paragraphs:

Teaching of Concepts : A concept is a class of stimuli which have some common characteristics. These stimuli may be objects, events or persons. A concept is not a particular stimulus but a group of stimuli. An effective teachers, dedicated person and beautiful women are the examples of concept. Concepts are not always congruent with our personal experiences, but they represent human efforts to classify-our experiences. The attribute and attribute values are distinctive features of a concept.

The teaching of concepts incorporates the four components of the basic teaching model. A series of nine steps are followed for teaching of concepts.

Nine Important Steps for Teaching Concepts

Step 1-	Describing the terminal behaviour. It refers to the expected behavioural outcomes of the students after the learner has understand the concept. This serves two purposes, first the teacher has a means for evaluating the level of student performance and second is to determine the need for remedial instruction.
Step 2-	Analysis of concept in terms of attribute and attribute values. The analysis reduces the complexity of concept to be learned. The analysis of concept determines the attributes and values to teach the students. It concerns with entering behaviour of the learners.
Step 3 -	Provide the student with useful verbal mediators. In this step, relationship between verbal and concept learning is determined because the student has pre-requisite of verbal learning before learner undertakes the learning of the concept.
Step 4 -	Provide positive and negative examples of the concept. In the teaching of concepts, the examples are used more frequently. A positive example involves the attribute of the concept and a negative example does not involve any of the attribute of the concept. Gage suggests that positive examples are useful in the teaching of the concepts.

Step 5 - Present the examples in close succession or side by side. This step provides the external learning conditions of contiguity and discrimination. The positive and negative both type of examples are presented to facilitate discrimination learning conditions. The negative examples should be followed by positive one for effective presentation of examples.

Step 6 - Present a new positive of the concept and ask student to identify it. This step presents both contiguity and reinforcement of learning conditions. If a student identifies the new positive example in successive presentation of examples, his, response should be confirmed or praised to provide the reinforcement.

Step 7 - Verify the students to learning concept. The step concerns with last component of performance assessment of basic teaching model. Both type of examples are presented and student has, to select only positive examples to verify whether expected learning outcomes have attained or not.

Step 8 - Require of student of define the concept. This step is also related to the last component of basic teaching model. The student is asked to define the concept or explain in his own words. It is difficult to formulate a definition of concept. The student's definition should be approved for providing the reinforcement to learner.

Step 9 - Provide an opportunity for practice and reinforcement of student responses. This step provides occasions for practice or students responses and these responses are reinforced. In this step, remedial instruction may be organized for poor students. This step facilitates for the understanding of the concept and can be retained for a longer time.

Teaching of Principles : Gagne has defined the term principle that it is statement of the relationship between two or more concepts, Principles are sometimes called termed rules or generalization. These are some examples: 1. Eight plus six equal to fourteen 2. Learning is result reinforcement principles are in the development and education of the students.

The teaching of principles involves the four components of the basic teaching model. A series of eight steps is followed for this purpose :

Eight Principles of Teaching

Step 1 -	Describing the terminal behaviour, after student has, learned the principle : The step refers to the expected behavioural outcome and the student is allowed to assess his own performance and to create his self reinforcement.
Step 2 -	Analysing the principle in terms of concepts: The principle is analysed in terms of concepts to reduce the difficulty and complexity of the principle. The entering behaviour of the learner is assessed to determine the strategy of instruction. The pre-requisites are determined for any given principles by asking questions. The sequence of concepts is also determined in this step, which are essential for understanding the principle.
Step 3 -	Assist the student in the real component concepts : In this step external learning condition of contiguity is provided for recalling the component of concepts. It refers to more than one object, person or place. The responses are reinforced.
Step 4 -	Assist the student to combine the concepts properly : Under this step contiguity learning conditions is generated for the proper .relationship of the concepts, the guidance is provided for the student's learning with the help of questions.
Step 5 -	Require the student to demonstrate the principle. In this step the principle is demonstrated fully presenting the serval positive and negative

examples. The student is asked to identify the plural form of examples. The singular and plural form of examples are presented.

Step 6 - Require the student to give full statement of the principle. The student is asked to define the principle with the help of full statement. The verbal mediator is used to define the principle.

Step 7 - Verify the student's learning of the principle. The step concerns with the last component of performance assessment of basic teaching model of Glaser. The student's learning is assessed to determine how well has he acquire the new principle.

Step 8 - Provide for practice of the principle and for reinforcement of student's responses. In this step, an opportunity is given to practice the principle so that it can be assimilated and retained for a larger period. The remedial instruction may be arranged for the poor performance of the students because instructional conditions for the principle learning is not always conducive. The student's responses are reinforced for practising the principle.

Uses of Teaching of Concepts and Principles : There are various ways in which concepts and principles are useful for the student's education :

- To reduce the complexity of the environment.
- To assist us to identify the objects of the world around us.
- To reduce the necessity of constant learning.
- To provide direction for instrumental activity.
- To make instruction possible.

Teaching of Problem Solving : Problem solving is a higher order of learning and it is closely related to principle learning. Gagne has defined the term problem solving that it combines to or more previously learned principles into a higher- order principles. Problem solving represents acquisition of substantive knowledge which can be applied to a wide variety of problems. The problem solving is highly individual and most complex learning. It involves divergent thinking and lower-order principles to form higher order principles. The instructions for problem solving are developed by using the following steps :

Five Steps of Problem Solving

Step 1-	Describing the Students—Terminal Performance which Forms the Solution of the Problems : It is the first component of basic teaching model. The description of the students terminal behaviour fulfils two learning conditions : reinforcement and discrimination. This step directs the student towards the solution of the problem.
Step 2 -	Assess the student's Entering Behaviour which They Require in the Solution of the Problem : This is the second component of basic teaching model. The teacher has to identify the lower-order principles which are the pre-requisites for the solution of the problem. He has to assess whether student fulfil them or not.
Step 3 -	Invoke the Recall of All Relevant Concepts and Principles: This step concerns with contiguity of external conditions of learning. The pre-requisite concepts of the principles must be recalled by the students in solving the problem must be recalled by the students in solving the problem and discover the relationship between them. This is the third concept of teaching model.
Step 4-	Provide Verbal Direction to Student's Thinking and Giving them the solution of the Problem : In this step the teacher provides some verbal directions towards the solution of the problem. Some challenges are given for stimulating thinking of the students. This step concerns with third component of the basic model of teaching.
Step 5 -	Verify Student's Learning by Requiring them to Give Full Demonstration of the Problem Solution : This is the last component of the basic model of teaching. The problem solving has high transfer-

ability. In assessing learning outcome of the students, a situation is presented for transfer of learning. He should be able to make use of lower-order principles to form higher-order principles. This step provides the feedback to the learner for the adequacy of terminal performance and the instruction.

Teaching of Creativity

Ausuble defines that creativity refers to rare and unique talent in a particular field of endeavour. He further states

"Creative achievement reflects a rare capacity for developing insight, sensitivity, and appreciations in a circumscribed content area of intellectual or artistic activity.

There are three aspects of creativity:

(a) Creative abilities.

(b) Learning of creative abilities.

(c) Development of creative abilities and their use in problem solving.

Guilford has advocated four distinctive aspects of creative abilities : 1. Originality, 2. Fluency, 3. Flexibility, and 4. Elaboration. These abilities form the creative thinking.

One of the earliest and important technique for improving the quantity of idea is best known as 'brain storming'. Osborn (1960) has given four basic rules for developing creative responses in a group procedure:

Criticism is Ruled Out: Adverse judgement of ideas must be avoided.

'Free Wheeling' is Welcomed : The wilder ideas are better for creative responses.

Quantity is Wanted : The larger number of ideas have more possibility for useful ideas.

Combination and Improvement are Sought : It concerns with the contribution of new ideas. The candidate is suggested how can two or more ideas be combined to produce novel idea.

Torrance (1963) reports that college students generate a significantly greater number of new ideas. They do not multiply as many ideas as possible relative to particular stimulus feature. Torrance has developed six principles for stimulating creative thinking.

1. Treat question with respect.
2. Treat imaginative unusual ideas with respect.
3. Show pupils that their ideas have value.
4. Give opportunities for practice without evaluation.
5. Encourage and evaluate self-initiated learning.
6. Tie in evaluation with cause and consequences.

The teachers generate original behaviour in students when all involve in the production of new ideas or original responses. The most powerful psychodynamic stimulant of creative functioning is an initiate model of creative process. The display of divergent thinking provides stimulation for any creative productivity.

The major educational question concerns with the possibility of developing whatever creative abilities the student may have. The teacher can provide certain learning situations which Mill develop originality, flexibility and fluency. These abilities can only be developed by solving various type of problems. The following steps may be used for developing creative abilities:

Various Types of Problems

Step 1 -	Classify the kind of problems which are to be assigned to the students : The problems can be broadly classified into two categories : (a) Presented problem (b) Discovered problem. The creative abilities are developed by providing learning situations from presented problems to discovered problems, i.e., known to unknown situation.
Step 2 -	Provide situation for the development and use of problem solving skills: The brain storming strategy is used for developing problem solving skills. The training of brain storming increases creative problem-solving, produce more problem solutions. The teaching of certain basic research skills may be second technique of developing creative abilities.
Step 3 -	Developing creative reading another useful problem solving skill: Torrance has provided some evidence

	that the student can be taught to read creativity with proper direction and encouragement.
Step 4	Reinforce creative achievement: It is difficult to reinforce the creative performance because the teacher fails to recognize it. Torrance has given five ways in which the teacher can encourage and reinforce to creative performance: (1) Asking usual question (2) Presenting usual ideas (3) Showing that their ideas are valuable (4) Giving credit for self-initiated learning (5) Providing an opportunity for students to learn, think and discover.

The teaching creativity is very challenging task for a teacher. The ultimate aim of education is to produce creative artists and creative scientists. The creative thinking is useful for all type of education practices.

Discovery of Learning

Discovery of learning refers to these teaching situations in which the student achieves the instructional objectives with limited or without guidance of the teacher. The following are the main characteristics of discovery learning:

(1) The teacher may give the principles and the problem solutions. It is known as an expository teaching.
(2) The teacher may give the principle which applies to the problem but does not provide the solution.
(3) The teacher may not provide the principle but gives the solution of the problem.
(4) The teacher may provide neither the principle nor the solution of the problem This is known as undersigned discovery.

The discovery of learning is received by the unguided discovery. An inquiry training method is used. It indicates amount and the nature of the instructional guidance provided. An inquiry training involves three phases. The first phase is presenting the problem, the second phase is the practice session and the third phase of the training session is the teacher's criticism or reinforcing the behaviour of the student.

The various teaching strategies have been tried out in the research studies. The expository teaching strategy. Way is found to be effective. The expository teaching is the situation in which the teacher gives both the principle and the solution of the problem. The discovery learning of higher order is received by unguided discovery. The research or discovery learning has provided information on the different type of effects and amounts of instructional guidance.

The expository teaching is more popular in our schools today because it is more effective and takes less time than discovery learning. It is very successful in teaching concepts and principles. The branching programming is an example of expository teaching. It provides an opportunity to the learner to organize the concepts or principles and verifies the correctness of concept learning. The remedial instruction is provided according to the needs of the students.

The discovery method is the best method for transmitting subject matter. The problem solving is the primary goal of education. It is highly democratic whereas expository teaching is authoritarian. The instructional and teaching procedures are useful for students. The instructional objectives direct towards the type of learning and learning condition required whereas entering behaviour reveals the students needs to be incorporated in the instructional procedures.

Teaching of Skills

The instructional objectives related to psychomotor domain are achieved by developing certain skills. A psychomotor ability is a general trait of an individual which is related to performance of a wide variety of skills.

The skill is a set responses or behaviour which involve some physical and manipulative proficiency A skill has three characteristics:

(1) It involves a chain of motor responses.
(2) It represents the coordination of muscular movements.
(3) It requires the organization of chain into complex manipulative response pattern.

The cognitive behaviour involves verbal and non-verbal responses whereas psychomotor behaviour requires motor responses which are manifested by muscular movements. A skill is a series of chain of muscular movements with each link of an individual's (S-R) unit which acts as a stimulus for the next link.

Phases of Skill Learning: The teaching of skill is organized in three phases : (1) The cognitive (2) the fixation, and (3) the autonomous.

In the cognitive phase, the students attempt to develop some cognitive map about skill which is to be performed.

In the fixation phase, the correct behaviour patterns are practised unit the chance of making incorrect responses is put to zero.

The autonomous phase is characterized by increasing speed of practicing the skills in which it is important to improve accuracy of the point.

The following steps are followed for the teaching of skills:

Skills of Teaching

Step 1-	Analyse the skill: The first function of teacher is to analyse the skill which a teacher plans to teach. The successful learning of skills is determined not only be the external conditions of learning but also by the entering behaviour of the students.
Step 2 -	Assess the entering behaviour of the students : The second function of a teacher is to determine the pre-requisites for developing new skills. The entering behaviour can be assessed at three levels : cognitive, fixation and the autonomous. The physical and manipulative proficiency may also be determined. The entering behaviour is more important for developing certain skills than the external conditions of learning.
Step 3 -	Arrange for training the competent unit's skills : The step serves two purposes : To develop the pre-requisite components of skills by providing an opportunity to acquire the skills components; To provide an opportunity for practicing new component of the skill at autonomous level of learning.

Step 4 -	Describe and demonstrate the skill to the student : This step provides an actual teaching situation for the desired skill. In describing the components of the skill, the student listens at cognitive stage mid in demonstrating the skill, the student observes the sequence of components at fixation level. The actual teaching of the skill gets under way with this step which requires to describe and demonstrate the skill and help the student for practicing the skill.
Step 5 -	Provide the three basic learning conditions : In the teaching of skill at autonomous stage, three external learning conditions : contiguity, practice and feed back are combined into a single teaching situation.

The contiguity external learning condition provides the awareness of chain of motor responses, proper coordination and timing. After that he should be given chance to practice the skill. The student's responses are reinforced to bring the excellence in the skills. In micro-teaching these three learning conditions are combined into one teaching situation for developing certain teaching skills. The autonomous phase of skill learning can be attained by integrating the first three external learning conditions in one teaching or training situation.

Teaching of Verbal Knowledge

The verbal learning is considered a process of forming verbal associations. According to Robert Gagne verbal learning is like skill learning that involves a chain of at least two links. The first link present the stimulus and second the response. The verbal learning is generated by internal and external conditions of learning. The meaningfulness and verbal association for the two internal learning conditions are essential and serval external learning conditions influence verbal learning : (1) instruction to learning (2) practice (3) reinforcement (4) interference and (5) method of measurement. The meaningfulness is an important condition for all verbal learning. The series of teaching steps are followed for the teaching of verbal learning.

Verbal Learning of Teaching

Step 1 - Describe for the student what is expected to learn : This step refers to task analysis. The teacher has to analyse the components of verbal learning or skills and should be arranged in a logical sequence which may facilitate student's learning. This step is derived from the research work conducted on incidental or instructional learning.

Step 2 - Assess entering behaviour for the availability of meaningful responses and verbal mediators: The meaningfulness depends upon the entering behaviour of the students. He has to assess the entering behaviour of the learners whether they can fulfil or not. The instruction for the teaching of verbal learning should function as bridge between old and new meanings. When a teacher introduces material, he should provide the additional time required for familiarization. This step involves three activities : (a) Determining verbal mediators which are useful for instructional components, (b) Assessing entering behaviour which is available. (c) Supplying mediators which may be useful in verbal learning.

Step 3 - Provide the appropriate practice conditions : This step concerns with the third component of basic teaching model. The second external learning condition is very useful for developing verbal skill. This step includes the following activities : (a) provide opportunity for emitting required responses (b) a schedule of practice for mass or individual may be followed (c) determining the degree of mastery of performance and (d) provide an opportunity for part or whole practice.

Step 4 - Provide knowledge of correct responses : This step provides the reinforcement to the students for their correct response. They should be given prompt for emitting correct responses and their responses should be confirmed. The confirmation provides the

	reinforcement to the students. The prompting situation is more effective than confirmation.
Step 5 -	Provide conditions which may reduce interference: In this step opportunities are given for practicing the new verbal learning. It reduces the interference of those factors which may cause forgetting. The teacher should identify those factors which are frequently the source of interference. The major source of forgetting is pre-active and retroactive inhibition. The pre-active inhibition concerns with entering behaviour of the learning whereas retroactive inhibition relates to terminal behaviour of the learner.
Step 6 -	Use of suitable methods of measurement for verbal learning : The last step concerns with the fourth component of basic teaching model, i.e., performance assessment. The method of measurement is used for ascertaining the level of performance of student or how much is verbal learning retained by the students. The decision may be taken about the instructional objectives whether these can be achieved. This step also provides the reinforcement to the students as well as to the teacher. He can improve and modify his instructional procedures.

Teaching of Language

The language is media of communication or vehicle of communication. The structural linguists analyse language into basic components: phonemes and morphenes.

The phonemes are the basic sound units of a language. A language unit consists of phonemes which convey meaning. A morphene is any from which cannot be into two or more forms. These components are combined in various ways to produce the grammar of syntax of the language.

Modern linguists have different relationship between language structure of syntax and grammar. They have given new concept of transformation grammar.

Noam Chomsky, (1957) has given the idea of transformational grammar. It assumes that language is a system of rules and that an application of these rules make possible the formation and comprehension of new sentences. The knowledge of language depends upon the mastery of the rules. Chomskey's transformational grammar is of major importance in studying the relationship between language and thought. The rules are the product of the syntax of the language and the psychological process within the teacher The phonemes of language are important in learning to read.

There are two basic teaching methods of language:

Audio-lingual Method: This method consists of two process : (i) speaking and (ii) listening. The speaking implies content first and expression later on. The process of listening is different from speaking, because speaking is the function of listening is different from speaking, because speaking is the function of lingual aspect and listening is the function of audio-aspect. In listening, expression comes first and content is received afterward. The communication abilities are developed by the audio-lingual method. It concerns with developing language skills.

Cognitive Code Method: This method is helpful in developing the thought aspect of the language. It has also two process : (i) reading and (ii) writing. The writing is similar to speaking that content or thought comes first and expression comes afterward in reading process, the expression comes first and content come later on. This method is an effective for developing thought aspect of language learning.

Both methods are essential in teaching of any language because every language involves four skills: (1) Reading, (2) Writing, (3) Speaking and (4) Listening. A complete language learning implies development of these four skills. These methods are useful for teaching the first language.

In the second language teaching., usually two methods are used : Direct method and Translation method. The direct method is an effective for developing speaking or fluency of the language and translation method is more effective for language comprehension.

The language laboratory is the most popular technical innovation in the field of language teaching. It provides more opportunity to students to hear and speak the second language. This is highly individualized strategy for language teaching. Every student gets an opportunity for speaking and listening according to his won need and requirement. This audio-lingual method is employed in language laboratory.

Importance of Instructional Procedures

The instructional procedures have the following advantages in teaching and learning process:

1. The instructional procedures tell us how to teach concepts, principle and problem solving.
2. It provide steps how to teach skills.
3. The instructional procedures provide us guideline how to teach verbal learning and language learning.
4. The learning objectives can be effectively achieved by employing proper instructional procedure.
5. The awareness and practice of instructional procedures for teaching various subjects may be useful for producing effective teachers. The quality of training can be maintained.
6. The instructional procedures are helpful for both pre-service and in-service teachers for improving their teaching efficiency.
7. The feedback devices for the modification of teacher behaviour are effective only for developing criterion pattern of behaviour but instructional procedures are effective for providing the basis for teaching specific skills, concepts, principles, etc.
8. The knowledge and understanding of instructional procedures is based upon planning and organizing teaching different components of learning subjects.

The concept of instructional procedures incorporates the principle of psychology and theories of learning which are important and useful in designing and practicing the teaching instruction.

Training Programmes

The Rehabilitation training programme mentioned below are being conducted by various institutes in the country have been standardized and approved by RCI. The Council keeps on updating and adding new training programmes as per requirement of the country.

New Training Programmes

Name of the Course	*Duration*	*Qualification*
Speech and Hearing		
a. M. Sc. Speech and Hearing	2 years	Degree
b. B. Sc. Speech and Hearing	3 years	Degree
c. Diploma Speech and Hearing	1 year	Diploma
d. B.Ed. (HI)	1 year	Degree
e. B.Ed. (HI)	1 year	Degree
Mental Retardation		
a. Bachelor in Mental Retardation	3 years	Degree
b. Diploma in Mental Retardation	1 year	Diploma
Visually Handicapped		
a. B.Ed. Special Education	1 year	Degree
b. Course for Training Teacher of Visually Handicapped Children at Primary Level.	1 year	Diploma
c. Course for Training Teachers of Visually Handicapped Children at Secondary Level	1 year	Diploma
d. Orientation and Mobility Training Course	6 months	Certificate
Locomotor Handicapped		
a. B.Sc. Prosthetic and Orthotic	3½ years	Degree
b. Diploma in Prosthetic and Orthotic Engers.	2½ years	Diploma
c. Multi-rehabilitation Workers	1½ years	Diploma
Multi Handicapped		
a. Post-graduate Course on the Education of Physically and Neurologically Handicapped Children	1 year	Diploma
b. Basic Development Therapy Course for Children with Cerebral Palsy	1 year	

National Institute for the Mentally Handicapped

The national institute for the mentally handicapped was established in the year 1984 as an autonomous body under the Ministry of Welfare, Government of India. The Institute serves as an apex body with specific emphasis on training and research in the field or mental retardation. The NIMH offers specialised services keeping in view the various requirements of the mentally handicapped persons.

The following are the objectives:

1. To develop appropriate models of care and habilitation for the mentally retarded persons appropriate to Indian conditions.
2. To develop manpower for delivery of services to the mentally handicapped.
3. To acquire relevant data to assess the magnitude, cause, rural urban composition, socio-economic factors etc. of mental retardation in the country.
4. To identify, conduct and coordinate research in the area of mental retardation.
5. To provide consultancy services to voluntary organisations in the area of mental handicap and to assist them wherever necessary.
6. To serve as a documentation and information centre in the area of mental retardation.
7. To promote and stimulate growth of various kind of quality services for persons with mental retardation throughout the country.

At the Institute's headquarter at Secunderabad, there are six departments namely as medical sciences, psychology, special education, speech pathology and audiology, information and documentation services and vocational training. The Institute has three regional training centres located at Mumbai, Kolkata and New Delhi, while Model School for the Mentally Deficient Children at New Delhi was taken over by the Institute in the year 1986.

Some of the Institute's training programmes are also carried by a network of supported and affiliated centres spread across the country.

The National Institute runs the following pre-service, in-service., seminar and other training programmes:

1. Three years bachelor's Degree Course in Mental Retardation (BMR) at Secunderabad.
2. Diploma Course in Mental Retardation.
3. Post-graduate Diploma in Mental Retardation.

Thakur Hariprasad Institute of Research and Rehabilitation of the Mentally Handicapped, Hyderabad

Thakur Hariprasad Institute of Research and Rehabilitation for mentally handicapped was established in the year 1968. If offers:

1. Special education programmes tailored to meet each student's special needs.
2. Modern Home like residential for care mother settings.
3. Health care services.
4. Transitional services from school to work and other programmes.
5. Extensive Vocational and Rehabilitation Programmes.
6. Therapeutic Recreational Activities.
7. Special programmes for children and young with antism and behaviour programmes.

It has made significant contribution in the field of MR in India over the last decades. More specifically, THPI runs the courses such as:

Programmes: (1) Diploma in MR. (2) Diploma in Medical Pedagogy,. (3) Diploma in Development Therapy. (4) Course for Paediatricians and Clinical Psychologists in Neuro Kinsiological Diagnosis. (5) Diploma in Vojta Therapy. (6) Training for para-professionals etc. (7) Need-based Training Programmes and (8) Certificate Course in Vocational Training.

Several Specialised Service Wings : (1) Rehabilitation of children under judicial custody. (2) Rural camps. (3) Training of school teachers. (4) Consultation services and (5) Resource services.

In Addition to General Services : (1) Behaviour Modification. (2) Speech Therapy. (3) Occupational Therapy. (4) Physiotherapy. (5) Family Therapy (6) Home Guidance Clinic. (7) Sibling Counselling. (8) Need-based Interventions. (9) Psycho-linguistic Therapy. (10) Developmental Therapy. (11) Vojta Therapy. (12) Medical Pedagogy Therapy. (13) Early Social Integration and (14) Cognitive Therapy.

National Institute for the Visually Handicapped, Dehradun

The National Institute for the Visually Handicapped. (NIVH) Dehradun, was established in July, 1979, amalgamating 9 Nationai Centres for the Blind. The latter was started in January 1950 with a training centre for the adult Blind, taken over from St. Dunstan's Hostel for the Indian War Blinded. Subsequently, other units such as a women's wing, a workshop for making Braille appliances, a sheltered workshop, a central Braille press, schools for blind and partially sighted children and a national library for the war blind added.

(i) to promote research.
(ii) to undertake the training of personnel, and
(iii) to provide certain national level services.

The national institute for visually handicapped is a registered society under the Ministry of Social and Women's Welfare. Its director is the executive head. The Institute has the following divisions : (1) school Division,; (2) Training division, (3) Aids and Appliances Division; (4) Research Division; (5) Book Division and (6) Industrial Psychology Division.

The activities of the Institute include operating schools for the blind, imparting occupational training, running of a sheltered workshop, a Braille press, a teacher's training centre, and conducting research on several aspects of blindness.

The Institute operates tow schools-one each for the blind and for the partially sighted children. These schools prepare the blind children for the secondary examination. It is the taken of these to school to try out new methods to teaching and equipment.

The Institute has taken up research studies on case study of various disabling conditions and preparations of reports for complete set of management; effect exercise in Physiotherapy treatment, innovative method of treatment in management of paraplegia/orthopaedic conditions; construction of indigenous activities of daily living use of simple methods in Occupational Therapy; develop simple method of treatment programmes in Occupational Therapy in the Zone of hand functions; and role of electromyographic studeies round the knee joint in different pathological conditions.

Ali Yavar Jung National Institute for the Hearing Handicapped, Bombay (AYJNIHH)

The National Institute for the Hearing Handicap has been setup in Bombay The foundation stone was laid in December 25, 1978. The Institute is functioning since 1981. It has its regional centres in the country.

There is also training centre for adult deaf which was established in 1962 at Hyderabad which continued to provide occupational training to deaf bays and girls in the area of sheet mental works, fitting, carpentry, electric worshipping, cutting and tailoring welding, photography turning. These students are drawn from all over the country. Recently the institute has made further studies by expanding education and training activities with latest audiological equipment to provide service facilities. Research programmes include early identification of hearing impaired. The courses run by AYJNIHH ie; D.Ed. (Deaf), B.Ed. (Deaf). B.Sc. (AST), D.C.E.

National Institute for Orthopaedically Handicapped, Calcutta

The Institute has been established in 1979 by the Government of India to:

1. Conduct research on early detection, prevention, medical and physical rehabilitation of orthopaedically handicapped children and adults;
2. Conduct education and training of orthopaedically handicapped children and adults training of teachers, and
3. Plan economic rehabilitation of orthopaedically handicapped.

The national institute in collaboration with Spastic society of West Bengal have conducted a course to train special teachers. The schools that are being started in the National Institute will primarily act as a model in teaching the handicapped as well as training special teachers.

Alimco has located a limb fitting centre in the Institute premises. An orthotic and prosthetic unit is also functioning. The physics therapy unit is also in operation.

The NIOH has taken up large number of research projects and studies. These include effect of exercises in physiotherapy treatment, occupational therapy, and several immature methods of treatment in the management of orthopaedic conditions.

National Institute of Rehabilitation Training and Research, Olatur, Cuttack

National Institute of Rehabilitation Training and Research (NIRTAR) came into existence when National Institute of Prosthetic and Orthotic Training (NIPOT) a unit of Artificial Limbs Manufacturing Corporation of India (ALIMCO) established in 1975, was converted into an autonomous body on 22nd February 1984 under Ministry of Welfare, Government of India.

Objectives

1. To undertake, sponsor or co-ordinate the training or personnel such as Doctors, Engineers, Orthotists, Prosthetic and Orthotic technicians, Physio-Therapists, Occupational Therapists, multi-purpose rehabilitation therapists and such other personnel deemed necessary for the rehabilitation of the physically handicapped.

2. To conduct, coordinate, sponsor or subsidise research into biomedical engineering, both fundamental and applied, leading to the effective evaluation of mobility aids for the orthopaedically disabled persons or suitable surgical or medical procedures or development of new aids.
3. To develop models of service delivery programmes for rehabilitation of the physically handicapped.
4. To promote or distribute or subsidise the manufacture of prototypes and distribution of nay or all aids designed to promote any aspects of the education and rehabilitation therapy of the physically handicapped.
5. To undertake vocational training, placement and social economic, educational and any form of rehabilitation and any activity to incidental to these.
6. To undertake any other action in the area of rehabilitation of the physically handicapped.

A regional Rehabilitation Training Centre is also attached to this Institute, besides a leprosy rehabilitation unit.

Rehabilitation camps are organised periodically in rural and tribal areas to make the rehabilitation service available to the physically handicapped almost at their doorsteps.

Rehabilitation Council of India, New Delhi

The Rehabilitation Council of India which was originally established in 1986 as a registered society has become as statutory body by promulgation of the Rehabilitation Council of India Act, 1992,- with effect from July 31, 1993. Its main function is to regulate training, its recognition and derecognition and quality improvement in special education.

Aims and Objectives

The main and objectives of the Rehabilitation Council are as follows:

1. To regulate the training policies and programmes in the fields of Rehabilitation of disabled people.

2. To bring about standardization of training courses for professionals dealing with disabled persons.
3. To prescribe minimum standards of education and training for various categories of professionals dealing with disabled persons.
4. To regular these standards in Government Institutions, Central as well as State, uniformally through out the country.
5. To recognise institutions training professionals in the field and recognise the Degree/Diploma/Certificates awarded by these institutions and to withdraw recognition.
6. To recognise Degree/Diploma/Certificates on reciprocal basis and to get Indian Degrees/Diploma/Certificates recognised abroad and to withdraw such recognition.
7. To maintain an Indian Rehabilitation Register.
8. To collect information on a regular basis, on education and training in the field of Rehabilitation of disabled persons from institution in India and abroad.

The council has standardised several courses for different categories of manpower requirement in the field of special education.

Exercise

1. Differentiate between teacher-training and teacher-education. Enumerate the objectives for teachers-training in special education.
2. Describe the role of N.C.E.R.T. in teacher training. Enumerate the teacher competencies.
3. Differentiate between skills and competencies. Enumerate the classroom teaching skills Indicate the components or activities in reinforcement skills.
4. Explain the term, 'Instructional Procedure.' Enumerate essentials for effective instructional procedures.

5. Explain the term 'Conditions of Learning.' Enumerate the conditions of learning. Describe the procedure for teaching concepts to disabled children.
6. Enumerate training programmes and institutes of special education in our country.
7. Describe the provisions of teacher training for special education in mainstreaming or integrated education.
8. Write short notes on the following :
   (a) Learner controlled strategy
   (b) Importance of instructional procedure.
   (c) Classroom teaching skills.
   (d) Teaching of Creativity.

3

Classroom Management

Kothari Commission of Education (1964-66) has very rightly stated in its opening sentence that 'Destiny of India is being shaped in her classroom. But it has not explained the meaning of classroom. The term 'Classroom' is very broad as well as very specific phenomenon. It is very difficult to explain. The knowledge of teaching training and instruction is applied for organizing classroom activities. There are several components, devices and techniques of classroom teaching which can be observed by entering into the classroom.

I. K. Devies has recently introduced the new approach 'Managing Teaching Learning.' The teacher is a principal component of classroom activities. Now he has to play the role of a manager. A teacher has to plan, organise, administer, supervise and evaluate or control his classroom activities. Devies has evolved the new concept of classroom management.

Classroom management is one of the two major responsibilities of a teacher, the other responsibility being instruction. Some instruction and others look upon the two as distinct features in a larger context. These two responsibilities need not be inter-dependent as instruction can take place without a group of learners and classroom can be managed whether instruction takes place or not. Management is an important function for any organisation and it concerns the co-ordination and cooperation necessary for goal attainment. Authority and leadership make co-ordination possible. Authority is the manager's ability to direct and control and leadership is the form of authority that brings about the need process.

A teacher has to play the role of a manager of planning and organizing his classroom activities. This approach is based on human organization—Modern Theory of Relationship Centred. The basic assumption of this theory is that a teacher has the ability to take decisions and solve a classroom problems. Classroom management is the main responsibility of the teacher. It is most difficult job of a teacher but has to direct and control the classroom activities. The main focus of classroom activities is to generate conducive learning situations. The quality of teaching and teacher training depends upon quality of classroom management. The teacher is as the management expert of the class, he uses his manager's ability, authority and leadership qualities which are the keys to classroom management. It is very dynamic complex and difficult process of education.

The Meaning

Classroom management is viewed as an organisational function in which tasks are performed in a variety of settings, resulting in the inculcation of certain values such as human respect, personal integrity, self-direction, group cohesion, etc. When tasks are performed tensions are be generated and these have to be solved. Tensions are related to or have a braining on certain situational factors and ideological in stances of schools and teachers.

In viewing classroom management from the conceptual point, one recognizes some of the recent approaches to management, such as management by objectives (MBO), behaviour modification. (positive and negative reinforcement), transactional analysis (TA) and Contingency management. A comprehensive theory of classroom management is as elusive as a theory of instruction.

A distinction between tasks and activities may be indicated. The concept of activities refers to distinctive patterns of overt behaviour of teachers and students in classrooms. A task is defined as the way in which information processing demands of an environment are structured and experienced. It is expressed in terms of a goal, and a set of operations designed to achieve the goals. A task gives meaning to an activity by linking various elements within an activity to a purpose or goal. In terms of classroom management, teachers perform various tasks such as planning, organising, coordinating, directing, controlling and communicating, behaviour, therefore, can be understood in terms of tasks accomplished.

The teacher's various tasks are related to certain variables such as time available for the teacher and students, space in the classroom, learning material and resources and the form of rewards and punishments generally adopted by the teacher. Further, the concept of classroom management is visualized, mainly in terms of instruction. It could also deal with an individual student's degree to develop self-control in connection with instruction, his behaviour with peer group and teachers outside the class or in the several activities that take place in the college. These, in turn, are affected by factors such as age and background of the students, solidarity of groups that exist in a college, the organisational setup adopted by college authorities and finally the educational goals at the tertiary level. Classroom management has a wide spectrum of tasks and activities involving mainly the teacher and the student with supporting factors such as resources available, the climate of the classroom and the those of the college. It doesn't limit itself of the management of the classroom alone but has a far-reaching goal of the development of individual students to be independent by a sound, scientific and value-oriented system of education.

The problems of classroom management are intimately linked to the larger concerns of teaching styles, motivation, interest, strategies for ensuring success, the effect of group forces and the incorporation of mental hygiene principles into daily classroom practice. However, many educators and administrators have not accepted the existence of the problems of management erupt the advice and guidance given to teachers will be to "establish rapport". 'make learning interesting' or manifest warmth, friendliness, understanding and patience for students These may be desirable attributes to develop but in themselves they will not help in managing the classroom. Other practical steps have to be taken to manage the classroom.

The Definitions

Teaching process is organized through classroom management. 'Classroom management' is defined operationally.

"A system of actions and activities are managed in classroom to induce learning through teacher-taught relationship or interaction."

This definition of classroom management is very comprehensive which includes the major components of teaching in classroom. Teacher and students are the basic components for managing classroom activities. The mode of relationship between them depends on several factors. The action of teacher means non-verbal behaviour or use of body language which creates the emotional climate of classroom. The activities of teacher means verbal interaction or verbal communication, skills and competencies. The focus of classroom management is to facilitate student learning.

The definition of classroom management indicate is the wide variation of its components. The following are the main approaches which are used in managing classroom activities.

The Concept

Management approach provides teacher with concrete suggestion about ways they can have a positive influence on the interests, learning, and social development of their students. Teachers are often unaware of what they do, and this lack of perception sometimes results in unwise, and self-defeating behaviour. It may be, therefore, reasonable to assume that the development of skills for observing and describing classroom behaviour is a prerequisite for improving classroom teaching. Teaching programmes traditionally have not trained teacher to recognize and use specific behaviours. Instead, they have given teacher's global advise without linking it to specific behaviours. We share the belief that "teacher must be provided with specific and concrete skill if they are to be successful in the classroom."

Classroom management is of major connected with education and includes teacher functions variously. Described as discipline, control, keeping order, motivation and establishing a positive attitude toward learning. It helps to focus on the teacher's role in shaping the learning environment. The most important determinant of classroom environment is the teacher's method of classroom management especially the techniques for keeping the class activity engaged and involved in productive, independent activity. It differs from discipline and control which is direct and extraneous. Management helps prevent problems rather than deal with problems once they have emerged. Studies conducted by J. Jouin (1970) reveal that the key to classroom management lies in the things the teacher does ahead of time to create good learning environment and a low potential for trouble.

The Principles

Something as complex as classroom management cannot be reduced to simple cook book recipes. There are general principles that apply to most situations and can be learned and practised systematically. Though not omnipotent, they handle most problems successfully as well as provide firm base to teacher for handling problems need specialized attention.

General Principles of Classroom Management : General principles are in the form of following assumptions :

(1) Students are more likely to follow classroom rules when they understand and accept them.
(2) Management should fix its sights towards maximizing the time students spends in productive work, rather than merely stressing control.
(3) Teacher's goal is to develop inner self control in the students, and not merely to exercise external control.
(4) Students engaged in meaningful work in accordance with their interests and aptitudes, have less discipline problems.

Specific Principles of Classroom Management : Specific principles are in the form of following assumptions :

(1) Establish clear rules when rules are needed.
(2) Minimize disruptions and delays.
(3) Plan independent activities as well as organized lessons.
(4) Let students assume independent responsibility.
(5) Encourage effort, and
(6) Cue and reinforce appropriate behaviours.

However, rules will not handle all situations, hence between need to know how to give on-the-spot instruction when needed, specify and reward desirable behaviour as a way of ensuring that students know what to do and are motivated to do it.

Besides general qualities and behaviour of teachers that help establish a good class atmosphere and maximize the time and effort.

Various Approaches

The following are the main approaches to managing classroom activities.

Herbartian Approach: It is very old and classical approach. It has five steps—preparing, presentation, comparison, obstruction and generalization. It is content-centred approach to classroom management. It employs teacher controlled instruction (TCI). All the classroom activities are managed and controlled by the teacher and students are the passive listeners. It stresses on the memorization of content. It is known as thoughtless teaching.

Evaluation Approach: B.S. Bloom has developed this approach to classroom teaching. It considers that teaching is tripolar process (1) Educational objectives, (2) Learning experiences and (3) Change in behaviour. The classroom management is to realize the educational objectives. The purpose of managing classroom activities is to provide teaching experiences. The students and objectives are measured with the help of change of behaviours. The classroom management is objective-centred. The classroom activities are managed for realizing the objectives.

Managing Teaching Learning : I. K. Devies has given the management approach to teaching learning. A teacher has to play the role of manager and has to manage classroom activities. This approach is based on the modern theory of human organization and relationships. Devies has given four steps for managing teaching (1) Planning (2) Organizing (3) Leading and (4) Controlling. The organizing and leading steps are related to classroom management. The controlling steps provide the feedback to classroom management. According to Devies five teaching structures are generated through classroom management from primary to higher stage. There is continuum and great variation in classroom management.

Organizing Teaching: This approach assumes that teaching is a continuum from more thoughtless to most thoughtful i.e., memory to reflective level i.e., (1) Memory level. (2) Understanding level and (3) Reflective level. At memory level classroom management is controlled and dominated by the teacher. At understanding level classroom management is controlled by both teacher and the learners. At reflective level, the learners dominate in managing classroom activities it is a problem solving stage of teaching. The classroom activities are managed in seminar and conference hall.

Modular Approach of Teaching : Teaching models are used in managing classroom activities. There are various families of teaching models each family has own classroom management. A model consists of four fundamental elements - focus, syntax, social system and support system. The format of classroom management can be studied and analysed with the help of these elements. The syntax of managing classroom activities indicates the structure of teaching. The variation of classroom management can be identified with this modular approach of teaching.

Operations of Classroom Teaching: It is also known as phases or stages of teaching in classroom. A general format of classroom management requires three stages of managing classroom activities. (1) Pre-active stage (2) Interactive stage and (3) Post-active stage. The interactive stage relates to managing classroom operations and activities, the pre-active stage activities are planned before the classroom. Thus, there is flexibility in managing classroom activities. This concept of operations of classroom is given by Karl Open Shaw.

The Dimensions

The approaches of teaching and classroom management reveal the great variation in the structure. These approaches provide the general format of classroom management. The classroom management consists of four dimensions.

In managing classroom activities, a teacher has to consider these four dimensions. A brief description of these dimensions have been provided in the following paras.

Physical Dimension or Environment: A classroom is a functional unit of an educational institution. The location, buildings lawns and classrooms are designed by the manager or founder of the institution. The classroom management concerns with seating arrangement., light air arrangement and black board facilities. A teacher as manager has to look into these facilities of classroom physical setting which should be conducive to learning,

Social and Cultural Dimension: A classroom is a miniatures of the society as well as of an institution. A classroom management involves relationship social and cultural environment which depends on following relations.

(a) Teacher and taught relation.
(b) Relationship among students.
(c) Relation between teacher and principal and
(d) Relationship among teachers.

It is a very classical phrase -John and Latin. Here John means students and Latin means content or subject matter. A teacher must know the background of his students and their entering behaviour and learning abilities and interest. Education is the creature and creator of the society. The new society is shaped in the classroom of an educational institution through its desirable social and cultural environment.

Psychological Dimension : It is said that no learning without motivation. The main focus of classroom management is to facilitate learning. Teacher motivates his students verbally and through actions (non-verbally). He also reinforces their desirable behaviours. In higher classroom teacher raises the level of aspiration of students. Teacher involvement in classroom management encourages the students participation. The psychological dimension plays a significant role in the students participation and their learning. It is a criterion for an effective classroom management.

Ethical Consideration or Value Dimension : It is most important dimension of classroom management- A teacher's role in classroom management is more than a manager. Teacher is leader of the class and ideal to his students. He influences the students behaviour. He should look like a teacher and behave like teacher. He has to maintain classroom code and conduct which should be value based. This dimension of classroom management concerns with feelings, attitudes and affective values aspect of the students.

Classroom Components

There is variety of classroom components which are essential aspects of classroom management. These components or variables play different roles in managing classroom activities.

Teacher as Principal Component : A teacher as manager is the principal components of classroom management. Most of classroom activities are managed and controlled by teacher. A teacher organizes his teaching activities to facilitate student learning by generating learning structures in the classroom management. He encourages and motivates the students in his classroom management. He also evaluates the effectiveness of his instructional procedure of his classroom.

Student as Dependent Variable or Components : The student as secondary or dependent variable in classroom. The purpose of teaching is to facilitate learning. The learning depends on teaching. If teaching is organized at memory level, then rote learning takes place. The understanding level teaching facilitate assimilation and mastery concept but students are more active at this level.

Intervening Components or Variables : Teacher and students interaction in classroom depends on several components or variables. These are known as intervening components or variables. The following are the main intervening variables of classroom management.

(1) Subject-content includes, terms, concept, facts, principles theories verbal language, problem, solving and creativity.

(2) Teaching objectives cognitive affective and psychomotor.

(3) Strategies or methods of teaching are of teacher controlled instruction (TCI), Learner controlled instruction (LCI) action oriented instruction and group controlled instruction (GCI).

(4) Techniques and maxims of teaching.

(5) Teaching aids or audio-visual aids of teaching.

(6) Motivational techniques.

(7) Teaching skills and social skills.

(8) Communication competency and skills.

(9) Instructional procedure.

(10) Supporting devices of teaching.

All these teaching variables are taken into consideration while managing classroom activities.

Managing Classroom Behaviour

Behavioural problems hinder the special students' academic achievement and leave a negative effect upon their acceptance by others. Hence it is important to mange these behavioural problems properly.

Two major type of behaviour problems may concern the teachers, (1) inappropriate classroom behaviour, and (2) poor study skills.

Inappropriate behaviour are taking out, fighting arguing., being out of seat, swearing, avoiding interactions with others, immature and withdrawn behaviours.

Typical study skills problems are incomplete assignments poor attention during lessons, failure to follow directions, and poor management of study time.

Behaviour problems do not occur in isolation. To understand and manage classroom behaviour problems, not only the behaviour of the target student but also that of the teachers and peer must be examined. From example sarcastic comment from a teacher can initiate a verbal retort from the student.

Principles of Behaviour

Principle of behaviour management are:

(1) Stating precise goals.

(2) Breaking behaviours into teachable sub-components.

(3) Instituting systematic management procedures.

(4) Collecting data to monitor student progress.

Briefly, goals should be realistic, specific and observable. The task should be broken up into simpler sub-tasks which can be taught easily. There should be consistency in providing re-enforcement to the students. Classroom teachers can collect information by informal techniques such as (i) Direct observation of behaviour, (ii) Informal behaviour inventories.

Improved Behaviour

Strategies for managing and improving behaviour include:

1. Stating behavioural expectations for all students;
2. Finding out of students meeting expectation are receiving reinforcement to encourage maintenance of those behaviour;
3. Determines if there are students who do not meet expectations. If so do they;
   - know and understand the expectations and
   - have the prerequisite skills for the behaviours;
4. Identifying target behaviour to be achieved;

5. Selecting an observation system and collecting baselines data on behaviour;
6. Analysing data to determine the need for an intervention programme;
7. Determining if the target-behaviour needs to be learn (increased or decreased if intervention is required;
8. Selecting an intervention that uses the most positive approach;
9. Implementing the intervention;
10. Collecting data on student performance;
11. Analysis the data to determine the need to continue, modify or terminate the intervention: and
12. Taking required action.

When the behaviour is at the desired level and no longer dependent upon the intervention, continue to collect maintenance data and return to step (4).

The need for intervention can be reduced through preventive planning. Expectations for behaviour should be communicated to student. They may be done in the following ways:

Establishing class rule. Rule for classroom conduct should clearly communicated the exact behaviour expected by the teacher.

Reinforcing appropriate behaviour. When appropriate behaviours occur, they should be rewarded.

Providing reinforcers that are valued by students. To find out what students perceive as rewarding, ask them or observe them.

Using token economics to deliver reinforcers. If students are presented with tokens rather than reinforcers after the occurrence of a desired behaviour, such a system can be used with one student, group or entire class. In setting up a token economy, the teacher should specify the behaviours that earn tokens.

Using contingency contracts with teenagers and older students. These are written agreements negotiated between the students and teacher that implicate what the student must do to earn a specific reward.

Teaching behaviour by shaping. Shaping involves the reinforcement of small progressive steps towards the desire behaviour.

Using modelling to improve student behaviour. It involves the reinforcement of another individual, the model for exihibiting the desired behaviour in presence of the target student. This should be done carefully to avoid any adverse effect on the child.

Decreasing in appropriate behaviour by positive and differential reinforcement approaches.

(i) Using negative procedures as a last resort. There may be time out or withdrawal of previously earned reinforcers.

(ii) Involving parents in behaviour management programmes to provide continuation of the programme at home.

Adapting the Environment

Classroom management elements that teacher should consider are:

Arranging the Classroom Environment : Various considerations for arranging the physical environment are:

1. Ensure a safe and barrier-free environment by removing objects cluttered on the floor desks, equipment, architectural barriers.
2. Make the working condition pleasant like temperature, light, noise level, ventilation and attractive furnishings.
3. Obtain furniture and special equipment that is comfortable, attractive, durable and functional.
4. Arrange space functionally for storage, working and performing activities.
5. Keep in mind the educational goals in making seating arrangements as social interactions may influence them.

Organising the Classroom Environment : The instructional environment of the classroom includes the procedures, materials performance. The teacher organises the curriculum, groups students, and sets up delivery system for the presentation and practice of skills and information. This structure directly affects non-academic performance as well as student achievement. Important principles to be considered are to:

1. Organise curricular skills and information sequentially, arrange skills and information according to subjects, activities of interest.
2. Group student for instruction according to type of disability keep it flexible.

3. Set up systems for monitoring practice. Provide auto instructional material which includes self-correcting material, programmed instructional and mediated instruction. These give a constant feed back to the child.
4. Provide guidelines for student behaviour. Frame classroom rules and routines that are short, specific, simple clearly stated, positive and enforceable by teacher, structure prompts and models.
5. Use systematic record-keeping procedures. These should be consistent and relevant.

Using Technology of Teaching : The current technology of education includes systematic instructional techniques, procedures for changing behaviour and technological advances in equipment, media, and learning resources. Electronic technologies such as television, radio, audio and video-tapes and computers have the capability to revolutionise the quality, productivity and, availability of education.

Managing Duration and Resources : The teacher as manager of the total learning environment, supervises the allocation, organization and use of essential learning resources:

Instruction Time: Daily schedules divide the day into time blocks and tell what activities will occur and when they will occur. Suggestions for scheduling are :

1. Move from definite to flexible schedules.
2. Proceed from short work assignments to longer ones.
3. Alternate highly preferred with less preferred activities.
4. Plan for leeway time.
5. Provide a daily schedule.
6. Schedule assignments that can be completed in a day.
7. Plan a variety of activities.

Instructional Materials : For choice of material consider its validity, cost, number of students with whom it can be used, its physical robustness, probability, difficulty level, presentation sequence, input modes, to modes of response and durability, and

Personnel Difficulties: If teacher feel it is difficult to handle it all by themselves. There may be tap two excellent sources of assistance viz. peer tutors and volunteers.

The Sociometry

An educational institution does not exist in a vacuum. The learners and the teachers reveal in their attitude and behaviour, the influences of the experiences they have had in their homes and community. As such, educational institutions—schools and colleges form part of society. They reflect it characteristics in many forms. Student's faculty members, both teaching and non-teaching, and administrators constitute the nucleus for the interactions that originate out of academic, psychological and social situations of educational institutions. The quality of the interactions that lead to human relations within the institution and between the institution and the community is determined by the social and psychological structure of the students body and the faculty, the organisation and administration of the institution, the impact of learning experiences of the students and the institutional climate. The strength of the relationship in terms of mutual understanding, friendliness spirit of give and take cooperative undertaking, democratic leadership and emotional stability envisages effective functioning of the educational institutions.

Teacher as the Focus

The teacher is the significant figure in any educational institution in communicating with the learners in the classrooms and holding joint responsibility with parents in the welfare of the learner's education. Actually, two-way communication is desired-A teacher understanding the learners better by means of the knowledge of their home background and the parents getting to know the programmes in an educational institution and the part played by their offsprings in them. The teacher, the parents and the community generate manifold waves of inter-relationships which call for the understanding of the nature of the services they render and the points of view they hold. The teacher, the pivotal point in this educational enterprise needs to develop himself professionally and maintain a wholesome personality and a nature mind in order to strengthen the bonds of relationships.

Human Relations : Human relations indicates the process by which individuals conceptualise and relate to each other as human beings and in turn, relate to others in their society, in specific contexts, such as educational institutions, medical institutions, industries, legal institutions, social institutions, etc.

Human relations in an educational institution is related to the interactions and inter-relationships generated by the personnel, directly and indirectly involved in the various activities of the institution. Some of the significant grouping of personnel whose human relations relate to the effective and efficient functioning of the institutions are: (1) Teacher-Learner relations. (2) Learner-Learner relations, (3) Teacher-Teacher relations, (4) Teacher-Administrators relations, and (5) Teacher-Community relations.

Some authors have divided the 'relationship' as academic, social and constitutional but opinion differs in regard to this division as it is difficult to accept any clear demarcation between social and academic relationships.

Teacher-Learner Relations

The learner's behaviour as an individual, and especially as an individual interacting with the teacher and the other learners, depends to a great extent on the kind of teacher the learner has. If the teacher can satisfy the social and psychological needs of the students, favourable, attitudes are developed in the classroom. This may be carried out by the teacher in such activities as listening to the learners, responding to their suggestions, accepting their feelings, involving them in the teaching and learning process and encouraging their efforts. Thus creating a warm, supportive and positive emotional climate in the classroom. Such a climate enhances emotional security, motivates learning and leads to a high standard of achievement. Being and understanding and considerate person is thus, one of the hall marks of an efficient teacher. Some of the components of human relationship which exist inside a classroom are open channels of communication, participatory decision-making, flexibility of the syllabus, 'we' feeling in groups, integrity, friendliness student leadership, etc.

Learner-Learner Relations

The human relationships among the learners/students can either stimulate or thwart the growth of each other in many ways. It is necessary for the teacher to understand the relationships operating among the students. The learners need a period in which they relate to each other as equals and so learn to stand on their own. A great amount of emotion is usually stimulated in peer group in regard to friendship relations during adolescence. In the peer group, there is a gradual shift from activity orientation to thought, feeling and personality orientation. The learners by exchanging ideas and feelings with peers, clarify interpersonal relationships. Conversation in peer groups is a medium through which social sensitivity and skills are developed.

The influences and the impact of the peer groups extend far beyond the outcomes of simple interactions and inter-relations. In his field theory approach, Kurt Lewin, further of the group dynamics movement, has referred to the effects of "the group atmosphere", which indicates that behaviour depends on the total field of forces in operation. The socio-metric movement has refined techniques for measuring the influence peers have on each other who influences whom, in what ways and on what occasions. Sensitivity education, which is a group-process by which people attempt to know one another better uses sensitivity to another's needs, interests and values. Learners are undoubtedly affected and influenced by their peer groups. Research is yet to find with certainty the conditions of such influence on learners and how exactly they are influenced.

Teacher-Teacher Relations

The teacher as an individual has great potential for professional improvement outside the classroom. One such situation is the working relationship among the teachers. The faculty of teachers differ widely in terms of morale or group cohesiveness: But whatever the nature of the groups the teacher has to find a place in it. He has to learn to relate and communicate adequately to his surroundings within their faculty group. As a member of this professional group, the teacher's different roles are responsible for his professional effectiveness and personal satisfaction within the institutional climate. There are many common areas for cooperation and mutual help such as marking, promotion, reporting of activities of students, inter-disciplinary topics, community and social science, etc. In fact an attitude of mutual helpfulness is contagious and favourable affects, teacher-learner and teacher-teacher relationships is especially decreasing staff conflicts and promoting harmony among them. Teacher education programmes should, therefore, lay stress on the importance of working with other teachers and developing skills necessary to work successfully with teaching peers, stressing on the need to communicate adequately and appropriately.

Teacher-Administrator Relations

Teacher get opportunities to come in contact with administrators in their daily routine of work and develop harmonious relations with them, as long as administrators do not indulge in authoritarianism and the teachers are aware of their role within a democratic set-up. However, when interpersonal difficulties are encountered it is natural for one of the persons to project the problem on the other. Instead of blaming the other, good human relations can be retained if each thinks in terms of the weakness on this part which could have been responsible for the problems created in working with the other. Self-assessment helps in eliminating many of the weaknesses and problems and develops interpersonal skills. Each becomes tolerant of the other as is acquainted with the other's point of view. Further, the administrator should exhibit a belief in the worth of all his faculty members, respect them and see to it that all live and work in harmony. He should have special skills to work with individual as well as groups in such a way that a good relationship is maintained.

Teacher and Community Relations

Teacher not only have to establish good rapport with learners, other teachers and administrators but have also to create sound relationships with parents and other community members. This sort of will have considerable effect on the success of the students efforts and on the effectiveness of the teacher. The teachers community relations extend beyond the parents group and enables them to participate as good citizens of the community. Since interacting with a community involves a number of interpersonal relationships caution should be the watchword. Realising his major responsibilities in the educational institution, the teachers relationship with the community should be cordial understanding and cooperative. An inter-play of a chain of relationship is anticipated in such situations and it is necessary for the teacher to avoid over-committing himself with the community activities.

Classroom Management Techniques

The teacher as management expert of the class adopts different strategies to manage it. In addition to authority and leadership, he has a repertoire of approaches which he applies depending on the behaviour patterns exhibited by the students and the situation on hand. Discipline when viewed as a component of classroom management indicates the need for guiding the students towards self-direction. If self-direction is the goal, the students and teachers should know how to move towards this goal. A knowledge of different models of discipline would enhance the efforts. Further there is a need to view classroom discipline in the larger context of the curriculum and instruction.

The teacher is successful in classroom management if he brings rhythm in everything he works with, develops a classroom culture and encourages his students to identify with the class but not to the extent of lighting the individual learning propensities.

Rhythm and Psychological Sequence: Rhythm in a classroom is satisfying, because it leaves no uncertainty about the activities that are to come up. It must guarantees what will be the sequence of events when there is rhythm in the class, the students look forward to the activity that is coming next and do not feel insecure. The teacher has to bring in a routine only in so far as a routine is essential to the rhythm. A chaotic, disturbing and insecure class is usually one in which routines have been neglected and in which programmes have not been followed. This does not mean that unplanned activities cannot be allowed to emerge in a classroom. These could be encouraged depending on the worthwhileness of the activities and the need and purpose to permit such activities but a sense of rhythm should be there in all the activities carried out in a class.

Class Culture and Code of Conduct: The purpose of a class culture is to make the members of the class secure. The teacher takes up the responsibility to encourage the development of a class culture, complete with sensible traditions, customs, and courtesies. The teacher helps the students to find their roles in this special culture of their class and play them well. This procedure develops a healthy way of viewing class discipline as students learn the accepted forms of behaviour.

A cohesive group offers its members both individual security and the confidence that comes with a common interest and a common purpose. The teacher must develop the concept of classroom wholeness but with unique, differentiated parts and give his students both the advantage of security and the right to recognition as individuals. The teacher thereby makes even students' purpose not subservient to, but compatible with those of his fellow members.

Perhaps a completely, routine and secure class cannot be aroused to become interested in a learning experience. A little insecurity is stimulating and enjoyable. For an experience to have educational value, it must be a challenge. The teacher has to stimulate questions and inject elements of doubt into seemingly secure situations. Too much rhythm without a break, too much attention to routine and too much group effort will be deadening and yet except by comparison with a standard of rhythm, routine and group effect, it is certain that a danger or a doubt cannot be seen for what it is.

Teacher Attention and Involvement in Teaching : Teacher attention is one of the most basic of all influences on student's behaviour. The teacher's smile, words of encouragement, praise, evaluation and silence powerfully affect student behaviour. Systematic use of attention makes the teacher successful in chanting the behaviour of students socially and academically. When a teacher responds to a desirable behaviour it usually tends to increase over time and when a teacher ignores a non-productive behaviour, that behaviour is likely to occur less frequently in the future. Effective and systematic use of attention requires skill and awareness on the teacher's part. An individual's behaviour will not change over night and will have to be shaped gradually. Praise should be as spontaneous and sincere as possible. Comments to the students should vary in content and specify the behaviours being praised. The effectiveness of the praise will be enhanced if student's improved behaviour is praised very shortly after it occurs. The teacher's acceptance or praise can be in the form of a smile pat or a nod or a note on the completed paper, depending upon the nature of response and how it is made. It is very difficulty to ignore consistently behaviour which is annoying. Many teachers who believe that they are "ignoring", misbehaviour, may inadvertently reinforce either by occasionally forgetting to ignore the response or by unwillingly attend to the behaviour often non-verbally.

Teacher's Verbal Control or Social and Emotional Climate : Verbal control is the most common form of resort of a teacher in a classroom. Verbal reprimand is quite understandable when, teaching is viewed as giving direction and redirection. Even though verbalisation is the strategy that teachers use most to control disruptive students, it is not always effective. It is suggested that a soft reprimand which is directed and heard only by the concerned student is more effective than a loud reprimand. Soft reprimands are very effective when combined with frequent praise for appropriate behaviour and when the intensity and tone of the teachers' reprimand are not severe. A soft reprimand should be one of the first type of punishment to use and can be exercised before trying loud reprimands. Reprimands audible to many students may be effective on particular occasions.

Self-management and Classroom Environment: An individual's behaviour is largely dependent on the reactions from others but in an educational institution the teacher is effective change agent, tries to reduce the amount of dependence a student has on him or his peer group. A fruitful purpose of the interaction between the teacher and the taught is for the leacher to guide the student towards self-direction.

Though some believe that all behaviour is ultimately determined by biological, chemical and social forces, others maintain that the individual's choices and thoughts control his own behaviour and these choices are made to some degree independent of any environmental forces acting upon him. Social institutions such as courts and schools punish people on the assumption that individuals do have choices and they have control over their actions to a great extent.

Self control involves not only the individual's ability to suppress desire and to delay gratification for his own welfare as well as that of the society but also any manipulation by him, designed to decrease or increase the frequency of his own behaviour. In the academic field, teachers should not only encourage students, who are inclined towards self-learning and self-evaluation which are fundamental for effective self-management but also place emphasis on student behaviour which is to be controlled by students own efforts. When a student realises his potentialities and not his limitations, he moves towards self-direction. Discipline is positive and it has to be looked up developmentally towards self-direction and self-management.

Students' Involvement and Students' Participation

The colleges can pursue several courses of action to direct student discontent and dissatisfaction into constructive channels. If students can be involved in daily activities, in annual functions and in co-curricular activities they will work within the college system rather than feel compelled to attack it. The following are some of the suggested programmes.

(1) Colleges should provide two-way communication channels. There should be regular opportunities for dialogue among students, teachers and administrators.

(2) Each college should design its own programme of student involvement and this will entail, more than giving a new life to student government. Students should be given an opportunity to lead group discussions to participate in departmental faculty meetings, to evaluate the academic progress of their peers and the class instructional programme. The mere knowledge of the availability of the such opportunities encourages the student body to work in close collaboration with the teachers and the administrators rather than to stand against them.

(3) College should offer courses on adolescent behaviour, understanding a college environment and how to bring about institutional changes. The widespread student unrest definitely indicates that there is something wrong with the system and that changes and reforms are necessary. Administrators and teacher must meet the challenges of the youth and solve their problems. They must help the students with non-violent and constructive programmes.

(4) Some of the students' demands may be anti-educational. Colleges can reform but it should follow its educative function. Colleges should stand firm on their professional prerogatives but at the same time concede to students, demands if they follow the general principles and purposes of education. Colleges should try to find a balance between responsiveness with responsibility.

(5) Consultative Councils when formed in colleges, would lend for student involvement. Generally a consultative council consists of elected parents, students, teachers and community representatives: five (or seven) members in each category, making a total of 20 members of the council. The Council could advise the Principal on a wide range of matters, especially regarding student affairs. The council could be of great help during crises also.

Group Management and Action Orientation

In suggesting classroom strategies to face the aggressive/ disruptive behaviour of adolescents. Kounin's classic study of teacher's techniques for classroom management and discipline takes a prominent place. Kounin's study resulted in the recognition of the famous. 'ripple effect'. The effects of disciplinary action against a particular student on the students in a classroom is called the ripple effect. Teacher's reprimands often result in disturbances of classroom activities and sometimes in more misbehaviour. Kounin (1970) found that when the teacher desists undesirable behaviour with clarity, it could produce more appropriate behaviour and less deviancy on the part of other students than desist without clarity. Desist with firmness is effective with the audience i.e. other students, who themselves are interested in irrelevant activity (deviancy) at that time. Desist with anger is not an intensification of firmness.

Classroom management is conceived by Kounin as dealing with the surface behaviour of students as measured by overt signs of work involvement and by deviancy. The following dimensions of teachers styles are related to discipline and management of the classroom.

1. Withitness indicates teacher's communicating ability of his knowledge of what is going on in the class in regard to student's behaviour.
2. Smoothness shows that the teachers keeps to a flow of classroom activities, which is a pointer to classroom management.
3. Group alerting refers to teacher's promptness in identifying students who are not performing their assigned tasks.

4. Overlapping denotes the teacher's ability to deal with one or more disciplinary problems at the same time.
5. Accountability marks the level to which the teacher holds responsibility for their performances and activities during the lesson.
6. Violence and challenge arousal denote the extent to which the teacher stimulates students intellectual curiosity and enthusiasm.

The mastery of classroom management skills should not be regarded as end in itself but these techniques are necessary tools. The mastery of techniques make choices possible. The possession of group management skills allows the teacher to accomplish his teaching goals, whereas the absence of managerial skills acts as a barrier.

The focus upon group management 'skills is not to be understood as opposed to a concern for individual students. The mastery only enables the teacher to programme for individual differences effectively and to help individual students. If there is a climate of work involvement and freedom from deviancy, different groups of students may be engrossed in doing different things and the teacher is free to help individual students. It can be said that a mastery of group management techniques enables the teacher to be free from concern for classroom management.

Determinants of Classroom Management

Factors Influencing Managing Classroom Activities: Classroom management is a dynamic and complex process which is influenced by various factors. Teaching and classroom management is a continum in several ways. Classroom Management is a continum based on the following factors or determinates.

Stages of Classroom Management : There is a continuum in educational institution from pre-primary stage to college management at pre-primary secondary, higher secondary, graduate and post graduate level. It indicates a continuum from closed climate to more open climate of classroom management.

Objectives of Teaching Learning: There is a continum in the B.& Blown taxonomy of educational objectives. There is continum from psychomotor objectives of affective objectives through cognitive objectives. Every domain has its own continuum. There is continuum within cognitive objectives It also indicates a continuums from trainable to educable classroom management.

Modes of Teaching for Managing Classroom Activities: Thomas F. Green has given modes of teaching as a continuum from conditioning to indoctrination. There are four modes of teaching conditioning, training, instruction and indoctrination. The first two modes of teaching are uses for developing habits, skills and conduct of the students. This area is known as trainable. The last two of teaching are used for developing knowledge, feeling, beliefs, attitudes and values among students. This continuum has great variation of managing classroom activities. Every mode of teaching has its own classroom management.

Conditions of Learning or Structures of Learning as Continuum: Robert Gagne has given eight conditions of learning as continum from S.R. learning to problem solving which is basic for managing classroom activities. I. K. Devies has used five learning structures for managing teaching learning the classroom activities are managed for generating either of these learning conditions or learning structures. The main focus of classroom management is to relate teaching to learning. The structure of classroom management is determined by the conditions of learning.

Organization of Teaching: Teaching is organized into three levels as a continum from memory level to reflective level. The memory level teaching is the pre-requisite for understanding level. The prerequisite for organizing reflective level is the understanding level teaching. It is a continum from throughtless teaching to most thoughtful teaching. Herbart emphasis is on presentation, Morrison classroom climate provides situation for assimilation or mastery of the concept. Hunt, model of teaching is more open for problem solving. Teaching is organized in three forms of classroom management memory understanding and reflective.

There are some other important determinants for managing classroom activities which are as follows:

School Subjects as Determinants : There are various school subjects which are taught in classroom. These subjects have their own nature and purpose. Science subjects requires demonstration and experimentation. There are three ways for classroom activities,

Knowing, doing and showing. Thus each subject has its own way for managing classroom activities. Classroom-management depends on teaching subject.

Components of School Subject as Determinant : The school subjects consist of different components such as terms, concepts, facts, principles theory, generalization, verbal language and creativity or problem solving. The classroom activities are managed for these components. Each components requires different activities to be managed in classroom. The instructional procedure is prepared for each component separately. The more meaningful and purposive activities are managed in classroom in view of these components of school subject.

Strategies of Teaching as Determinants : There are several strategies of teaching which are used in classroom. These can be classified in several ways such - Teacher Controlled Instruction (TCI), Learning Controlled Instruction (LCI), Group Controlled Instruction (GCI) and action oriented instruction. This classification is based on management approach of teaching. The lecture strategy is know as Teacher Controlled Instruction (TCI). The question answer strategy is interaction or dialogue between teacher students. It is mainly used in democratic form of government. This project strategy is action oriented instruction or group controlled instruction (GCI).

Form of Motivation as Determinant : The motivational techniques of classroom are of three types - external motivation, external-interval motivation and self motivation or internal motivation. The level of aspiration is significant for higher classroom management. It has also a continuum for managing classroom activities the form of motivation determines the structure of classroom management.

Type of Discipline in Classroom as Determinant : There are various models of discipline. These are classified broadly into two categories (1) Behaviour modification model and (2) Emergent models of discipline. Behaviour modification is a systematic way of reinforcing procedure to increase probabilities of desirable behaviour. Emergent models of discipline are-psychodynamic model, group dynamic model and the personal social growth. The highest model is self-discipline classroom.

Supporting Devices

Classroom management, is not sufficient enough to realize the objectives of education. Therefore, supporting devices of classroom management are used in this context. The following are the common supporting devices of classroom management.

(1) Laboratory experimentation (2) Field work (3) Library study (4) Educational excursion or field trips (5) Home assignment (6) Self study or Assimilation (7) Tutorials for remedial teaching (8) Action research and (9) Guidance services.

These supporting devices are required in different school subjects. The laboratory experimentation is needed in science subjects physics, chemistry botany and zoology. The fieldwork is done in agriculture science and geography subjects. Educational excursions are organized for historical places, geographical and religious places. The home assignment, self-study and library study are done for assimilation process. Tutorials classes are arranged for remedial teaching for weak students. The classroom management is for normal students and tutorials are organized as supporting device for remedial teaching. It is individualized teaching activities of students and problems of teaching-learning are solved by using action research and guidance services.

Teacher's Roles in Classroom

Teacher is the principal component of classroom management. He has to play the several roles-as manager philosopher, guide and friend. He has the authority, responsibility, accountability and leadership in managing classroom activities. He has to employ an appropriate model of discipline, strategies and techniques of teaching. He has-to maintain rapport with students and social relation with his colleagues and principal. Some of the important roles have been discussed here.

Role as Teacher: Teaching is a noble profession. Teacher is an ideal for his students as well as to society. He should look like a teacher and behave like a teacher. The important role which influences most to students. How he dresses in classroom and how addresses to his students ? He must know his students i.e. entering behaviours and social and cultural back ground.

Role as Philosopher: The main job of a teacher is impart knowledge of his subject content. He must have the mastery of subject and latest development of his subject. He should have the interest is has subject. Research studies have found that mastery of the subject in a powerful predictor of teacher-effectiveness.

Role as Guide: Teacher job is to help students in their personal and learning problems. He has to deal the students problems scientifically for providing the awareness of causes of the problem. The remedial teaching is arranged for weak students.

Role as Researcher : Teacher should have the ability deal the problems of classroom management. He should have the knowledge and skill for using action research. Classroom management problems can be solved with the help of action research project.

Role as Manager : Teacher should know the functions, authorities, and responsibilities of a manager. The main functions of a manager are planning, organizing, supervising, directing, coordinating and controlling the teaching process. Now a teacher has a very wide area of responsibilities.

Role as Leader : A manager should have leadership quality. A teacher functions as a leader of his class. Academic leadership is the most important function of a teacher.

In the modern era, a teacher has enumerable responsibilities as our society becomes very complex. Teacher has to play the several roles in classroom management. The most important qualities of teacher are sincerity, honesty and involvement in teaching, He enjoys his classroom teaching. It brings excellence in classroom management. The knowledge of teaching, training and instruction can be effectively used by a teacher in managing classroom activities.

The Evaluation

The controlling is an important function of classroom management. It provides the basis for evaluation and improving the classroom management The classroom management is the process as well as product, therefore, two criteria-process and product are used for evaluating classroom management. The following techniques of evaluation are used for classroom management.

Techniques Used for Process Criteria : Classroom management is a complex process which involves various types components and activities. Flanders interaction analysis technique is used for measuring social emotional climate with the help verbal categories. The actions of classroom are measured by non-verbal interaction techniques. The decoding process of this technique indicates the directness and indirectness of the behaviours. It is content free technique, therefore content analysis technique of observation is also used for evaluating the quality of content presentation. The observation schedules are used for measuring teaching skills and competency.

Techniques Used for Product Criteria : The learning outcomes or achievements and attitudes of the students are used as product criteria of classroom management. The criterion-referenced tests are used for measuring learners attainment. Flanders and Amidon used achievement and attitude as product criteria for assessing the effectiveness of classroom interaction. A pooled criteria of process and product have been used in a number of research studies of classroom management.

Exercise

1. Define the term 'classroom management'. Explain the meaning of classroom management. Enumerate the characteristics of classroom management.
2. Enumerate the various approaches for managing classroom activities. Describe I. K. Devies approach of managing teaching learning.
3. Indicate the types and dimensions of classroom management. Describe the social and cultural dimensions and ethical consideration or value dimension of classroom management.
4. Indicate the determinates of classroom management. Describe the continum factors and other determinants of classroom management.

4

INTEGRATED EDUCATION

The term 'Education' is commonly used. The meaning or the term is very broad. It has several meanings. It has its literary as well as technical meaning. There is separate dictionary of Education. Some important meanings of this term have been enumerated and stated in the following paragraphs.

THE MEANING

The term 'Education' is commonly used in various fields of knowledge. The meaning of the term is very broad. It has several meanings. Therefore, it is difficult to define the term Education comprehensively. It has its literary as well as technical meaning. Which have been enumerated and stated in the following paragraphs :

1. Education as process of development.
2. Education as Teacher-training.
3. Education as independent field of study or own content or subject of study.
4. Education as an investment rather best investment.
5. Education as an instrument of social change and social control.
6. Education as a creature and creator of the society.
7. Education as filtering process in democracy.
8. Education is for future or future or futurology.

9. Education is an art as well as science and
10. Education is the positive science.

The above meanings of the term, 'Education' have been explained in brief in the following lines. The third meaning 'Education' as an independent field of study or subject is important from research point of view. In the research an independent field of study is known as discipline which is commonly denoted by term subject. The subject word is used for an individual in the research terminology.

Process of Development: The education is mainly considered as a process of human development. All the educational institutions or schools and colleges have the focus to impart the knowledge to the students for their development. In most of the institutions, education subject is not taught but these are known as educational institutions.

The educationists and philosophers have defined education as process of development. Some definitions have quoted here for this purpose.

"Education is process by which a child makes his internal and external."

Forbel

"By education I mean all round drawing the best in child and man body, mind and soul."

M.K. Gandhi

According to Gandhi, education is a process for training of hand, head and heart, i.e., 3H of child and man.

- Education is a dynamic process.
- Education is a continuous process or life long process.
- Education is tripolar process and
- Education is a purposeful or objective-oriented process.

In this way education means a process for developing child's abilities by imparting knowledge.

Teacher-training: The term 'Education' is also used for preparing teachers. i.e., teachers' education. All the teachers' training institutions are known as college of Education or Department of Education. In these colleges of Education, theory and methodology of teaching are taught to the pupil-teachers and teaching practice is organized to prepare effective-teachers. These colleges of education were called training colleges but now the term 'training' has been replaced by the term 'Education'. Thus, the second meaning of Education is training for teachers or preparing teachers.

Independent Field of Study: The term 'Education' refers to an independent field of study or course of study like other courses or subjects, e.g., History, Geography, Psychology and Sociology, etc. It is taught at Intermediate, B.A., and M.A., level. M.A., degree in education is awarded like other subjects. There is separate faculty of education in most of the universities. B.Ed. and M.Ed. degree refer to Bachelor of Education and Master of Education respectively. In this way the third meaning of Education is the independent course of study like other courses or subjects or independent field of study.

Education as an Investment: The meaning of investment is that the return of invested money in the context, is higher than that. The product in terms of quality and quality is higher than invested cost in a particular aspect, is known as good investment.

The return of education is in terms of quantity and quality, is always higher than invested cost in education. Every parents intends to educate their children by investing money according to their financial conditions. The outcomes of education are both qualitative and quantitative. The qualitative outcomes are difficult to measure. Thus the fourth meaning of education is as a good investment.

Education as an Instrument of Social Change and Social Control: During ancient times the social change was brought about by social war and battle. After Mahabharat Bhismpitamha has expected for the new change in society. But today the social change and social control are possible peacefully by changing the education. Mahatma Gandhi had tried to reform the untouchability of cast system in society but he could not succeed. Education could reform the evil of untouchability by introducing uniform system in the schools. In this way the fifth meaning of education is as an instrument of social change and social control.

Education, the Creator and Creature of the Society: The society establishes. The education institutions to create new society according to its ideals. Thus society creates education and education creates new society. It is an effective agency for developing and forming new society. In this way sixth meaning is that education is the creator and creature of the society.

Education as a Filtering Process: In India democratic from of government has been adopted. Abraham Lincoln defines the term 'democracy' as, "The government of the people, for the people and by the people." The government by the people means that such people would be prepared by the education who can provide the leadership in the various fields. In education system, there are tests at every stage—primary, secondary, college and university. The function of test is to filtering the people who can reach at the top level which may provide the leadership and will govern the people. Thus, education is a filtering process in the democracy.

Education is for Future or Futurology: The purpose of Education is to prepare people for future not for today. Those who are admitted or entered into Education at elementary stage whole come out after 16 or 20 years to enter into their lives or in society. They would be capable to adjust, acquire the place and can pace with the world. Thus, the education is given for future always. The orientation of education is towards future life situation.

Education as an Art as well as Science: The art is concerned with doing aspect of a phenomenon whereas science tries to understand its nature and structure. The science involves the observations and experiences regarding a phenomenon. The doing aspect of education is to have all round development of a child make him complete man or most civilized and cultured man, but education also tries to understand his abilities and potentialities and the requirements of society and needs of a nation. The frame of reference of the development these environment and nature of child is to evolve education process for this development. Hence education is both science as well as art.

Education as Positive Science: Education involves observation experience and understanding process of child development. The educational process creates conducive environment—physical, biological, social and cultural for the modification of desirable behaviours which are socially acceptable. Therefore, desirable behaviours are always positive. The discipline of psychology includes both type of learning positive as well as negative whereas education is concerned with positive learning. Similarly the environment contributes in the development of man material but sometimes it has the adverse effect on man and material. Most of disciplines of the human edifice involve both type of knowledge positive as well as negative, but education discipline concerns with only positive as well negative, but education of the child and the environment. It has the clinical or remedial function for improving the environment for the desirable change of the behaviour of child.

According to Indian philosophy, Education means 'mukti' i.e., to get rid of from the cycle of death and birth, i.e., Savidya Vinarmukata. Education means to achieve the highest aim of life, truth, beauty and goodness. It is the ultimate aim of life and also the values of life.

Thus, the education has several meanings of this term. In the context of social, education means as an independent field of study or course of study like other course of study or subject content of education.

The Discipline

A discipline in the generally accepted sense of the word means field of study which has a well defined content and a technique of its own together with a unique system of values. It is implicit in this concept of a 'Learned discipline that it constitutes an important part of man's cultural heritage and that its pursuit results in a specific enrichment of the human mind. Most of the subjects taught in universities and college are 'discipline' in the sense. These have been traditionally accepted by the academic world and will continue to be accepted for some time to come.

When new directions of thought emerge from man's struggle and effort with life and environment or through his creative mental efforts and acquire in time a degree of stability, a new discipline but during the course of its development it evolves its own distinct characteristics and acquires status in the intellectual world. Sometimes two or more branches of knowledge merge at their upper reaches and this merge at the highest point works downwards to the lower levels and may even after the whole pattern of the parent discipline. The newly evolved pattern sometimes proves its validity in practice, and may become a nucleus for a new discipline.

There may be a social and professional activity which on account of its importance becomes an area of application for several disciplines, and this common area in course of time may come to be recognized as an independent field of study. Examples of such bodies of knowledge developing round and important professional or social activity are medical science growing round the art of healing, agriculture growing round the farmers occupation, technology developing from craft and education growing round teaching.

The important thing to realize is that the necessary conditions for the growth of discipline are:

Freedom to Develop : New ideas or new thinking; New synthesis and analysis; New horizons and new field.

Increasing Opportunities to Experiment with Them : When a number of discipline converge into an important field of social activity, this activity gives a new meaning a two-way-flow of ideas and resulting in the enrichment of both. It is an inter-disciplinary approach in different disciplines.

The Characteristics: Every discipline has some specific features. It may be distinguished from other disciplines on the basis of these features. Every discipline has the following characteristics:

1. Every discipline has own specific content or subject-matter or course of study at different levels of teaching.
2. It is related to some professional and social activity. For example, agriculture is related to 'farming'; psychology deals with the 'behaviour'; chemistry is related to 'matter'.
3. Every discipline has its own method of study. For example, physics and chemistry's content matter is studied through laboratory or experiment method. History requires another method such as library method.

4. Each discipline has its own field of investigation For example, researches of botany are concerned with plants and zoology with animals.
5. Each discipline has its own method of investigation. Science subjects employ the experimental method whereas social sciences employ survey method.
6. Scholars of every discipline have unique ideas and horizons of thinking and have impact of the discipline on their life style.
7. Every discipline has its own conduct.

Education as a Discipline

Mainly two criteria can be used to examine that Education is the full-fledged discipline in edifice of human knowledge: (1) General criteria and (2) Specific criteria. The details are as follows.

General Criteria: These criteria are of three types- (i) Preservation, (ii) Transmission, and (iii) Advancement of the content.

(i) The preservation of content of each discipline is being done in the social and institutional libraries. In each type of library, we have separate section of Educational books, Journals, Hand-books, Encyclopaedia etc.

(ii) The transmission of content of each discipline is being done in the schools, colleges and universities. There are B.Ed., M.Ed. and M.Phil. classes for teaching Education content. The content of Education is taught at two levels professional at B.Ed. M.Ed. levels and as academic subject at Inter, B.A. and M.A. levels.

(iii) In very discipline content is not only preserved and transmitted but also enriched or advanced through research work. The research works are being done in education at individual level for Ph.D. D Phil. and D. Litt. degrees. The N.C.E.R.T. is an organization at national level to conduct research work and provides financial help for research projects.

In most of the Indian universities, there is separate Education faculty because its nature is both theoretical as well as practical. Therefore it can not be placed in Science faculty nor Arts faculty, hence separate faculty.

Specific Criteria: The following are the main types of the criteria:

(i) Education has its own independent content like other disciplines. Education includes: Aims of education, Theory of education, Curriculum, Teaching method, Co-curricular activities, Teacher and students, Discipline, Text-books examination, Teaching theory, Teaching models, Teacher behaviour, Teacher education, Educational administration and organization, etc. The main areas are schools and classroom teaching.

(ii) The whole content of Education is directly or indirectly related to 'Teaching activities'. Teaching is both social as well as professional activity. It is science as well as art. Therefore, education has its own faculty at university level.

(iii) Education content is both theoretical and practical. Therefore its methods are scientific as well as descriptive. A student of education has to prepare theory and he has to practise in classroom teaching situation.

(iv) Education has its own field of investigation. A scholar of education has to select a problem from school and college or teaching learning situation. The purpose of educational research is to contribute new knowledge which can be applied to the development work of teaching.

(v) Education has its own methods of research. Scientific and non-scientific methods are employed in educational researches. The experimental survey and historical methods are used in educational research.

(vi) Education has its unique impact on student and research workers. They have the main concern of developmental process.

It is evident on the basis of above criteria that Education is also a full-fledged discipline of human knowledge, though it is an emerging discipline. But persons do not admit it as discipline, because Education content mainly includes : Educational psychology, educational philosophy, educational sociology, economics of education etc. Thus, education has borrowed the contents of other disciplines. Secondly education refers to a teacher education programme in which teachers are trained for their profession of teaching.

The content of education is being enriched through inter-disciplinary approach. The above content is the contribution of this approach. The approach of inter-disciplinary is being employed in other disciplines also e.g., Bio-chemistry, Geo-physics, Economic-Geography, Agriculture-Botany, Econometrics, Social-psychology, Industrial-psychology, etc. This approach has been discussed and illustrated in the following paragraphs.

Inter-disciplinary Approach

This is a recent approach for advancing new knowledge in the edifice of any discipline. This approach is now being used in teaching as well as research activity. The term 'Inter-disciplinary approach' refers to the interaction of two or more disciplines.

In the present time our social and professional problems are too complex. They cannot be solved by the experts of one discipline. It requires that the experts of various disciplines should work jointly to provide workable solution of the problems. The solution of the problem will be common contribution of the disciplinary which have worked together.

This approach can be understood by an example in the field of behavioural sciences. After independence education has been made compulsory for all. An expert of sociology has pointed out that the mass education has created a problem as a result of social change. The young generation is leaving their parental profession after acquiring education. In this way social process would be distributed. The expert of Sociology refers this problem to the educationists to find out the solution of the problem. The experts of education have included a new vocational aim of eduction. The vocational institutions are preparing the personnel for various jobs : engineers, doctors, mechanics, teachers, etc. The mechanical engineers are working in the factories of Bata and Tata. This knowledge will be considered as sociology of education. It will be included in both disciplines: Sociology and Education.

Another example which illustrates the interaction of three disciplines in the area of behavioural sciences. The education is for both boys and girls and they would like to serve in any department. Thus, husband and wife both are in job who will look after their children during office time. This problem has been identified by an expert of sociology and refers to an educationist to provide the solution. He has proposed a new ladder to the system of education. There should be pre-primary education, it is meant for 2 to 6 years children. A child psychologist can suggest the method, content and technique to deal with 2 to 6 years children. Thus, the experts of three disciplines : Education, Sociology and Psychology are interacting on this problem. The solution of the problem will be the new knowledge of these disciplines. It will be termed 'social psychology of education and special education.'

The financial aspects of these problems can be suggested by the expert of Economics. The Nursery and KG. schools have been started. These are self-supporting institutions. The parents can afford to pay fees. This knowledge is termed as economics of education.

The education has its foundation on other disciplines. The aims of education are given by philosophy and methods of teaching and techniques are devised by psychology.

Concept of Integrated Education

Integration is another expression used to mean mainstreaming. Integration cannot be reduced simply to an educational issue or employment issue. Its achievement will require the successful coordination of a whole series of transitions for the handicapped, ranging from early identification, to early intervention, to school programme to community, jobs and finally to community living.

An approach to integration that takes the individual needs of the special child into full consideration may result in one or more of following:

Physical Integration : Planning for the location of special programmes in school buildings with regular education programmes.

Social Integration : Planning for regular personal interactions between students who are handicaps and those who do not.

Academic Integration : Planning to ensure students with an without handicaps simultaneously use school resources.

Societal Integration : Planning designed to enable students with moderate and severe handicaps to work, live, and spend issuer time with their fellow non-handicapped citizens.

Meaning of Integration

The term 'integration' means:

1. Providing special services within the regular schools.
2. Supporting regular teachers and administrators.
3. Taking parents' concerns seriously.
4. Having students with disabilities follow the same schedule as non-disabled students.
5. Involving disabled students in as many academic classes and extra-curricular activities as possible including music, art, field trips, assemblies and exercises.
6. Arranging for disabled students to use library, playground, and other facilities at the same time as non-disabled students.
7. Encouraging helper and buddy relationships between disabled and non-disabled students.
8. Arranging for disabled students to receive their education in regular community environments when appropriate.
9. Teaching all children to understand and accept human differences.
10. Enrolling disabled children in the same schools they would attend if they did not have disabilities.
11. Providing an appropriate individualised programme.

The Priority

The National Policy on Education, 1986, has given priority on an equity basis in the field of education and recommends to provide equal opportunity to all not only for access but also for success. "Equalisation of educational opportunity" includes the opening of schools within walking distance, providing communities to schools, reducing the dropout rate and increasing the retention rate of children through various measures. Besides all the above facts, provisions should be made for non-formal education centres for non-attending children and various ancillary services to facilitate schooling of children.

The very term integration signifies the process of interaction of disabled children and normal children in the same educational setting. Of course, there are two separate terms which are, very often, synonymously used with integration. These terms are: (i) Mainstreaming and (ii) Normalisation.

Basically Integrated education is the result of Mainstreaming movement in America. This movement makes provision for mainstreaming the disabled children, in other words, mainstreaming refers to integrating handicapped or disabled children into regular classes and helping them through specialized techniques.

Again, sometimes integration is interchangeably used with Normalisation. The reason is that in integrated education, the disabled children are treated with normal children. There is every limitation to think that these two groups are different from any aspect.

Moreover, integrated education is an educational programme in which exceptional children attend classes with normal children on either a part of full-time basis. Such a combination may be taken as social integration or academic integration or both. Some educationists think that integrated education is the placement of the disabled children in ordinary schools with some specialised educational help and services.

The definition given by Stephens and Blackhurt reveals "Mainstreaming is the education of mildly handicapped children in the regular classroom. It is based on the philosophy of equal opportunity that implemented through individual planning to promote appropriate learning achievement and social normalisation."

Meaning of Integrated Education: Integrated education movement flows directly from the recognition of equal rights for all citizens and equal educational opportunity for all children with special needs, their education should be provided in the least restrictive and most effective environment. The least restrictive environment which disabled children need can only be provided in general schools. Thus, integrated eduction refers to education of disabled children in common with other in general schools with provision for extra help for the disabled. It refers to integrating the physically and extra help for the disabled. It refers to integrating the physically and mentally handicapped children with the non-disabled children in regular classroom and providing specialized services to meet their special needs.

Four key process are important in integrated education

(1) Normalization,

(2) Deinstitutionalisation,

(3) Mainstreaming, and

(4) Inclusion.

The details of these process are given below :

Normalization is the process of creating a learning and social environment as normal as possible for the exceptional child and adult.

Deinstitutionalization is the process of releasing as many exceptional children and adult as possible from the confinement of residential institutions into their local community.

Mainstreaming is the process of bringing exceptional children into daily contact with non-exceptional children in an educational setting.

Inclusion is the process of bringing exceptional children of whatever condition into the general classroom for their education.

Integration is the opposite of segregation. Segregation is the process by which a special group in society is identified and gradually the social and physical distance between this group and the rest increases. A feeling of otherness develops in the group which alienates the former group.

Integration is the process of bringing the 'part' (the handicapped to the 'whole' (the society). The indicators of integration are that (i) handicapped persons enjoy the same right as the rest; (ii) have equal opportunity for growth and development in environmental conditions available to the rest; (iii) have access to the quality of life like any other citizen and (iv) are treated as equal partners in the community. The process begins by physical proximity, i.e., reduction of physical distance. It continues with mutual sharing of the physical facilities and progresses towards reduction of social distance. The reduction of the physical and social distance results in social integration in which the groups become equal partners in the community.

The Characteristics: It has the following main features:

(1) Integrated education is an education setting in which disabled children receive education along with non-disabled children in the regular classroom with provision for extra help for the disabled. Thus, integrated education is a practical solution to the problem of segregation of disabled children.

(2) Integrated education is not alternative to special education. Rather it is complementary to special education. Only mildly and sometimes moderately handicapped children can be enrolled in integrated schools. Severely handicapped children who are enrolled in special schools can also be admitted in integrated schools after they acquire communication skills, daily living skills, study skills, and other pre-requisite skills.

(3) It is designed to provide equal education opportunity to the disabled and to prepare them for independent living like other members of the society.

(4) It provides the least restrictive and the most effective environment to disabled children so that they may grow and develop like other children.

(5) It is an educational setting which promotes a healthy social relationship between the disabled and the non-disabled children and reduces the physical distance between them through equal participation in social activities.

(6) It is an arrangement in which disabled children are considered as important as their non-disabled peers.

(7) It accepts the disabled child as an individual in his own rights.

(8) It ensures civic rights to the disabled in order to raise their standards of living.

(9) It is an economic system for the education of disabled children and solves the psychological problems which these children face in special educational settings.

(10) It is based on cooperative efforts of regular classroom teacher, the specialist teacher, parents and community members.

(11) It is a viable approach to attain the goals of universalisation of elementary education by providing equality of educational and development opportunities to the disabled who have been denied equality so far.

Needs of Integrated Education: Many educationists nullify the idea of special education on the grounds that in never equalises educational opportunities, rather it creates a feeling of differentiation among children. Special classes create a feeling of inferiority complex among disabled children. Recently, psychologists think that integrated education should be introduced in our school system to provide equal opportunity for education of all children. Educationists justify this type of education under following points.

Normal Mental Growth is Possible: Psychological complexes are prominent under special educational settings. The disabled children think that they are inferior to others for which they are being treated separately. In integrated educational system, the disabled get the chance to enjoy along with normal children from developing psychological complexes. Every child feels that he is, in no way, inferior to anyone. Thus, the integrated educational system leads to normal mental growth of children.

Social Integration is Ensured: Certain social qualities are very much pertinent with the disabled children when they tend to get education with normal ones. Children get wider community integrated set-up and this is conducive for the disabled ones to learn social virtues along with normal ones. These social virtues include love, affection, cooperation, sympathy and adjustments etc. The students in integrated settings not only get special attention but are also taught in a wider educational arena.

Integrated Education is Less Expensive : No doubt, special educational set-ups are very costly and expensive. Besides that, training programmes for special teachers and teaching experts are time-consuming. Considered from another angle, integrated education is less expensive and advantageous. To establish a special school, generally we seek the assistance from various comers, i.e., trained personnel, experts, physiotherapists, doctors etc. Again, keeping a disabled child in a normal class is less expensive than placing him in a special set-up.

Integration is Possible through Integrated Education : Social interaction is pronounced in integrated educational set-ups in comparison with special educational set-ups. A natural environment is created for interaction of the disabled with non-disabled peers. Learning to adjust in this environment, to accept and to be accepted by their friends are possible through integrated education. The students in normal set-ups also acquire a sense of competency and emotional adjustment.

Academic Integration is Possible : Academic integration is possible through integrated set-ups. Educationists believe that once a child is placed in a special school, below par academic abilities of the disabled ones under the teacher are developed. The teaching experts always have the idea that the students in the special schools or the disabled children are under-achievers. Owing to the placement of children in special schools, they fail to score well in academic studies. In a way, we can say that, with a sophisticated environment and up-to-date curriculum, integrated education brings academic integration.

Principle of Equality is Maintained : Particularly in India, constitutional provisions were made to universalise the elementary education and to provide educational facilities to the disabled children. The very objective of equality should be maintained through integrated set-ups, so that no student would think himself inferior to the other.

Various Levels

Various types of integrated education for disabled are found. Among them seven important types of models are worth noting here.

(1) The first category of integration is the full time integration in normal schools. In regular classes, the teachers teach the disabled children throughout the day. Students also get support from teaching experts only when they are in need.

(2) Another category of such children attend regular classes. But some classes are suspended due to the arrangement so special classes.

(3) The third category includes the education of the disabled in a special class. But the students are required to maintain their attendance at normal classes. Again, they have to engage themselves in co-curricular activities of the normal school. .

(4) The fourth category of integration includes the education in residential schools with some lessons in neighbouring normal schools.

(5) The fifth model integration includes reverse integration. Here a large number of normal children are placed with the disabled children to ensure academic and non-academic participation among themselves.

(6) Education in normal classes with home tuition or home-bound programme is included in the sixth category of integrated education.

(7) The seventh category of integration is the short term education in hospitals or in other establishments.

The Scope

Integrated education is proposed to provide educational facilities to the following types of disabled children.

1. Children with locomotor handicap (orthopaedically handicapped).
2. Mildly and moderately hearing impaired.
3. Partially sighted children including one-eyed children.
4. Educable mentally retarded.
5. Children with multiple handicaps (blind and orthopaedic, hearing impaired and orthopaedic, EMR and orthopaedic, visually impaired and hard of hearing).

6. Children with learning disability.
7. Blind children who have completed preparation in braille reading and writing, orientation and mobility training.
8. Deaf children who have acquired communication skills and learnt speech reading.

The scope of integrated education includes pre-schools training for the disabled, counselling for parents, primary education, secondary education, +2 levels of education and vocational courses.

Concepts of Mainstreaming

The concept of mainstreaming owes its origin in the work and ideas of Samuel Gridley Howe, an American Physician, who took keen interest in the education of blind and deaf children. As early as 1851, Howe had stressed that blind children should be educated in regular schools because of the social advantages of such a setting. He was advocating in favour of "exposing the disabled to an educational experience as close to that of non-disabled as possible." In other words, he was advocating in favour of mainstreaming the handicapped children in the general schools. It was in (1975) that the concept of mainstreaming was introduced in the "Education for All the Handicapped Act (USA)."

Mainstreaming refers to an educational placement procedure and process in which disabled children are educated in the least restrictive environment to satisfactorily provide for their educational and related needs. The concept of mainstreaming is based on the following convictions:

1. Disabled children have a wide range of special educational needs.
2. The special education needs of disabled children very greatly in intensity and duration.
3. There is a continuum of educational settings which may be appropriate for an individual child's needs.
4. Disable children should be educated with non-disabled children.
5. Special classes, special schools and other ways of segregating the disabled from the non-disabled may be necessary only when the special needs of disabled children

cannot be satisfied in general schools even with the provision of supplementary aids and services.

According to Kauffman et al (1975) "Mainstreaming refers to the temporal instructional and social integration of eligible exceptional children with normal peers based on an ongoing, individually determined, educational planning and programming process and requires clarifications of responsibility among regular and special education, administrative, instructional and supportive personnel."

Components of Mainstreaming

According to this operational definition, there are three components of mainstreaming:

Integration in Education : Integration is the opposite of segregations. Segregation is the process by which children with special needs or the disabled children are identified as a separate group and are educated in special schools in the company of other disabled children of the same category being alienated from the parents, siblings, non-disabled peers and their own community. Gradually the social and physical distance between this group and the rest increases. A feeling of 'otherness' develops in the group. Integration is the process of bringing the 'parts' (the handicapped children) to the whole (the society). The indicators of integration are that disabled children enjoy the same right as the rest, have equal opportunity for growth and development in the least restrictive and most effective environment, have access to the quality of life like any other children, and are treated as equal partners in the school and community. The process begins by reduction of physical distance. It continues with mutual sharing of the physical facilities and proceeds towards reduction of social distance. The education of the physical and social distance results in social integration in which the groups become equal partners in the community.

Integration is basic to mainstreaming. Integration should be temporal, instructional and social. The child with special needs should be placed in a regular class with other children for a period of time which may vary from two periods to six periods, every day. Along with temporal integration there should be social and instructional integration. The special child should be accepted by his peers, regular teachers and should participate in all social activities of the school. Instructional integration is the most difficult component for mainstrearning. The special child's instruction should be so designed that he participates in classroom activities with normal peers yet does not have difficulties in learning. The efficacy of mainstreaming depends in part upon the amount of time the special child spends in the regular classroom, the extent to which he is accepted by normal peers and participates in social activities, and the success of instruction in the regular classroom.

Educational Planning and Programming : Simply placing the special child in the regular classroom with other children is not enough for mainstreaming to succeed. The educational programme of the mainstreamed child needs to be planned carefully. Special efforts must be made to plan the programme for the unique needs of such children so that they can achieve the maximum benefits of participation in the regular classroom. For this to occur, supportive personnel and services should be provided both to the child and the regular class teacher.

Clarification of Responsibilities : In some mainstreaming situations the regular teacher must assume total responsibility for the special child. But usually resource teachers are appointed in mainstreaming situations. When both regular teachers and the resource teachers are working with the child, there may be confusion regarding who is responsible for what. The child's total needs can be met when their respective roles are clearly and carefully delineated. The efficacy of mainstreaming depends upon both the regular teacher and the resource teacher discharging their respective responsibilities sincerely.

Characteristics of Mainstreaming

In summarizing what has been discussed above it can be said that the effectiveness of mainstreaming depends on the following conditions:

(1) There should be temporal, social and instructional integration of handicapped children.

(2) Educational programmes for the mainstreamed handicapped children should be planned carefully to meet their special educational needs.
(3) Supportive services and personnel should be provided both to the children and the regular class teacher.
(4) The responsibilities of the regular teacher resource teacher should be clearly delineated.
(5) The regular class teacher should ultimately take the responsibility of educating the handicapped children in the general school.
(6) Only mildly handicapped children should be exposed to mainstreaming situation. Severely handicapped children who have completed their preparation and learnt the pre-academic skills, daily living skills, communication skills, and other pre-requisite skills in special school settings may be later mainstreamed in the general schools.
(7) The regular teacher must accept and agree to implement mainstreaming in their classroom and schools.
(8) The regular teachers must prepare themselves for their new and difficult role. The authorities must arrange to provide in-service and pre-service training on characteristics and special educational needs of handicapped children to the regular teachers.
(9) In all cases parents should be involved in the care, training, and placement of their handicapped children.

Over the years, things have improved, diagnosis has become multi-disciplinary, education has become the emphasis, trained professionals are available. Hence, the need for integration and mainstreaming is more felt. Mainstreaming is an approach that emphasizes integration and as such it is the antithesis of the earlier institutionalisation movement which emphasized segregation. But not until the 1970s it was thought fit to integrate retarded children, even though it was known earlier that special classes were not superior to regular classes, and that placement in special classes stigmatised those children. Hence, efforts are directed toward a less restricted educational environment.

The Council for Exceptional Children (CEC) has specified the essentials of mainstreaming the mildly disabled.

1. Providing the most appropriate education for each child in the least mainstreaming the mildly disabled.
2. Concentrating on specific educational needs than on labelling.

DEINSTITUTIONALISATION

'Deinstitutionalisation' means that removing retarded persons from institutions and placing them in other environments. 'Mainstreaming' means educating retarded persons as much as possible in classes with non-retarded persons. 'Integration' basically means mainstreaming. 'Normalisation' means that the individual's total environment should be as close as possible to that of non-handicapped person's environment Segregation is only desirable when the nature of the handicap is such that education in regular classes with the use of supplementary aids and service cannot be achieved satisfactorily.

Deinstitutionalisation includes three process (1) reversing institutionalisation by finding alternative placement, (2) returning to that community all residents who have developed the skiils necessary for successful transition, (3) establishing residential environments that protect rights and reports on deinstitutionalisation; (a) placement in nursing homes where the quality of care is less than at institutions, (b) primarily medication was the treatment, (c) readmission to institutions since community facilities are not available, (d) poor medical diagnosis, (e) regression in adaptive behaviour, and (f) incompetent staff to look after the inmates.

Deinstitutionalisation is a trend which grew in reaction to institutionalisation. In institutions, disabled children were considered physically or mentally ill and received treatment but no care and education. Around 1800 such institutions sprouted and as they grew in size they become less cost, effective and housed people without much of treatment. The trend continued. In the 1950s and 1960s a number of social movements took place to help the retarded e.g. President Kennedy's approach to mental illness which led to the establishment of community centres which provided impatient and outpatient care, treatment, consultation and education.

INNOVATIONS IN SPECIAL EDUCATION

Innovative steps have been taken and are in operation in recent years to make mainstreaming and/or integration effective. Teachers who know how to individualise instruction will have little difficulty, integrating disabled pupils in the classroom. Individualised instruction in a classroom does not mean 30 students doing 30 different things at the same time. It means that after general discussion, the class can be divided into three to five small groups for part of their instruction. It is in the small groups that the most pressing needs of the children can be met.

According to LK. Devies, "Teacher should be managers of learning, facilitators or of the learning experience rather than disbursers of information. All teachers need time to work with individual pupils or groups of pupils. Experienced teachers keep catch up time in the few minutes before recess during lunch, or after school to help those pupils who need extra instruction, During this time they also help children to begin homework."

Group Instruction for Teaching: Using small group instruction is another way to make mainstreaming more effective. Before using this technique the teachers should have sufficiently developed their classroom grouping skills to enable small pupil groups to function smoothly. They should be taught how to work in groups. The following instructions could be a starting point.

1. Choose your two most trustworthy pupils.
2. Assign them each a specific task to be completed outside class, such as preparing for science demonstration.
3. Excuse the pupils from regular class work. Make the assignment a choice one.
4. Have the pupils put on their demonstration.
5. Compliment pupils for a job well done.
6. Get ready for complaints from others for such choice assignments. Now the stage is set.
7. Select a reliable pupil and one of the less reliable ones.
8. Gradually extend this procedure over five or six weeks to more and more small groups.
9. Make sure that having a group assignment remain a privilege, this will encourage good behaviour.

Mastery Learning Strategy: Mastery learning techniques offer a systematic way to give pupils longer periods of time to master skills and concepts without penalty. In the long run mastery learning can save time by reducing the time for revision. Hoom (1964) has found that mastery learning hinges on pupil preserverance and aptitude, and on the clarity of the teacher's instructions. Pupil's perseverance tends to increase as pupils realise that they are learning.

In order to use mastery learning the following steps may be used. Use Mastery Learning by:

1. Restricting mastery learning to the basic curriculum.
2. Beginning with the most essential basic skills.
3. Providing pupils with a short list of skills to learn.
4. Having each pupil study, practice, self-test, recycle with final checking (testing) by the teacher until mastery is achieved.
5. Initially, allowing about 10 to 15 percent more time for handicapped children.
6. Drawing on assistance of tutors from other grades or the same grade, teacher aids, parent volunteers, programmed instructional units, micro computer drills.

Mastery learning is an optimistic theory about teaching and learning that any teacher can virtually get all students to learn excellently, swiftly and self-confidently. Both exceptional and non-exceptional children can benefit from the system of instruction if it is systematic, if the tasks are broken into small steps, its goals are clearly stated, if sufficient time is given to the learners, and there is some criteria of what constitutes mastery.

Bloom asserts that native intelligence matters in learning. But when instruction is matched to learner's present level of functioning, all students can learn fast. Mastery learning programmes are used successfully in special education programme under IER. Some of the materials used in special education programmes under IER. Some of the materials used in special education classes are based on mastery learning principles. In order to make it more effective a resource room with a resource teacher are required.

Role of Teacher

A teacher always tries to bring out the best in each child. When children stay away from their family, the teacher is the person who contributes a lot for them. Again teachers for deaf and disabled children have special roles in schools. Besides some additional qualities, they must have the primary aim of teaching and guidance. To make the children interested in the class is very important for a teacher. The teacher must try to satisfy the needs of the children as far as practicable, so that the relationship becomes strong. He should remain alert always in order to meet the needs of the students.

Again, the teacher should have pleasant personalities. They must try to develop a tendency to understand the child and the situation. Readiness to work hard is highly appreciated. Good teachers always have knowledge of up-to-date methods of teaching. Some teachers must develop skills in teaching and handling the problems of exceptional children.

No doubt, the education of exceptional children either in special school or in an integrated set-up depends on the efficiency of the teacher. The following steps are noteworthy for effective teaching:

(1) Problems of children should be intimated to the parents by the teacher within a minimum span of time.

(2) Records of every child should be maintained properly by the teacher, so that a programme of action can be executed immediately.

(3) A teacher must have a clear concept of special education and integrated education.

(4) Remedial teaching programmes should be worked out by the teachers which may be conducive for children with specific educational needs.

(5) A teacher should prepare instructional materials to teach in integrated set-ups.

(6) Cooperation of other faculty members must be sought by the teacher to provide best possible eduction for disabled children.

Emphatically speaking, education of exceptional children either in special schools or in common schools, is a tough task. Their early identification, assessment of disability, enrolment in school, specialised help and successful placement in a vocation and life is not limited to primary schools or secondary schools only. Through joint effort and in collaboration with various departments, effective implementation of integrated education is possible.

EXERCISE

1. Define the term 'Education.' Justify that education is an independent field of study.
2. Explain the term 'Independent Field of Study.' Justify that special education is the result of this approach.
3. Define the term 'Special Education'. Enumerate the characteristics and scope of special education.
4. Define and explain 'Integrated Education'. Enumerate the characteristics and levels of integrated education.
5. Compare among Special Education Integrated Education and Mainstreaming.
6. Explain the term 'Inter-disciplinary Approach' to education. Illustrates with rentable examples.
7. Justify that 'Special Education' is the result of interdisciplinary approach. It is an interaction among the disciplines: Psychology. Physiology, Anatomy, Medicine, Sociology, Social Welfare and Education etc.
8. Write short notes on the following:
   (a) Special Education
   (b) Integrated Education
   (c) Mainstreaming
   (d) Deinstitutionalization.

5

Historical Background

The education of disabled children never received such amount of consideration and special efforts were made by government and non-government agencies in past as in present days. The attitude of the community in general and the attitude of parents in particular towards the education of the disabled have undergone change with the development of society and civilisation.

In the first phase, disabled children were treated with hostility and were neglected. They were considered as 'Curve of God' and a burden for the parents. They were often killed by their parents.

In the second phase the disabled children were kept in protection and wardship. Mankind was subjected to a health that "the disabled are useless, incapable of doing anything on their own, a species to be pitied and looked after as long as they are alive." Thus, no attempt was made for their education, training, habilitation, and rehabilitation.

In the next phase, an attempt was made for their education. But disabled children were considered distinct from their peers. They were considered to be incapable of receiving education in general schools. Thus, for the first time special schools and institutions were established in different countries for the education and training of such children. They were educated in special schools being separated from their parents and their non-disabled peers.

In the second half of the twentieth century, new thinking and new realization have opened new directions for education of disabled children. It is now realised that a disabled child is not a different kind of person. He is a child with special needs. Like all other members of the society, the disabled must have the same rights to education, work and full participation in the society. It is also recognised that the disabled, particularly those with mild to moderate degree of disability and the orthopaedically handicapped, can be educated along with their non-disabled peers in general schools with provision for extra help. Moreover, education of disabled children in common with non-disabled children in general schools has been found to be an economical system in terms of expenses and coverage. These realizations, recognition and thinking on the part of educationists, planners and teachers have led to the conceptualisation of integrated education for the disabled children.

Special Education in other Countries

There have always been exceptional children, but there have not always been special educational services to meet their needs. The historical roots of special education are found in Europe and America primarily in the 19th century. In ancient civilization handicapped children were either killed or subject to abuse and neglect. Prior to the 19th century there were isolated instances of acceptance, kindly care, and education of disabled children.

Systematic efforts to provide special education to handicapped children started in the 10th century in Europe and America. Most of the originators of special education were European physicians. But the Americans who were initially concerned with the care and training of the handicapped kept themselves informed about the development that took place in Europe. Even some Americans used to visit Europe to get first-hand knowledge about the education of handicapped children. It is a fact that the European physicians were initially concerned about the education of mentally retarded children. Similarly much of the initial work in the field of special education in America entered around deaf children and blind children.

'The history of special education does not indicate "Europe good, America bad". But it is true that important ideas in special education found their way for Europe to America. Many Europeans and American physicians and educators contributed greatly to the development of special education, most prominent among them were:

1. J.M. G. Itard, Physician
2. Samuel Gridley Howe
3. E. Seguin, Teacher of MR
4. T.H. Gallaudet
5. Sigmund Freud
6. Phillipe Pinel,
7. Ann Sullivan

Development of Special Education in Europe: J.M.G. Itard's contribution. Itard, a French physician, is the person to whom most historians trace the beginning of special education. In the beginning years of 19th century, Itard set about to educate a wild boy of 11 or 12, named Victor. The boy was apparently abandoned in a forest in Southern France at the age of 3 or 4. He managed to survive until his capture. At the time of capture was animal like in appearance and behaviour. He was naked, dirty, scarred, and unable to speak, and he selected food by smell. Itard could not make him normal, but did dramatically improve his behaviour through patient and systematic educative procedure.

Itard was the originator of instructional devices, the inventor of behaviour modification techniques, the first speech specialist, creator of oral education of the deaf, and father of special education for the mentally retarded and the physically handicapped. His work with Victor firmly established that the retarded could learn and improve.

Seguin's Contribution : Seguin is known as the greatest teacher of the mentally deficient. Being influenced by the achievements of Itard he established the first public school for the feeble-minded in Paris in 1837. In 1846 he published his classic textbook 'Idiocy and its Treatment by the Physiological Method.' His concept of education was the promotion of the harmonious physical, intellectual, and moral developments of the child. His techniques and materials later became the basis for the so-called Montessori Method. Seguin migrated to America and worked in collaboration with Samuel Howe for the education of mentally retarded.

The sensational discoveries and revolutionary ideas of Itard, Seguin and their successors during the 19th century which have formed the foundation for present day special education are as follows:

(1) Individualised instruction for the mentally retarded children.
(2) A carefully sequenced series of educational tasks for the MR.
(3) Emphasis on stimulation.
(4) Meticulous arrangement of the child's environment.
(5) Immediate reward for correct performance.
(6) Tutoring in functional skills.
(7) A belief that everyone should be educated to the greatest extent possible.
(8) An assumption that every child can improve to some degree.

Development of Special Education in America: It is true that much of the initial work in the development of special education took place in Europe. But there were many Americans who contributed greatly during those early years.

Louis Braille's Contributions: Louis Braille was the most important figure in the history of education of the blind. Braille, who became blind due to an accident during his early childhood, developed a revolutionary system of reading and writing for the blind. The Braille method is still recognised as the most appropriate method of reading and writing for the blind.

Howe's Contribution : Samuel Gridly Howe was one of the first physicians in the United States to develop keen interest in the education of blind and deaf children. His phenomenal success with one of his pupils, Lattra Bridagmen, a deaf-blind-mute, earned him international fame.

Anne Sullivan's Contribution : Sullivan was a student of Howe. She was greatly influenced by her teacher's training methods. Although she was visually handicapped, she served as Helen Kellers tutor. Helen Keller was deaf-blind-mute. Sullivan's dedicated efforts could bring astonishing results. Helen quickly learned the names of objects and events in her environment. By the age of ten, she learned to say aloud "I-am-not-dumb-now". Later she became a graduate and wrote a number of books.

Gallaudet's Contribution : Thomas Hopkins Gallaudet had keen interest in the education of the deaf. He established the first American residential school for the deaf in 1817 in Hartford. The Gallaudet College in Washington D.C., which is the only college for the deaf was named in his honour.

Fall and Rise of Special Education

There were many other Europeans and American physicians and educators whose fascinating and brilliant careers helped to shape special education. In fact, the early years of special education were vibrant with the pulse of new ideas of great physicians and educators. The results they achieved with handicapped children were truly remarkable. But despite the energy, optimism, and achievements of these early leaders, special education lost its momentum during the last part of the 19th century. Pessimism took hold, humane and effective treatment turned to ineffective institutionalisation and human warehousing, hope turned to despair. The special schools which were opened in the late 1800s became dumping grounds for all kinds of misfits. Many factors were responsible for the decline of special education such as:

(1) Too much expectation of parents for their disabled children to achieve miraculous cure too soon.

(2) Total failure of special education personnel in some cases.

(3) Disagreement among professionals about the appropriate method of education.

(4) Lack of financial support for providing special education services to a large number of disabled children.

(5) Social, political, and economic turmoil resulting from the civil war.

(6) The idea that the handicapped were inherently inferior and not amenable to improvement thought education.

(7) The influence of Charles Darwin's theory of Evolution, the survival of the fittest.

After the World War II special eduction made a come back with wealthy and powerful people like President Kennedy and President Johnson taking interest in the education of all handicapped. Education of the handicapped was initialy considered as a privilege. With the development of democracy and socialism in different countries of the world education was considered to be a basic right of the child. This realization paved the way for mainstreaming disabled children.

Provision in Legislation

Over the years, the objective of the struggle has changed from survival to equality. The concept of equality includes the rights of the disabled as approved by the United General Assembly in 1975.

Despite inclusion in the U.N. Charter, these rights have not become a practical reality for millions of handicapped persons throughout the developing world.

India is committed to the welfare and uplift of its less privileged citizens. Towards this goal, several provisions have been included in the Indian Constitution for care and protection of disadvantaged groups.

Exploratory efforts began in 1980 to suggest a comprehensive law for the disabled. These continued and intensified in this decade. The goals of 1981 which was declared as an International year for Disabled Persons (IYDP) with equality and full participation.

The Baharul Islam Committee (1989) felt that the rights of the handicapped should be protected. The general purpose of the proposed legislation is to promote the welfare of physically and mentally handicapped persons so that they can lead a dignified, full and productive life by giving them equal opportunities enshrined in article 16 and 46 of the Constitution of India.

Through the proposed legislation, the state should be made responsible with regard to the fundamental policies for the physically and mentally handicapped through proper medical care, habitation, rehabilitation training, protection, education and vocational training, recreation, promotion of employment, social security etc. by providing various benefits and provisions. Rehabilitation Council of India Act, 1992 has been enacted which authorises the Council to control quality of special education.

Different western countries have instituted statutory provisions in favour of integrated education of the disabled.

In India, however, there is no such law but policies of education from 1964 on wards have recommended placement of these children in regular schools with adequate support system.

The centrally sponsored scheme for Integrated Education for Disabled Children (IEDC) was initiated in early seventies by the Government of India in various states. The scheme has been revised and now covers the following types of the handicaps

(1) Mental Retardation
(2) Learning Disability
(3) Visual Impairment
(4) Hearing Impairment
(5) Speech Impairment
(6) Physical Disabilities

Education, Care, Training and Rehabilitation of exceptional children has a long past, but a short scientific history. An understanding of the origin and development of the special education movement would help to understand where we stand now in the field, particularly in India. Children with defects were not cared for in pre-historic societies. Defects like mental illness in the good old days were considered the result of some kind of sin. Children suffering from them were either killed or punished. The physicians and scholars in ancient Greek, and Roman societies made some efforts to treat and preserve the lives of the handicapped and provided asylums for them. The Renaissance brought a small change in the earlier attitudes. This was the state of affairs until the late 18th and early 19th centuries.

The early history of special education started with the hearing handicapped as early as 1555 when the Spanish monk Pedro Ponce de Leon (1520-1584) taught a small number of deaf children to read, write and speak and learn academic subjects Jnan Pablo Ronet in 1620 wrote the first book on the education of the deaf and developed a one handed manual alphabet that is being used even today. In England John Bulwer published another book on the education of the deaf in 1644, followed by the Deaf and Dumb Man's Tutor by George Dalgarno in 1680 which set out instructional methods.

The first school for the deaf in Great Britain was established in 1767 in Ediburgh by Thomas Braidwood. Braidwood's method combined oral and manual method teaching alphabets and signs.

At about same time Samuel Heinicke (1729-1784) developed the oral method emphasising up reading and speaking skills in Germany at Leipzig in 1778 which was further developed by FM. Hill (1805 -1874).

In France, Michael del Epee (1912-1789) who established the first school in Paris in 1755, and Ambrose Sicard (1742-1822) were developing sign language The French system also emphasised training of the senses of sight and touch which became the forerunner to Montessorie's sensory training approach.

Education of deaf children was started with Gallandet (1787-1851) using the French method. Gallandet established the first school of the deaf in 1847 (which is today known as the American School for the deaf). The New York School for the deaf opened the next year. By 1863 there were 22 schools for the deaf in USA. The first oral school of the deaf in Massachussets was established in 1867. Day school classes for the deaf were started in 1869 at Beston. Adult education for the deaf began in New York City in 1874.

Subsequently Grahma Bell (1847-1922) worked tirelessly for the deaf. Helen Keller (1880-1957) who was deaf and blind herself from early childhood, was a living example of the effectiveness of special education in overcoming the disability. The development of services for the deaf were hindered because of the conflict over oral and manual method of instruction, but these have been reconciled over the years. In 1880, an international congress of education of the deaf was held in Milan, Italy. It made two recommendations.

(1) Oral method must be preferred to the manual method.
(2) Oral method must be preferred to lip reading/sign language.

In Europe, oral method continued to prevail unchallenged during more than half the 20th century. After World War II the progress in electoacoustic technology gave new impetus. The increased belief that early education and intervention would allow, most deaf children to attend ordinary schools for normal hearing or special unit to these schools. The mainstreaming movement progressively gathered more and more strength in great Britain, then in the United States, and continental Europe.

In France Education of the blind began with Valentin Hany (1745-1822) a French philanthropist who in 1784 founded the national Institution for the blind in Paris. It is an integrated school and its success led to the establishment of seven schools in Europe during the next 15 years. The first school for the blind in Watertown, Massachusset was instituted in 1829 by Samuel Graindley Howe (1801-1876). This gave rise to residential schools for the partially sighted until the development of special classes in public schools in 1900 at Chicago. Special classes for the partially sighted was begun 13 years later in Boston. Hany developed embossed letters to be read with fingers and using this he printed the first book for the blind. Louise Braille (1809-1852) blind from childhood himself developed the system of Braille using raised dots to represent letters or alphabets, manually prepared for many years. The Braille typewriter was developed by Frank Hall (1943-1911), and a Braille: printing system was standardised internationally in 1932.

Education of children with mental retardation began with the attempt by a French physician Itard (1775-1835) to educate an 11 year old boy who had been found living as a savage in the woods. This was documented in the book "The Wild Boy of Aveyron". Edward Seguin (1812-1880) followed the technique in France and United States and Maria Montessorie (1870-1952) in Italy. Seguin published his book "Idiocy and its treatment by the physiological method" in 1866. It contained ideas which are relevant even now— total education of the child, individualisation of instruction, beginning instruction at the child's current level of functioning, and rapport between teacher and pupil. These were included in the famous method of Montessories for the eduction of the handicapped and non-handicapped.

Decroly (1871-1932) in Belgium developed a curriculum for mentally retarded children early in the 20th century and established schools throughout Europe. Rinet (1857-1911) made and immense contribution with the invention of intelligence testing.

In 1839 the first blind and mentally retarded (MR) child was enrolled in the Perkins Institute for the Blind in the USA. In 1848 the first residential school for the MR was opened in Massachusetts. By 1917 all states except four provided instructional care for the mentally retarded in the USA.

The first public school with special classes for children with mental retardation was formed in Germany in 1859 and thereafter in other European nation in the next decades. In the USA the first public school with special classes for the MR was opened in 1896 at Providence, Rhodes Island.

There ware very few special treatment and provisions for the orthopaedically handicapped and the health impaired prior the 20th century. In the USA the first special class was established in Chicago in 1899, for children with low vitality in 1908 at Providence, Rhodes Island, and a class for children with epilepsy in Baltimore, Maryland in 1909.

Esquirol (1772-1840) published the first description of childhood psychosis in 1838 in a volume on scientific treatment of mental illness. For the first time in 1871 the New Haven Connecticut Public Schools provided a class for emotionally disturbed (ED) boys in New York City in 1874. These were first attempts niade in USA. It was not until the 1930s that ED children were studied in a systematic way. Since world War II these have been characterised by the rapid development of services for handicapped children.

Special education services expanded rapidly after World War II both in numbers and types of children served. Legislative measures, Parental involvement, early education or pre-school education for handicapped children all took off, including the education of those suffering from cerebral palsy, the learning disabled and the physically handicapped. By the 1970s facilities were available for all categories of the handicapped in the advanced countries of the world, and after 1981 in the developing nations.

Vocational Rehabilitation, occupational therapy, physical therapy were brought into the services for the handicapped. Expanded technology, use of computers, transportation devices, learning and visual aid technology, telecommunication systems, tele-typewriters for the deaf all came into use. Talking boons for the blind, which convert print into vibrating images that can be read with fingers were invented. The Kurzwell Reading Machine which converts print into spoken English, mobility aids etc. have further revolutionised the education of the disabled.

Besides, the 1970s have seen the emergence of mainstreaming and least restrictive environment as dominant concepts in special education. The special class has doubtful efficacy and that is why there is a shift from placement in residential schools and special day schools and increased enrolment in regular classes. Segregation is now discouraged unless the handicap is very very severe.

Special Education in India

The Kothari Commission (1964-66) observes that the coveted goal of universalisation of elementary education depends upon the extent of success in bringing special groups of children within the eduction network. Unless educational services are extended to this group of children on mass scale, the universalisation of elementary enrolment of the handicapped children in relation to total children at the elementary stage is 0.07 percent. This figure of enrolment has gone up to one percent as per review of NPE (1992) This low percentage of enrolment speaks volumes for the serious neglect and denial of educational opportunity for millions of disabled children in the country even though the constitution of the country prescribes compulsory education for all children upto primary level. Most of the special groups of children are either not enrolled at all or drop out due to one reason or the other after stagnation. The slow progress towards bringing the disabled within the education network has been due to liner provision in special schools despite the fact that about 90 percent of them can be catered to in regular schools.

Integration of the handicapped, into the regular school programme enunciated by the Kothari Commission leads to (i) reduction of costs of education and (ii) promotion of mutual understanding between the handicapped and non-handicapped. However, many handicapped children find it difficult to cope with normal ones as they tend to be neglected. It is increasingly felt that every attempt should be made to bring in as many children into integrated programmes as possible.

He has been reinforced in the National Policy on Education, (NPE) 1986 stipulates that wherever possible education of children with locomotor handicaps and other mild handicaps will be common with that of others. The children with severe handicaps are proposed to be enrolled in special schools with hostels at district headquarters.

The ideal scenario for education of the handicapped is universalisation of primary education along with other children by 1995.

The Programme of Action (POA), 1986 and 1992 suggest pragmatic placement principles. It postulates that a child with disability who can be educated in a general school should be educated in general school only and not in a special school. Even those children who are initially admitted to special for training in plus-curriculum skills (that are required in addition to their regular school curriculum) should be transferred to general schools once they acquire daily living skills, communication skills and basic academic skills.

For achieving equalisation of educational opportunities, POA (1992) also envisages that children with disability should have access to quality education comparable to other children. It postulates-

(1) For children who can be educated in general primary schools.
(2) For children who require to be educated in special schools or special classes in general schools.
(3) Reduction of drop out rates at par with other children.
(4) Providing access to disabled children of secondary and senior secondary school with resource support and

making special provision for vocational training of these children.

(5) Reorienting pre-service and in-service teacher education programmes to meet special needs in the classroom.

(6) Reorienting adult and non-formal education programmes to meet educational and vocational training needs of persons with disability.

LEGAL PROVISIONS

The persons with disabilities (Equal Opportunities, Protection of Rights and full Participation) Act, 1995.

The Gazette of India: Extra ordinary, Part-II, Section-1 No. I of 1996, 1st January; 1996, Ministry of Law, Justice and Company Affairs, New Delhi Chapter-V of Education p. 12-13.

1. The appropriate Governments and the local authorities shall—
   (a) ensure that every child with a disability has access to free education in an appropriate environment till he attains the age of eighteen years :
   (b) endeavour to promote the integration of students with disabilities in the normal schools;
   (c) promote setting up of special schools in government and private sector for those in need of special education, in such a manner that children with disabilities living in any part of the country have access to such school.
   (d) endeavour to equip the special schools for children with disabilities with vocational training facilities.
2. The appropriate Governments and the local authorities shall by notification make schemes for—
   (a) conducting part-time classes in respect of children with disabilities who having completed eduction upto class fifth and could not continue their studies on a whole time basis;
   (b) conducting special part-time classes for providing functional literacy for children in the age-group of sixteen and above;

(c) imparting non-formal education by utilizing the available manpower in rural areas after giving them appropriate orientation;

(d) imparting education through open schools or open universities,

(e) conducting class and discussions through interactive electronic or other media;

(f) providing every child with disability free of cost special books and equipment needed for his education.

3. The appropriate Governments shall initiate or cause to be initiated research be official and non-governmental agencies for the purpose of designing and developing new assistive devices, teaching aids, special teaching materials or such other items as are necessary to give a child with disability equal opportunities in education.

4. The appropriate Governments shall set up adequate number of teacher's training institutions and assist the national institutes and other voluntary organisations to develop teachers' training programmes specialising in disabilities so that requisite trained manpower is available for special schools and integrated schools for children with disabilities.

5. Without prejudice to the foregoing provisions, the appropriate Governments shall by notification prepare a comprehensive education scheme which shall make provisions for handicapped.

(a) transport facilities to the children with disabilities or in the alternative financial incentives to parents or guardians to enable their children with disabilities to attend schools

(b) the removal of architectural barriers from schools, colleges or other institutions imparting vocational and professional training;

(c) the supply of books, uniforms and other materials to children with disabilities attending school;

(d) the grant of scholarship to students with disabilities

(e) setting up of appropriate fora for the redressal of grievances of parents regarding the placement their children with disabilities.

(f) suitable modification in the examination system to eliminate purely mathematical questions for the benefit of blind students and students with low vision;

(g) restructuring of curriculum for the benefit of children with disabilities;

(h) restructuring the curriculum for the benefit of students with hearing impairment to facilitate them to take only one language as part of their curriculum.

6. All educational institutions shall provide or cause to be provided amanuensis to blind students and students with low vision.

Equalization of Educational Opportunity

From 1950 onwards India has switched over to democracy. Its main tenets are equality, liberty, fraternity and justice. Equality implies equality of opportunity. In a democratic system all men are born equal and enjoy equal rights without any differentiation and discrimination of poor and rich and high and low. It is the prime duty of the government to minimise inequalities, disparities and imbalances as far as possible. To get education on equal footing is everybody's right in a democracy and hence should have full opportunity to develop his mental faculties. In this the interests of minorities, backward classes and deprived sections of the community need special consideration. People living in hills, rural areas and remote place need greater attention. Facilities of freeship, mid-day meals books assistance and scholarships etc. should exist for poor but meritorious children in schools and colleges. There is need to devise ways and means tó identify the talent and help it grow to its full stature without economic impediments and hurdles. Rich persons and philanthropists should also contribute generously towards their education and the help the government in all possible ways. Any discrimination between the education of boys and girls is improper. Both have equal rights to develop their individuality This will go a long way in the evaluation of an egalitarian, democratic and socialistic pattern of society in the country and develop a healthy social and economic order.

National Policy on Education (1986, 1992)

The objective should be to integrate the physically and mentally handicapped with the general community as equal partners, to prepare them for normal growth and to enable them to face life with courage and confidence. The following measures were to be taken in this regard:

(1) Wherever it was feasible, the education of children with motor handicaps and other mild handicaps would be common with that of other.

(2) Special schools with hostels would be provided, as far as possible an adequate arrangements would be made to vocational training to the disabled.

(3) Adequate arrangements would be made to give vocational training to the disabled.

(4) Teacher's training programmes would be reoriented in particular for teacher of primary classes, to deal with the special difficulties of handicapped children and

(5) Voluntary effort for the education of the disabled would be encouraged in every possible manner.

Recommendations of Ramamurthy Committee, 1991: The Government of India set up the Ramamurthy Committee to comment upon NPE/POA stipulations. Some of the specific observations made on the handicapped as stated in the NPE 1986 were as follows.

NPE advocated the policy of integrating the physically and mentally handicapped with the general community as equal partners.

The POA mentioned the detailed measures to be taken, important amongst them being massive in-service training for teachers, orientation programmes for the administrators, development of supervisory expertise in the resource institutions like the SCERT and DIET, etc. It also called for provision of incentives like supply of aids, appliances, text books and free uniforms.

The causes for the low coverage of handicapped children in education are the following.

1. Education of the handicapped is viewed as a social welfare activity.
2. Child to child help leading to sensitization of the future generation, child to parent help for community sensitation and special and general pedagogy reinforcement were missed.
3. Most of the special centres for the handicapped are located in metropolitan cities and urban centres. The non-government organisations barring a few exceptions have not significantly begun to operate at district or sub-district levels. Reportedly, 215 districts in the country do not have special schools for any disability though there are over 1000 documented special schools.
4. The scheme of Integrated Education for Disabled children which was conceptualised by the Department of Social Welfare in 1974 was implemented for several years in terms of running Mini Special Schools within general schools. The reason was that there was no provision of sensitisation and involvement of all the teachers.

The NPE, so far as it relates to education of the handicapped, is inadequate in the following respects:

1. It has not stressed the mobilisation of the total general education system for the education of the handicapped.
2. Special schools have been treated in isolation from other educational institutions from the point of view of providing the educational supervisory infrastructure, leaving it to the Ministries of social welfare and HRD to co-operatively develop the same.

The merit of the POA is in its call for establishment of special schools a district and sub-district levels: curriculum development a part from provision of infrastructural facilities; and specific target setting for universal primary education of the handicapped. While special schools for the eduction of those with sever handicaps are rightly emphasised by the POA, they have not laid emphasis on multiple delivery of services in special schools. While single disability mode is required for research, development and rehabilitation work, for delivery of educational services, multi-service mode in special schools should be given importance. This is particularly so because doctors, dispensaries, public health centres and development functionaries are multi-purpose in nature. The POA has not called for redefinition of the role of special schools.

The Department of Education has been implementing a scheme for the integrated education of the disabled under which 100% assistance is given to the states. The scheme is at present being implemented in nineteen States and Union Territories. The annual provision under the scheme is of the order of Rs. 2 crores and as of now 20,000 children are being covered. Assistance provided to the states under the scheme is expected to be utilised to provide for salaries and incentives for teacher, setting up of resource rooms, carrying out assessment of handicapped children, training of teachers, provision of instructional material, etc.

Recommendation of the Committee (1992): Having comprehensively taken into account the problems faced in providing education to the handicapped with reference to their special and diversified needs, and having studied the history of implementation of the educational programmes for the handicapped, the Committee gave the following recommendations:

1. People should be made aware of the problems of the handicapped. The media should be effectively used for this purpose.
2. Every family with handicapped child should be provided support through incentives, dialogue and periodic training and evaluation. Parents groups and community education group should be formed.
3. The educational system of the handicapped should be flexible. It should offer a range of educated in general schools, special classes in general schools and integrated education for the disabled, vocational centres, etc.
4. Educational packages should be offered for hearing impaired children in a differentiated way—

Purely oral oriented programmes for profoundly deaf children.

Combined oral-manual programme for profoundly deaf children for the education of who pure oral programmes will not be adequate. Segregated programmes for those children from whom such programmers are essential.

Integrated programmes for those whom this modality promises better emotive cognitive, social and linguistic development.

5. For making boys and girls of impaired hearing economically independent, vocational training has to be specially organized. Vocational training which is job-oriented and matched to the abilities and aptitudes of the hearing impaired, should be organised in a significantly diversified way.
6. Bharati Braille has been developed, at the National Institute for the Visually Handicapped (NIVH), Dehradun. This should be utilised maximally.
7. While work has been initiated for the development of Braille notations for mathematics and science, not much progress has been made.
8. For the moderately mentally retarded, special curricula should be developed and standardised-not merely for the purpose of base education in the three R's but also for training in self-care skills lip motor integration, perceptual and motor skills, language communication and conceptual skills.
9. Vocational schools for mentally retarded adults are not many. For their benefit jobs in sheltered workshops, farms and industries should be provided.
10. In the pre-service teacher training programme, education of the handicapped, should be made part of the pedagogy and methodology,
11. A programme of sensitisation should be implemented, for inservices teachers as well. This should include various components, namely Non-formal Education, Vocationalisation of Education and Distance Education.

12. Teacher training colleges should have special courses for teaching handicapped children; a special component on the education of the handicapped should be included in the B.Ed. courses as well.
13. At last one resource faculty should be provided in each DIET to provide teacher training inputs in the context of education for the handicapped.
14. The role of the special schools should be clearly redefined as spelt below:
    (a) Early identification of children with handicaps and formulation of stimulation programme for them.
    (b) Education of the handicapped children who cannot be educated in general schools up to the point when they can be integrated-thus breaking the insulation between the general and special schools.
    (c) providing service as resource agencies for implementing the integrated education programmes in general schools.
15. A lot of development is taking place in the application of technology for the benefit of the handicapped. Several technological aids all already available, e.g., Brailleix produced in Germany which facilitates recording of whole encyclopaedia on cassettes, printing conversion devices like tectacon which facilitates presentation of printed material in vibro-tactile form so as to enable blind persons to read, devices facilitating mobility of blind persons, etc. The technologies and techno-aids available for meeting the special needs of handicapped children should be reviewed, and measures for dissemination of information should be formulated.
16. Sustained researches should be undertaken to determine the needs of the physically handicapped and produce technological aids capable of helping in overcoming handicaps.

These recommendations were very comprehensive to shape the programme planning effectively. Subsequently another Committee was set up by the government, the Janardan Reddy Committee, which submitted its report in 1992.

The NPERC, 1992 felt that the NPE was inadequate in the following respects :

(1) NPE had not stressed the mobilisation of the total general education system for the education of the handicapped.

(2) Special schools had been treated in isolation from other educational institutions from the point of view of providing the educational supervisory infrastructure, leaving it to the Ministries of Welfare and HRD to co-operatively develop the same.

The NPERC made very useful recommendations relating to the modelities of implementing programmes for the education of the handicapped, Inter alia, it had advocated the use of media in creating awareness about the problems of the handicapped, providing support to every family with a handicapped child through incentives, dialogue and training and adopting a flexible approach to the education of the physically handicapped. The NPERC examined at length the needs of different categories of the disabled such as the deaf, the blind and the mentally retarded, and made specific recommendations. The NPERC had also made important recommendations on the role of training, and of technological development in the education of the physics all handicapped.

The Programme of Action which was formulated in 1992 by MERD, Government of India took all these historical antecedents into account and focused on an operational framework for implementing the plan of education handicapped.

Programme of Action (POA) 1992: The POA made a state of the art analysis of the situation. At the end of 1991-92 about 30,000 children with disability were availing special benefits under the scheme of Integrated Education for Disabled Children (IEDC). In addition, about 60,000 children with mild disabilities received resources support without special benefits. A large number of children with disability were also receiving education in special schools which numbered about 1035. The Project Integrated Education for Disabled (PIED) is being implemented, as a field of demonstration , in one block each in ten States and Union Territories. In the blocks about 90 percent of children with disability are receiving education in general schools. The cost per pupil in these blocks is now around Rs. 2000 but is likely to come down as the number of beneficiaries increases. General teachers feel confident and motivated as their status in the community has improved due to the services they provide. The innovative multi-category training of resource teachers has been found to be effective and has been institutionalised in the Regional Colleges and the training programmes organized by Non-governmental Organisations. Each DIET has been provided a resource centre for orienting elementary teachers and establishing field demonstrations in lab areas. Faculty from 102 DIETs have so far received induction training at the NCERT.

The ministry of social welfare had taken steps to ensure supply of trained manpower to special schools and improve standards in these schools thought the National Institute for the handicapped and increased support to NGOs.

The ministry of labour manages 17 Vocational Rehabilitation Centres (VRCs) for the handicapped and helps in their placement. About 66,000 persons with disabilities had been rehabilitated under this schemes by September, 1991. Three percent of seats for admission to TTIs and under the Apprenticeship Training Scheme are available for handicapped persons. These seats are being fully utilised.

The evaluation of special schools and the scheme of IEDC has revealed some grey areas. The general education system has not yet been mobilised, to a noticeable extent, for education of handicapped either at the Central or State level. Inputs from different schemes like CBR, DRC, ECCE, non-formal education, adult education, vocational and technical education, etc. are not being brought together for the education of the physically handicapped. Some states are still reluctant to implementing it rather indifferently. Few NGOs are active in rural areas. The standard of education in special schools needs improvement.

Facilities for the education of children with multiple handicaps are yet to be developed. The early detection and intervention programmes so essential for education of these children have yet to be started. The goal of an unachievable dream unless concerted and urgent measures are take.

FINANCIAL RESOURCES

For achieving equalisation of education opportunities, children with disability should have access to quality education comparable to other children. However, considering the financial resources likely to be available the targets for education of disabled children should be as follows :

(1) Children who can be educated in general primary schools:
   (a) Universal enrolment by the end of ninth Five Year Plan.
   (b) Ensuring achievement of minimum level of learning through adjustment and adaptation of curriculum and teaching to special needs.

(2) Children who requite to be educated in special schools or special classes in general schools:
   (a) Universal enrolment by the end of the ninth Five year Plan.
   (b) Ensuring achievement of level of learning commensurate with their potential.

(3) Reduction of drop rates to level on par with other children:

(4) Providing disabled children access to secondary and senior secondary schools with resource support and making special provision for vocational training of these children, particularly those with intellectual disabilities.

(5) Reorienting pre-service and in-service teacher education programmes including pre-school teachers training programmes to meet special needs.

(6) Reorienting adult and non-formal education programmes to meet educational and vocational training needs of persons with disability.

The strategy of area-specific and population specific micro-planning for UEE is equally relevant for this disadvantaged group.

Planning for ULE, and adult literacy at the levels-centre, state, district, state, district, block and project should provide for the educational needs of this category of children.

Education of children with disability will be a component in the training of educational planners and administrators as well as pre-service and in-service teachers. District Institutes of Education and Training (DIETs), Colleges of Teacher Education (CTEs) and the Institute of Advanced Study in Education (IASE) which have been provided with facilities for this component will have to pay particular attention to this aspect of teacher training. While drawing up schemes for strengthening SCERTs, cells for education of the handicapped may be considered as envisaged in IEDC.

The material supplied under Operation Blackboard will have to take into consideration special needs of these children. School buildings will have to take note of architectural adjustments needs to ensure access to children with disabilities, at the construction stage itself so as to avoid expenditure on modifications later on. Special schools need to be opened in the districts which have no special school facilities. The education of the handicapped should form essential component in all externally assisted basic education project being implemented or proposed to be implemented.

The following actions are needed for achieving the targets laid down:

(1) Adequate allocation of resources.
(2) Provision for education of persons with disabilities should be made an integral component in externally assisted basic education projects.
(3) Provision for education of the disabled should be made in the Centrally Sponsored Schemes of Operation Blackboard, Vocationalisation of Education and Non-formal Education.
(4) The NGOs have to be encouraged to implement IEDC, particularly in rural areas. The NGOs involved in other educational activities should be encouraged to work in this area also and should be assisted in developing their expertise.

The Ministry of Labour is providing vocational training for the handicapped through the Craftsman Training Scheme (CTS), the Apprenticeship Training Scheme and separate Vocational Rehabilitation Centres (VRCs). Three percent of the seats for admission to ITIs under the Craftsman Training Scheme and Apprenticeship Training Scheme are reserved for candidates who are handicapped but have the aptitude and are otherwise fit to undergo the required training. The state UTs have been advised from time to time to implement this reservation for the handicapped which will be continued during the eight plan also. Seventeen VRCs will continue to provide training to a large number of handicapped persons during the eight plan. The instructors in ITIs will receive orientation to meet special needs of handicapped persons. This component will be added in M instructor's training programme. Adjustment and adaptation of equipment provide full access to disabled persons will be ensured.

School Education

The first attempts at educating handicapped children were made in the last two decades of the nineteenth century with the establishment of the first school for the hearing impaired in Bombay in 1885, Followed by the first school for the visually impaired in Amritsar in 1887. Growth of schools for the handicapped in the sixty years until the advent of independence was extremely slow and sporadic. By 1947 India had just 32 schools for the blind. The number rose to 170 in 1980. Now there are 243 schools for the visually impaired in the country. Prior to independence there were only eight codes available in the country but Bharati Braille has replaced all other codes now. Thirteen Braille presses are available in the country.

The number of schools for the hearing impaired was only 35 in 1947 but had risen to 180 by 1980. The present figure of schools for the hearing impaired is about 478 as per the Rehabilitation Council of India (RCI) directory of which 97 are secondary schools. The largest number are in the state of Maharashtra (139 schools).

Schools for the mentally retarded were just three in 1947, but rose to 200 by 1980 and at present there are 600 schools for mentally retarded children. The first school for the cerebral palsied was started in 1973. There are 12 schools run for the cerebral palsied at present, but no facility is yet available for autistic children. As regards the orthopaedically handicapped most of them go to ordinary schools.

Teacher Training

Since 1981, systematic attempts have been made in the field of teacher training for handling special needs children. The leadership in this direction has been taken up by NCERT in designing courses of short term duration, mainly to implement the integrated education (IED) scheme floated by the Government of India under centrally sponsored schemes which has been now named as project integrated education of the Disabled (PIED). NCERT has designed three level courses which are;

Level I: One week training of all primary teacher in the project area,

Level II: In-services training for six weeks for selected teacher,

Level III: One year multi-category training of teachers since 1987 in its Regional Colleges of Eduction.

Besides, a six months training course has been given to key persons at the NCERT headquarters. Several courses have been designed by the Rehabilitation Council of India. Degree courses have been started in some universities leading to B.Ed and M.Ed in special education.

The Rehabilitation

Vocational Rehabilitation Centres (VRC) have been established. National Institutes have started functioning. A three percent job reservations for the handicapped and special employment exchanges have been set up. National Awards, Tax concessions, self employment schemes, sheltered workshops are also available for the handicapped. District Rehabilitation Centres (DRC) have been set up.

Community Based Rehabilitation (CBR) are in operation, where it is the responsibility of the community to rehabilitate the disabled of all categories. Each level is equipped with Trained

Personnel. Regional Research Training Centres (RRTC) have been set up in the four regions of the country. A rehabilitation technology centre and the National Information Centre on Disabled and Rehabilitation (NICDR) have been set up at Delhi. The NGOs have done commendable work in the area of disability over the years.

The Documentation

The National Information Centre on Disability and Rehabilitation (NICDR) undertakes collection, classification and storage of data on 12 different aspects of disability.

1. Concessions and facilities provided to the disabled by the central and state government.
2. Organisations and institutions working for the disabled.
3. Professionals working for the disabled.
4. Statistics about beneficiaries of various rehabilitation schemes and programmes.
5. Demographic statistics about the disabled.
6. Aids and appliance available for the disabled.
7. Statistics about national awards and awardees.
8. Schemes of scholarship-beneficiaries.
9. Scheme of assistance for purchase/fitting of aids/appliances.
10. Scheme of organisations working for the disabled.
11. Employment statistics.
12. Research and Development Projects.

It is proposed to have Regional Centres of NICDR too.

Non-Government Organisations (NGOs) have contributed substantially to the care, training and rehabilitation of the disabled in India. There are 315 voluntary organisations working for the disabled in the country at present. Among them, prominents are the Mahavir Viklang Kendra, Jaipur, Nevedic Prosthetic Centre, Chandigarh, Thakur Hariprasad Institute of Mental Retardation, Hyderabad, Amar Jyoti School, New Delhi. Pandey and Advani (1995) have given an exhaustive list of the voluntary organisations in this sector.

An All India Federation of the Deaf has also come up. The Rehabilitation Council of India is now regulating the training, recognition and derecognition of the special education centre institutes.

Training programmes for physiotherapists, occupational therapists, prosthetic and orthotic professionals, speech therapists, audiologists, mobility instructors of the blind, vocational instructioners and counsellors, placement officers, clinical psychologists, rehabilitation workers and other are being held in various National Institutes and Universities as per the norms of the Rehabilitation Council of India.

The major changes as regards exceptional children have been changed from medical diagnosis to multi-professional assessment and treatment, treatment to education, meeting categorical needs to individual needs and change from category specific curricula and methods to appropriate variations in curriculum for all. There is a growing recognition of special education needs, training services development of much close relationships between the staff and pupils with special needs.

Present Facilities in our Country

The responsibility for implementing welfare schemes is being shared between the Central and State Governments. The responsibility of Centre rests with the Ministry of governments. The responsibility of Centre rests with the Ministry of Welfare, and its activities are carried out through five bureau, viz. Handicapped Welfare, Social Defence Administration and Minorities, Tribal Development, and Scheduled Castes and Backward Classes. According to estimates of national survey organisation the number of disabled persons is about 120 lakhs.

Institutions of Special Education: The Government of India has established several special institutes for the handicapped. There are four national institutes, each for one special field.

(1) National Institutes for Visually Handicapped at Dehradun.

(2) National Institute for the Hearing Handicapped at Mumbai.

(3) National Institute for the Orthopaedically Handicapped at Kolkata.

(4) National Institute for Mentally Handicapped at Hyderabad.

Besides, the National Institute for Rehabilitation, Training and Research at Olatpur (Cuttack), the Institute for the Physically Handicapped at New Delhi, the School for the Mentally Retarded Children at New Delhi and the Training Centre for the Adult Deaf at Hyderabad also assist in implementing the various programmes. The Artificial Limbs Manufacturing Corporation at Kanpur manufactures aids and appliances for the handicapped. These institutes have the main responsibility for training research workers, development of designs for finding and incentive. They should conduct research also.

There are 800-1,000 special schools for blind and deaf children, and for the mentally retarded. The majority of them are run by voluntary organisation. It is estimated that there are two million disabled children who will need special care, viz., improvement of health service, nutrition standards, mother care, and effective measures to prevent disability. The NPE plans to establish 10,000 schools for these children with 150 to 200 children in each.

There cannot be one model for special education programme. One can however, suggest a few alternatives. These models are : (1) Hospital Model, (2) Full time residential or Day school, (3) Home bound model with peripatetic teaching, (4) Part-time special schools resource room help, and the like.

Influence of Other Disciplines : Special education did not suddenly spring up as a new -discipline, nor did it develop in isolation from other disciplines. In the 20th century, members of the medical profession has continued to play important roles in the field of special education. The emergence of the disciplines of psychology and sociology and the widespread use of mental tests in the early years of the 20th century had enormous implication for the growth of the special education profession. Psychologists' study of learning and their prediction of success or failure in school learning helped focus attention on children with special educational needs. Sociologists and social workers drew attention to the ways in which the family and the community affect exceptional child's learning and development.

Contemporary special education draws heavily on all disciplines concerned with child development-medicine, psychology, sociology and social work. Special education, which was initially the concern of physicians and later of psychologists, is growing very fast to become an independent discipline. Opening up of M. A. (Special Education), M.Ed. (Special Education) and B.Ed. (Special, Education) in different University Departments and Colleges is an indication of this trend;

Exercise

1. Indicate the origin of special education. Comment on the statement. 'It is true that significant idea in special education found its way from Europe to America.'
2. Describe the development of special education in Europe and U.S.A name the father of special education.
3. Describe the legal provisions of special education in India and other country.
4. Describe the history of special education in our country referring Kothari Commission and NPE (1986) and Programme of Action (POA - 1992).
5. Explain the Equal Opportunities of Education. Indicate legal provision in our constitution. Describe the shift of handicapped education from social welfare to mainstreaming of education.
6. Write short notes on the following:
   (a) Recommendations of Rama Murthy Committee (1992)
   (b) Programme of Action (1991)
   (c) Institutions of Special Education.
   (d) Financial Resources for Special Education.

6

Particular Requirements

In a democratic country like ours every child has the right to eduction—the right to receive help in learning to the limits of his capacity, whether that capacity be small or great. It is consistent with a democratic philosophy that all children be given equal opportunity to learn whether they are average. Bright, dull, retarded, blind, deaf, crippled, delinquent. Emotionally disturbed or otherwise limited or deviant in their capacities to learn. Equality of opportunity denotes two deviant in their capacities to learn. Equality of opportunity denotes two things—equality of access to school education and equality of success in school.

In every classroom there are some children who have some learning problems. They need a little extra help from teachers to learn. Sometimes teachers understand their problems while at other time they are not able to understand their problems. The help they provide may not be sufficient. Their learning problems may persist and even accumulate despite special help by teachers. If teachers cannot understand the special needs of such children they will experience failure and frustration and later drop out from the school. In fact our failure to understand the special needs of such children have been major factors for our failure to reach the target of universalization of elementary education within the stipulated period. These children with special needs are called exceptional.

The Definition

The term 'exceptional' means different things to different people. Some use it when referring to the particularly bright children or the child with unusual talent. Others use it when they refer to any typical or deviant child. Telford and Sawrey (1972) said, "To be exceptional is to be rare or unusual."

According to Crow and Crow: "The term 'exceptional' is applied to a trait or to a person possessing trait upto the extent of deviation from normal possession of the trait is so great that because of it the individual warrant or receives special attentions from his fellows and his behaviour responses and activities are thereby affected.

According to W.M. Cruichshank (1974): "An exceptional child is who deviates physically, intellectually and socially so marked by from normal growth and development that can not be benefited from regular classroom programme and needs special treatment in school.

According to Kirk (1972): "An exceptional child is he who deviates from the normal or average children in mental, physical and social characteristics to such an extent that requires a modification of school practices or special educational services or supplementary instruction in other to develop to his maximum capacity."

Hewett and Forness (1984): "An exceptional learner is an individual who because of uniqueness in sensory, physical, enurological, temperamental or intellectual capacity and/ or in the nature and range of previous order to maximize this or here functioning level." All children traditionally labelled as exceptional fall under this definition.

The Characteristics

1. It is applied to a trait of a person possessing upto the extent of deviation from normal.
2. It is commonly applied to children who differ notable from the average children.

3. An exceptional child deviates physically, mentally, emotionally and socially from normal growth and development.
4. An exceptional child is he who can not be benefited from regular classroom teaching programmes.
5. An exceptional child requires a modification of school practices and needs special treatment in school to develop his maximum capacity.
6. An exceptional child belongs to both the extremes of physical, mentally, social, emotional and educational achievement.

Types of Exceptional Children: Exceptional children are of various types such as the following:

(1) Children with Hearing Handicap
(2) Children with Visual Handicap
(3) Children with Mental Retardation
(4) Children with Learning Disability
(5) Children with Emotional Orthopaedic Handicap
(6) Children with Emotional Disturbance
(7) Children with Speech Handicap
(8) Children with Special Health Problems
(9) Children with Multiple Handicaps
(10) Gifted Children
(11) Children with Creative Talents
(12) Socially Disadvantaged Children

Children with Hearing Handicap : The hearing handicapped are those children who have a damaged hearing mechanism and face difficulty in speech and language development. There is loss of hearing. The degree of hearing loss is less in some children while it is more severe in others. The hearing handicapped children may be hard-of-hearing or deaf.

The hard-hearing children are those children who have hearing loss but who can hear if spoken too loudly without a hearing aid. A hearing aid will enable them to hear better. For such children education in general schools is common with other children is not difficult. Most of them are already studying in the general classroom.

The deaf are those who cannot hear even if spoken to very loudly They require preparation in basic skills through special techniques before they are admitted in general schools. Hearing aids help them to become more functional.

Children with hearing impairment need hearing aid auditory training, more of visual cues in the teaching-learning situation, services of audiologist, ENT specialists, special needs of such children differ depending upon the type and nature of hearing loss. .The quality of previous training received in the home and pre-school centres etc.

Children with Visual Handicap: The visually handicapped children are those who have problems with vision. Some visually handicapped children can read large print and are functional in their environment whereas some have severe vision loss and cannot be taught through visual methods. The visual loss is measured with the help of Snellen Chart. Depending upon the degree of loss they may be partially sighted or blind.

The partially sighted are those who require large print or magnified print materials. Their visual acquity (sharpness of visual image) is very low (20/70 in the better eye). This means that the child can see at 20 ft. distance what a normal child sees at 70 ft. Their eye-sight may be weak due to short sightedness, long sightedness, astigmatism, glaucoma or muscle detachment.

The blinds are those who need to be taught through braille or through aural method. Their visual acquity (sharpness of visual image) may fall at 2/20 9. Such children must be prepared in pre-academic before they are admitted in general schools. They need orientation training, mobility training and more of oral instruction depending upon the degree of loss of vision.

Children with Mental Retardation : Mentally retarded children are those who have a lower level of intellectual functioning and have problems in social adaptability. There are various degree of mental handicap. Consequently there are various categories of mentally handicapped children - the educable mentally retarded (EMR), the trainable mentally retarded (TMR) and the custodial mentally retarded (CMR).

The educable mentally retarded are those who have minimum educational retardation in school subjects. Such children have problems of social adjustment, but are usually not recognised as mentally retarded at the pre-school level. The need is repetition of instruction. They are adaptive so that they can be identified in the early stages.

The custodial mentally retarded need help in develcping daily living skills. They can be educated in special institutions/ special classes. They are very poor in adaptive behaviour. They need constant care and attention.

Children with Learning Disability : These children are like other children in intellectual functioning. They are not mentally retarded, nor spelling, reading writing, arithmetic, listening and comprehension. Their problems may be due to cerebral dysfunction/emotional/behavioural disturbance, but it is not due to mental retardation, sensory handicap children may be categorised into mild learning disabled and severe learning disabled.

Such children have, a severe discrepancy between their achievement and intellectual ability. Such children may have the following specific problems—Reading disability, Writing disability, Problems in comprehension and communication, Problems in numerical ability.

Such children need repetition and drill, cognitive modelling, process training, multisensory experiences and remedial instruction.

Children with Speech Handicap : Speech handicap refers to minor and major speech and language problems. There are children with mild language and speech disorders in our classrooms, and they often go unnoticed. While speaking and writing they tend to omit, distort, add or substitute words, phrases, letters of the alphabet etc. The stammers are quiet or have long gaps in speaking full sentences. Their problems should be corrected before they start school. The major types of speech disorders are

(i) Vice disorders,

(ii) articulation or pronunciation disorders, and

(iii) fluency disorders.

Children with Special Health Problems : Under this category we have children whose poor physical condition makes them inactive and who require special health precautions in school and adequate medical check-ups and support. Such children can be categorised into two groups

(1) Children with mild health problems, and

(2) Children with severe health problems.

Epilepsy, diabetic problems, asthma, pain in the joints and anaemia are some of the special health handicaps.

Children with Multiple Handicaps : Multiple handicap refers to more than one handicap in the child. A child may be blind and deaf, blind and orthopaedically handicapped, deaf and orthopaedically handicapped, mentally retarded and orthopaedically handicapped and so on. In case of multiple handicap one handicap may be primary handicap and the other secondary or one handicap may be more severe than the other handicaps. It is therefore, important to identify the primary medical care, superior instruction from the teacher and a little love and affection from the parents and teachers.

Children with Orthopaedic Handicaps : Some children have orthopaedic handicap or locomotor handicap. Locomotor handicap refers to problems with the functioning of bones, joints and muscles. In some cases the problems are so severe that they require artificial limbs to compensate for their crippling conditions. In other cases they need wheel chair or crutches. They need removal of architectural barriers and some environmental modifications in the schools. Usually mildly orthopaedically handicapped children do not have learning problems. They can be integrated in the regular school without much difficulty.

Children with Emotional Disturbance : Children with emotional disturbance are very often considered as problem children in the school. An emotionally disturbed child has certain inner tensions which create anxiety frustration, fears and impulsive behaviour. Such a child may find excuses for this inner tensions in some physical difficulty. An emotionally disturbed child may attempt to solve the anxiety by behaving in a premature or childish way, becoming aggressive towards other people, or withdrawing himself to the world of fantasy. Such children need love and protection, security and recognition, pleasant and success experiences in the home and the school.

***Gifted Children* :** Gifted children are in some way, superior in intellectual ability to other children of the same age. Gifted children are those who have demonstrated high ability (including high intelligence), high creativity and high task commitment - a high level of motivation and the ability to see a project through its conclusion. A variety of terms have been used to describe individuals who are superior in some way such as 'talented', 'creative', 'genius', and 'precocious' (remarkably early development in partiicular areas like language, music, mathematical ability). Most of these children remain unidentified in the class. Specific efforts are also not made to meet the special needs of such children. Such children who do not profit much from the regular school programme need early admission in schools, skipping grades, telescoping grades, early admission in secondary schools and colleges and enrichment activities and materials.

***Children with Creative Talents* :** In a school teachers may come across few students who have the ability to produce something new—a composition, a system of ideas or a material or a process which is essentially new or novel, and previously unknown to them. Such children behave differently. They are courageous in their convictions. They have independent thinking and adjustment. They become absorbed and preoccupied in what they are doing. They are curious. They take risks. They are flexible in their opinions. They are intellectually self-confident. The prevailing school practices and situations create hindrance for their creative expressions. Teachers need to modify their attitudes towards such children and employ suitable strategies for promotion of their creativity.

***Socially Disadvantaged Children* :** Most teachers encounter a group of children in their classrooms who appear lifeless, incurious, and deceptively unintelligent. They show lack of interest, involvement, and motivation for academic success. The underachievement and the cumulative deficiencies in learning ultimately lead to their wastage and stagnation. These children are socially, economically, and educationally disadvantaged. School readiness programmes in pre-school centres, enriched experiences, and remedial instructions are very useful for them.

School Provisions

General school admitting disabled children should be arranged to provide the following aids and appliances for.

Orthopaedically Handicapped Children: Adjustable furniture. Special writing material (thick pen). Artificial limbs, Wheel chairs and Crutches.

Blind Children: Braille slate and stylus. braille sheets. Abacus. Taylor frame. Mobility canes. Cassette and talking books. Braille text books. Bulletin board. Flat desks. Embossed graph sheets with rubber band push pin tactile maps. Concrete objects to teach shape size, thickness, weight, ascending and descending, etc. number, texture and motor coordination.

Partially-sighted and Low Vision Children: Magnifying glass, Spectacles. Portable reading lamps. White borad in place of black board and Large print materials.

Hearing Impaired Children: Hearing aid (group hearing aid and individual hearing aid). Speech trainer or voice trainer. Mirror (big and small). Special learning materials like flash cards, educational games and toy materials, hand-outs of classroom instruction.

Mentally Retarded and Learning Disabled Children: Educational games and play materials. Concrete objects for teaching different concepts. Picture cards and pictures. Day, Date and Month. Calender Tool bom. Aids for sensory-motor coordination and Alternate learning materials (simplified).

Concept of Impairment

In the field of special education the three terms Impairment, Disability, and Handicap are very often used interchangeably. Thus, we come across expressions like hearing-impairment, hearing- disability, and hearing- handicap to refer to hearing loss. These three terms actually mean different things.

An impairment is a permanent or transitory psychological, or anatomical loss and/or abnormality. This may be so from birth, or, acquired later. Example : a hole in the ear drum, a missing or defective part of the body, paralysis after polio, myopia, low level of intelligence, etc.

Impairment may cause functional limitations. Functional limitation means partial or total inability to perform those activities - necessary for motor, sensory or mental functions within the range and manner of which a human being is normally capable such as walking, lifting loads, seeing, speaking, hearing, reading, writing, taking interest in and making contact with surroundings. A functional limitation may last for a short time, be permanent or reversible. Limitations maybe progressive or regressive.

Impairment leads to disability. Disability is defined as an existing difficulty in performing one or more activities which are generally accepted as essential components of daily living. Due to the impairment there is a reduction in functional ability. For example, due to the hole in the ear drum, the child is unable to hear, normally. A visually impaired child cannot see properly because of faulty image formation. An orthopaedically handicapped child cannot use the arms and fingers for gipping. A learning disabled child cannot calculate or understand number relationship like a normal child. Depending in part on the duration of the functional limitation disability may be short term, long term, or permanent.

Medically, disability is physical impairment and inability to perform physical functions normally. Legally, disability is a permanent injury to body for which the person should or should not be compensated. Disability can be divided into three periods:

(1) Temporary total disability,

(2) Temporary partial disability and

(3) Permanent disability.

Temporary total disability is that period in which the affected person is totally unable to work. During this time he may receive orthopaedic, opthalmological, auditory or speech or may other medical treatment. Temporary partial disability is that period when recovery has reached the stage of improvement so that the person may begin some kind of gainful occupation. Permanent disability refers to permanent damage to or loss of some part of the body even after any medical treatment.

The difference between these three terms can be summarised as follows: Impairment is structural, disability is functional and handicap is social psychological.

Difference between Impairment, Disability and Handicap

	Type of Disability	*Impairment*	*Disability*	*Handicap*
1.	Hearing Impairment	Damage in the ear mechanism (e.g. hole in eardrum)	Difficulty in transmission of sound .	Unable to hear normally.
2.	Visual Impairment	Detachment of Cay muscles (e.g squint /cross eyed)	Difficulty in focussing the eyes on a particular image.	Unable to from single image.
3.	Orthopaedic Impairment	Paralysis in ear	Difficulty in using arm for grasping and manipulating.	Unable to use the ear like others.
4.	Mental Impairment	Deficiency in mentat ability	Difficulty in doing things like others. Difficulty in un understanding abstract concepts	Unable to behave like others.
5.	Learning Disability	Dysfunctioning of specific brain faculty (for example motor area	Difficulty in writing only Can speak and read normally	Unable to read and Write like others

Just as impairment leads to disability, disability handicaps the individual. Handicap means a restriction imposed/acquired by the child's disability which affects the efficiency of his/her day-to day life activities. The term handicap refers to the problems a person with a disability or impairment encounters in interacting with the environment. A disability may pose a problem in one environment. A disability may pose a problem in one environment but not in another. The child with an artificial limb may be handicapped when competing against non-disabled peers in a football match but experiences no handicap in the classroom. Thus, a disabled person is not handicapped, however, unless the physical disability lead to educational, personal, social vocational or other problems The handicapping effects of a disability can be reduced by corrective services like hearing aids, artificial limbs, medical interventions, etc.

The Definitions

An impairment is defined as a loss of or damage to sensory organs. This may be so from birth, or acquired later. The impairment disturbs the normal functioning of the organ in its respective area. For example, a child with a hole in the car claim cannot hear properly because of the disturbance in the sound transmission. Similarly, due to visual problems, there is improper formation of images and the child has difficulty in reading. An orthopaedic impairment also refers to the loss of organ, or abnormality in any part of the organ or body which interferes with its normal functioning. For example, missing fingers or a polio infected arm. Such a child loses the grip of the fingers or the use of arm for manipulation of objects in his/her learning environment. A child with a mental impairment is unable to learn things as quickly as others can. Even the psychological process can be impaired. Impairment in the perceptual process can lead to learning disability, Emotional insecurity may also result in a disability. This implies that impairment leads to disability. Due to the impairment there is reduction in functional ability. For example, due to the hole in the eardrum the child is unable to hear normally, A visually impaired child cannot see properly because of faulty image formation. An orthopaedically handicapped child cannot use the arms and fingers for gripping and a learning disabled cannot calculate or understand number relationships like a normal child. Thus, a handicap is a restriction imposed acquired by the chiles disability which affects the efficiency of his/her day-to-day life activities. Summarizes the differences between these terms.

Thus, impairment is loss or damage in an organ with result that the person is handicapped. The handicapping of a disability can be reduced by corrective services like hearing aids, artificial limbs, medical intervention, etc.

Now let us define the disability areas specifically. This will provide guidelines for identification, as manifestation of behaviours and characteristics will become clear.

(1) The hearing impaired are those children who have a damaged hearing mechanism and face difficulty in speech and language development. There is loss of hearing. The degree of hearing loss is less in some children while it is more in others.

(2) Children with speech disorders are those who have difficulty in articulation, voice, and rhythm. In other words, we can say that they omit, substitute, distort and add sound while speaking a particular word or sentence. These problems can be due to organic defects or due to defective environmental feedback. Misarticulation leads to poor quality of speech. Such children have low and high pitch problems and do not conform to the normal speech patterns. They may break the rhythm of sound while speaking which may lead to stuttering. It is also known as fluency disorder. For more information see page 30 of this chapter.

(3) The visually impaired are those who have problems with vision. Some children can read large print and are functional in their environment whereas some have severe vision loss and cannot be taught through visual methods.

(4) The orthopaedically impaired are those who have problems with the functioning of bones, joints, and muscles, to such an extent that they require artificial limbs to compensate for crippling conditions, and some environmental modifications to be able to adjust in the classroom. Some children suffer from brain dysfunction and because of this, they have problems in performing motor activities.

(5) Children with special health problems are those, whose weakened physical condition makes them inactive. They require special health precautions in school.

(6) Mentally impaired children are those who have a lower level or intellectual functioning and have problems in learning, social and emotional behaviours. The degree of delayed development differs from one group to another. For identifying these children their adaptive behaviours should be assessed along with intellectual assessment.

(7) The learning disabled are defined as those having disorder in one or more of the basic psychological process involved in understanding, or using spoken or written language. They show imperfect ability to listen, think, write, read, spell or do mathematical calculation. These children however are above average in intelligence and do not have hearing or visual impairment.

The definitions, given in brief, will help us in understanding the classifications of disabled children. Let us learn about the classification of disabled children which will facilitate the placement and education of these children in IED settings:

Needs and Problems

All children have certain basic needs. The needs of children are often accompanied by or result in certain problems. The needs and problems of exceptional children are similar to and at the saw time different from those for non-exceptional children. The needs and problems of exceptional children also very depending upon the direction and degree of their deviation from normal children and their type of exceptionality. For example, the needs and problems of mildly and moderately handicapped children are different from those of severely handicapped children. Similarly the needs and problems of handicapped children are different from those of children with superior ability. Even though the needs and problems of exceptional children are related to their characteristics they have certain, common needs and problems such as, need for appropriate education, need and problems such as, need for appropriate education, need for independent functioning, need for respect for their individuality, etc.

Disabled children are like non-disabled children except their specific disabilities. For example, a blind child is like any other sighted child except his loss of vision. Disabled children have a fundamental right to live and participate fully in all settings and programmes that are as normalized as possible. But consciously or out of ignorance we tend to treat them, differently in school, at home, in the work place and in the community. Our differential treatment creates in them and among their peers a feeling of 'otherness'.

Disabled children have a strong desire for independent functioning. Instead of assisting them to maximize their independent functioning in normal environments we make them dependent on others. It is perhaps for this reason that many blind and orthopaedically handicapped children resort to begging. One of the objectives of special education is to teach the disabled children self-help skills, daily living skills, vocational skills, and to assist them to manage their own affairs independently during adulthood.

An exceptional child, whether he is handicapped or gifted, has an individuality of his own. He thinks, learns acts and adapts in his own way. He has the capabilities to live a better life and to improve his functioning level in the community. Teachers need to have confidence on his capabilities and respect for his individuality. In schools exceptional children do not have the opportunity to express themselves fully. Their individuality is suppressed and at times punished by teachers.

Exceptional children need free and appropriate education to maximize their capabilities. Such education should not be provided to them out of sympathy or as a privilege granted to them. Education is a basic human right and this must be granted to them just as we provide free and compulsory education to non-exceptional children. India is under pressure from international agencies to make education a basic right of the child. But it is surprising that the bill making education a basic right of the child is in the cold storage of the MHRD.

Many exceptional children and their parents experience difficulties relating to appropriate education. Appropriate education for exceptional children can only be provided in regular schools. But most teachers are reluctant to admit handicapped children in, the regular schools on the false impression that educating handicapped children in regular schools will adversely affect the education of non-handicapped children. In most cases, the blind, deaf and MR children in regular schools. The principle of "zero reject" stipulates that no in a school of his choice, Moreover there is no provision of appropriate; education for gifted and create children in our school excepting providing the, same type of education that are provided to average students. There are also no special schools for gifted, creative, emotionally disturbed and even the learning disable children.

The handicapped children-need equality of educational opportunity. The indicators of equal education opportunity for the handicapped have been spelt out by NCERT (1987) as follows:

(1) Equal access to educational institutions, in common with others.
(2) Access to special education institutions where needed.
(3) Resource facilities to support educational programmes.
(4) Equal access to curriculum.
(5) Curriculum adjustment to the needs arising out of a disability wherever needed.
(6) Adaptive aids and equipment to ensure optimal access to curriculum.
(7) Adjustment of instructional methods and materials to ensure optimal access to curriculum.
(8) Adjustment of evaluation and examination procedures to offset handicapping effects of the disability.
(9) Trained manpower for equal educational opportunity in general and special institutions.
(10) Educational administrator's response to the needs of the disabled children.
(11) Commitment to education and rehabilitation of the disabled.

The Programme of Action (NPE, 1986) also stipulates above mentioned measures for appropriate education of handicapped children. But handicapped children experience problems of access to and success in educational institutions. There are a limited number of general schools enrolling handicapped children along with normal children. Even these schools are not properly equipped with materials, and special education provided in such schools is not appropriate to the needs of handicapped children. Special needs of such children.

Exceptional children need special education and related services. This requires proper assessment and classification of exceptional children. The problem is that in most cases the assessment procedure is not objective and systematic. This is why many children with temporary learning problems are classified as mentally retarded or learning disabled. Moreover, what is cutoff points between a mildly understanding about these children we tend to classify them and label them as retarded deaf, handicapped, crippled, disabled, etc. Labelling itself is not a healthy practice for a number of reasons.

(1) Labels usually focus on a child's negative aspects. Once a child is labelled we tend to think about the child only in terms of this inadequacies or defects.

(2) Labels lead to low expectations from teachers, parents and others about what a child can do.

(3) One a child is labelled teachers tend to explain the child's poor performance only in terms of his disability and not in terms of instructional failure.

(4) A labelled child may develop a poor self-concept.

(5) Labels create a sense of helplessness, inferiority and stigmatization.

Exceptional children need special aids, equipment and learning materials to profit from regular and special education programmes and to meet their special needs. The blind children need braille materials and other aids; the low vision children need large print materials and magnifying glasses the deaf children need hearing aids, speech trainer, visual materials, etc. the MR children need games and play materials and other concrete objects; the LD children need alternate learning materials, work books, etc.; and so on. Gifted children need advanced learning materials, encyclopaedia, etc. In most school aids, equipment and learning materials are not able to maximize their capabilities. Discrepancy between what they are capable of doing and what they do gradually widens. This also causes a hug wastage of human resources.

Exceptional children, particularly the disabled ones, need incentives and financial assistance—conveyance allowances, allowances for purchase of learning materials, uniform dress, etc. The state Governments are not in position to provide such assistance to disabled children. They simply depend on the assistance provided by the MHRD, Governments of India. In most states the education of disabled children has been neglected due to withdrawal of assistance by the MHRD. Government of India. This is a recurring problem for most disabled children.

The Procedure

There are various types of exceptional children. Educational programmes should vary from one category to other categories of exceptional children. In this section a general discussion on their identification, assessment, placement and education has been made.

Identification and Assessment : Many exceptional children remain unidentified whether they are in the school or out of school. Consequently they are not able to maximize their potentialities. This calls for early identification of such children. Regular teachers should observe the behavioural characteristics of children suspected to be exceptional and refer them to specialists for medical and psychological assessments. In our country, particularly in rural areas, school authorities have been facing diffficulties for medical and psychological assessment of exceptional children due to non-availability of specialists. In such cases teachers can conduct functional assessment which indicates what a child can do and what he cannot do. Functional assessment is to substitute for medical and psychological assessment. In every case exceptional children should be subjected to medical and psychological assessment if intervention programme is to be effective.

Placement Services: After medical and psychological assessment exceptional children should be placed in a suitable grade in a suitable educational institution. The degree of deviation of an exceptional child and the nature and range of his previous experiences usually determine his placement in an educational institution. So far as handicapped children are concerned the following placement programmes are followed in our country:

(1) Full time placement in regular class.

(2) Part time placement in regular class with part time placement in special class.

(3) Full time placement in special class.

(4) Full time placement in special schools.

(5) Full time placement in residential schools.

Since we do not have special class and special school provision for gifted, creative, emotionally disturbed and socially disadvantaged children, they are usually educated in regular schools. However, various type of scholarships such as NRTS, NTS, Merit scholarships, etc., are available for bright students.

Emphasis on Individuality : Exceptional children constitute a heterogeneous group. There are various categories of exceptional children. Each category of exceptional children has unique characteristics. Again in each category there are various classes of children depending upon their degree of uniqueness. Education of exceptional children should match with their individual characteristics. In fact the individuality of each exceptional child should be the basis of all that we are doing and all that we want to for his education.

Emphasis on Learning : It is worth noting that children are required to learn in the way the teacher teaches. Since emphasis is being shifted at present from teaching to learning, teachers should teach in the way the child learns best. This emphasis on learning rather than teaching is rightly justified while planning any educational programme for exceptional children, whether they are disabled, disturbed, disadvantaged or gifted.

Special School Setting: In our country a large number of special schools have been established for education for severely handicapped children, particularly the blind, the deaf and the mentally retarded children. In special schools severely handicapped children are educated by specially trained teachers with the help of special aids and equipment and a curriculum adapted to their needs. Excepting a few Government institutions, education in special schools is very expensive. Thus, many handicapped children are forced to out of schools as their parents are not in a position to meet the expenses of their children's education in special schools.

Integrated Setting : The recent trend in the education of disabled children is to educate them in common with non-disabled children in general schools. The National Policy of Education (1986) envisages that "wherever it is possible, education of children with locomotor handicap and other mild handicaps will be common with that of others. Special schools with hostels will be provided, as far as possible at district headquarters, for severely handicapped children. Voluntary efforts for education of the disabled will be encouraged in every possible way."

Provision of Incentives: Government of India have made certain provisions of incentives for the education of disabled children. These include transport allowances, uniform allowances, purchases of books, escort allowances, attendance scholarships,- etc. Disabled children should be guided to take advantage of such incentives. In addition to these, gifted and talented children should be also guided to take advantage of NRTS, NTS and other scholarships.

Preparatory Classes : Disabled children should have some preparation before they receive formal education in a school. Such preparation can be made either in a special school or in ECEC centre, anganwadi, balwadi or preparatory classes in a primary school. For this purpose the teacher should conduct a screening test first, and then administer individual tests, interview parents and their disabled children to assess what the child knows and can do and what does not know or what he cannot do. A blind child must receive mobility training, orientation training and training in daily living skills and braille writing. A learning disabled child must be trained to sit and be attentive. Many disabled children need preparation in pre-academic skills. Such preparation is very essential for successful progress in primary grades. But once a child has completed preparation in pre-academic skills, communication skills, daily living skills, mobility training and orientation training he should be encouraged to receive education in a general school in common with others.

In integrated settings disabled and non-disabled children are taught by the regular class teacher with support from the resource teacher, and instruction in the resource room in areas of their deficiencies. "The objective should be to integrated the physically and mentally handicapped with the general community, to prepare them for normal growth, and enable them to face life with courage and confidence." (NPE, 1986)

Resource Teacher Support: Every school admitting exceptional children should have a resource teacher for every 8 to 10 exceptional children. The resource teacher may be a full time resource teacher or an itinerant resource teacher. He is the person to provide support services to exceptional children in the resource room. Since he is an expert in the methodology of educating exceptional children he can also act as a consultant to other regular teachers.

Aids and Equipments: Exceptional children who do not profit from the conventional instructional materials, teaching aids and equipment should be provided 'With aids and equipment in the resource room keeping in view their special needs, Braille materials, large print materials and magnifying glasses for the visually impaired, hearing aids, speech trainer, and visual materials for the hearing impaired, play and toy materials for the mentally retarded, alternate learning materials for the less abled ones, etc., should be made available in schools for proper education of exceptional children.

Special Health Problems

Are those whose poor physical condition, make them inactive and who require special health precautions in school. Such children can be categorized into the following groups.

(1) Children with mild health problems: Come under the educable IED group. Their health problems do not interfere with educational learning. But precautions need to be taken in terms of getting adequate medical checkups and support.

(2) There are children with severe health problems who cannot be integrated in regular schools. The severity of their health problem interferes with educational planning. They will need constant medical care and are therefore not able to participate in the academic and non-academic activities of general classrooms. Children with severe problem, like heart problem, diabetic, epilepsy, need to rest after 10-15 minutes of studying. It is difficult to accommodate them in general classroom since they require constant medical care and the full attention of the teacher. Such children need to be educated either at home/ hospital or in special classes in general schools. Some health problems are discussed below:

The problem may occur in disabled children hence, the knowledge of the symptoms and their implications can help the teacher in minimising these problems and helping the disabled to develop their talents like others.

Epilepsy : This is one of the special health problems which is generally faced by children. The symptoms of this problem are: (i) the child shakes violently as if in the grip of hysteria, (ii) there is constant recurrence of fits, (iii) the child loses consciousness, (iv) falls and moves arms and legs violently, (v) the child may become pale. (vi) he falls mid moves arms and legs violently, (vii) purposeless activities such as rubbing of arms and body parts, (viii) the child starts taking off his clothes. The problem is due to brain injury or an extra growth in the brain. Some drugs are available to control the fits and the extra growth can be removed by surgery. Epilepsy is treated as a special health problems.

Since the fits are painless to the victim, it is important that the teacher should remain calm and not attempt to restrain the child's movements. All sharp objects that may injure the child should be removed from around but the movements must not be interrupted. If the mouth is open some soft objects such as a handkerchief should be placed to prevent the tongue from being bitten. The child should be allowed to rest after the fit and the parents and doctor should boycott among peers and to protect the child from such treatment. The teacher can use this opportunity to explain the problem to the entire class. The teacher should also explain to the other staff members and the community that the cause of epilepsy is not evil spirits but injury of the brain. The child is normal in his/her intellectual functioning. This will help in better social, emotional and academic integration of such children.

Children with Diabetic Problems

Children with the problems show the following symptoms: Frequent urination, abnormal thirst, extreme hunger, frequent change in weight, generally rapid loss, sleepness, weakness, usual disturbances are felt more acutely and frequent skin infections such as boils and itching.

This problem can occur in both normal and disabled children studying in your school. As a teacher you are expected to identify these symptoms at an early stage. The problem is because the body not producing sufficient amount of the hormone called insulin and can be controlled by given insulin in the proper dose at the proper time. The teacher's role is to help the child to get medical examination and to take medicine and diet according to the doctors' prescription.

Asthma (Bronchical Problem): Generally, the problem of asthma is overlooked in our classrooms but since it creates some social and emotional problems for the child so it is better if the teacher is made aware of it. The child suffers from breathing trouble due to allergy. The commonly seen symptoms are: difficulty in breathing, the child takes large gulps of air becomes pale, breathes noisily and perspires too much. Asthma is caused by allergens such as dust and the pollen of some plants. It may also occur due to excessive physical activity or emotional reaction. Drugs can be given orally or by injection, which help to control the problem, but it is not completely curable. Teachers who have such children in their class should help these children by keeping them away from dust and pollen. They should not be asked to do strenuous exercises. The teacher is also required to help the affected child to adjust to the problem and to involve in social activities that are not too rigorous.

Juvenile Rheumatoid: Pain in the joint which occurs in younger children is known as Juvenile Rheumatoid. Such children have a skin rash and swelling and redness of the eyes. There could be some retardation in growth since it is a disease that attacks the joints. It may cause stunted growth. Swelling and pain occur in the fingers, wrists, elbows, knees, hips and feet. In severe cases, it left untreated the joints become stiff making movements difficult and painful. Juvenile rheumatoid is a chronic infection of the connective tissue of the body. Drugs and special exercises can prevent the disease from becoming too severe. In the case of such children the role of teacher is very important. The teacher must be understanding and at the same time, not overprotective. Such children require more time to finish their assignments. Various adjustments such as children require more time to finish their assignments. Various adjustments such as writing aids and special paper and pencils can be provided to the children who have stiffened upper limbs. Since such children are physically weak, the teacher should not insist on their participating in all activities.

Anaemia: Health problem is a condition in which the child suffers from sever loss of blood. Children who suffers from anaemia, have periodic attacks of acute pain, may be weak and prone to jaundice and leg ulcers. They have pain in the abdomen, knees, elbows and other joints in the body. They suffer from constant headaches and may occasionally faint, feel ringing in the cars and see spots before the eyes. The major cause of this loss of blood is the loss of the red pigment of blood cells known as haemoglobin. The shape of the red blood cells change to sickle-shaped. A complete cure is not possible in server cases of the disease. Children afflicted with the disease need to rest frequently and be protected from further infection. The teacher should allow them more time to finish their assignments. Since it also leads to lack of oxygen, frequent hospital treatment is required. Teachers should get the children medically examined if they suspect any such problems in them. The children with mild type of anaemia need only periodic medical check ups and medicines according to doctors' prescription. They can be integrated without any problems.

Exercise

1. Define the term, 'Exceptional Children'. Enumerate the characteristics and needs of exceptional children.
2. Classify the exceptional children and indicate the types of exceptional children. Enumerate their problems.
3. Describe the educational and school provisions of exceptional children and role of teachers and parents.
4. Differentiate among handicapped, disabled and impaired children with reference to types of disabilities.
5. Describe the procedures for educating exceptional children with reference to individually, integrating selling and aids and equipment for teaching in classroom.

7

Emotional Disturbance

Emotional disturbance can be viewed for a variety of perspectives. In the past emotionally disturbed children were viewed as autistic. They were confined to institutional programmes and were under residential care. Very few of the received schooling, if at all. After 1975 when the Handicapped Children's Act was passed in USA there developed a new interest in the education of the emotionally disturbed in a separate school. The other view which is prevalent is mainstreaming or integrating the emotionally disturbed into a normal environment. In many cases there is no such clear-cut decision regarding the care, treatment, education and rehabilitating of emotionally disturbed. Some children in the classroom are mischievous. They are hyperactive or hypoactive. They have temper tantrums and display unruly behaviour and self injurious behaviours quite often. These children pose problems for the classroom teacher.

Meaning and Definitions

The term Emotional Disturbance' has different meanings. For teachers, an emotionally disturbed child is one who is shy, withdrawn, or who is too aggressive. Emotionally disturbed behaviour was considered synonymous with misbehaviour or deviancy. By deviancy it is meant that "a student takes actions which are prohibited by the teacher." In this definition the locus of the problem was on the norms of the school. A different kind of definition was also given in terms of the ecology of the child. According to this, emotional disturbance is viewed in terms of environmental variables which create maladaptive emotional reactions. For example, the frustrating environment in the school or such other unfavourable circumstances lead to emotional disturbance. From the view point of the peer group certain behaviours are problem behaviour. According to this, a child who cannot make interpersonal adjustment with his age mates is considered as an emotionally disturbed child. When the child's sociometric relationship declines, he becomes emotionally disturbed.

There is no universally accepted definition of emotionally disturbed children. Professional groups and experts dealing with disturbed children have constructed individual working definitions to fit their own professional purposes. Defining the disturbed child is like defining experiences such as, anger, loneliness, or happiness. One can understand what these experiences are but defining these experiences is far from simple.

The American Psychiatric Association (APA) defined emotional disturbance as follow: "It is a type of Psychiatric disturbances without clearly defined physical cause or without structural damage to the brain."

In general, emotional disorder or disturbance in children can be defined in terms of certain observable characteristics such as : "hyperactivity, withdrawn behaviour, failure to achieve at a level reasonably commensurate with ability, tendency towards fighting and other aggressive behaviour, resentment and antagonism towards authority and rules and regulations, and general problems in learning and concentrating, not associated with known organic or sensory defects." Hence, an emotionally disturbed child is one who shows to an extreme degree, one or more of the characteristics listed above .

Emotional disturbance is not distributed evenly in all age groups, sex and social class groups. The behaviour problems are maximum during early puberty and these are found earlier among girls than among boys.

The Characteristics

The following characteristics over a long period of time and to a marked degree that adversely affects educational performance.

(1) An inability to learn that cannot be explained by intellectual, sensory or health factors.

(2) An inability to build and maintain satisfactory interpersonal relationships with peers teachers.

(3) Inappropriate behaviour of feelings under normal circumstances.

(4) A general and pervasive mood of unhappiness or depression.

(5) A tendency to develop physical symptoms of fear associated with personal or school problems.

This particular term 'emotional disturbance' with all the emotional and behavioural characteristics does include Schizophrenic and autistic characteristics. It does not include the socially maladjusted unless serious emotional disturbance is accompanied with social maladjustment.

Emotionally disturbed children may be either of mild and moderate type or of sever type. Teacher in regular schools are expected to manage the mildly and moderately disturbed children in their classrooms. Hence, it is imperative for them to be familiar with the behavioural and psychological characteristics of mildly and moderately disturbed children. Wen will discuss the behaviour and psychological characteristics of mildly and moderately disturbed children under these heads :

Intelligence and Achievement

1. In general, mildly and moderately disturbed children are found to be dull. Their IQ falls around 90. Very few disturbed children are found to be bright.

2. Most severely disturbed children are untestable. Those who can be tested are found to be retarded, their IQ falling around 50.
3. There are some disturbed children who are extremely bright, but they are not representative of disturbed children as a group.
4. The lower IQ scores of disturbed children are consistent with their impairment in other areas of functioning.
5. Most disturbed children are underachievers at school. A disturbed child does not achieve at the level expected for his mental age. It is relatively seldom that some finds an academically advanced disturbed child. Most severely disturbed children lack even the most basic reading and arithmetic skills. Those who appear to be competent in reading or arithmetic are usually unable to apply their skills in any useful way to everyday problems.

Social and Emotional Factors

1. Conduct disorders are the most common problems exhibited by disturbed children. Hitting, fighting, yelling, refusal to comply with requests, crying, destructiveness, vandalism are most commonly exhibited by such children.
2. They drive adults to distraction with their bad temperament and nastiness.
3. They are not popular among their normal peers. They are not good at making friends. Their most obvious problem is a failure to establish close and satisfying emotional ties with other people.
4. Some disturbed children are withdrawn. Their drawing back from interaction with others-their social isolation is clearly self-imposed. When will meaning adults and others care about them and try to help them, such children strike out with hostility and aggression. It is easy to see why they are friendless. They are abusive, destructive, unpredicatable, irresponsible, bossy, quarrelsome, irritable, jealous, defiant - anything about pleasant and

nice to be with. Naturally other children and adults choose not to spend with this kind of person.

5. Their behaviour is not only extremely troublesome but also resistant to change through the usual means of discipline. Often they are so frequently reprimanded and punished that punishment means little or nothing for them.

Behavioural Factors

The following behavioural characteristics are very effective in screening emotionally disturbed children.

1. Needs an unusual amount of providing to get work completed.
2. Is inattentive, indifferent, or apparently lazy.
3. Exhibits nervous reactions such as nail-biting, sucking thumb or fingers, stuttering, extreme restlessness, muscle twitching, hair twisting, picking and scratching, deep and frequent sighing.
4. Is actively excluded by most of the children wherever they get a chance.
5. Failure in school for no apparent reason.
6. Is absent from school frequently or dislike school intensity.
7. Seems to be more unhappy that most of the children.
8. Achieve much less in school than his ability indicates he should.
9. Jealous or over competitive.

Emotionally disturbed children are often seem as unpredictable that present serious problems. Emotionally disturbed children in contrast to the normal group have no close emotional proximity with their parents. Failure in school is often thought to be symptom of neurotic behaviour. Further. the self of the disturbed child is invariably negative. When self-evaluation questionnaires are given to emotionally disturbed children, they saw themselves as less likeable, and less able to arouse affection in others. They are either psychotic or emotionally indifferent. For this reason, quite a few programmes have been designed on classroom organisational pattern so that these children can function to their maximum but the research evidence on the learning characteristics of the emotionally disturbed children show lack of interest in academic matter and school performance, lower I.Q. and achievement. Their reading and mathematics achievement are significantly below the average. The majority of the studies demonstrate however, that emotionally disturbed children as a group have little less than average intelligence. But primarily their personality and behavioural traits contribute maximum to discrepant achievement in reading and arithmetic achievement.

The emotionally disturbed children lack most to these attributes, such as:

(1) Ability to handle anxiety.
(2) Feeling of self work.
(3) Conformity to demands.
(4) Peer acceptance.
(5) Less conflict over independence.
(6) Engagement in activity of academic nature, and
(7) Setting of realistic goal.

In fact, we sometimes overlook the emotional disturbance of gifted children over very bright children whereas we become more concerned about the learning disabled child who has emotional problems.

In the area of academics, most students with emotional or behavioural problems have considerable difficulty. Kauffmann, Cullinan and Epstein found that academic deficits specifically reading were related to the students aggression, defiance, and violation of the social rules.

The several other characteristics have been identified that are observed in behaviour disordered students.

(1) Disrupts other children.
(2) Is compulsive behaviour ?
(3) Does not compete the required task ?
(4) Is destructive to own and other's belongings ?
(5) Does not follow commands ?
(6) Is undependable behaviour ?

(7) Exhibits inappropriate behaviour.

(8) Is unhappy or depressed behaviour and ?

(9) Exhibits poor interpersonal relationships.

Mattison, Humphrey, Kales, and Wallace also noted the characteristics of behaviour disorders which are conduct disorders than anxiety, or withdrawal. However, anxiety disorder, avoidance behaviour, separation anxiety over anxiety, withdrawal, depression are typical behaviour emotional problems.

They have slightly less than average intelligence. Kauffman and Kauffman, Cullinan and Epstein found intelligence of emotionally disturbed children to be less than average or low average i.e., around 90 IQ, varying from 60 to 130 IQ.

THE CLASSIFICATION

Emotional disturbance cannot be classified on a continuum as MR, Hearing handicapped, or visual handicapped. It varies according to clinical symptoms which are grouped to define a type of emotional disturbances such as Autism, Psychosis, Childhood Schizophrenia etc.

Autism : Autism in children is one of the most severe forms of emotionally disturbed. This is also otherwise known as childhood schizophrenia. This condition is presented with and is followed by delay in speech development, non-communicative use of speech, and withdrawal tendencies. Such children do not use language to convey meanings.

Kanner described that an autistic child has:

(a) severe withdrawal of contact from other has

(b) an intense need to preserve sameness

(c) an inability to deal with people

(d) apparently good intellectual potential

(e) severe disturbance of language functioning.

Rutter emphasized delayed and deviant language, respective speech, stereotype behaviour (body movements while speaking), scholaliac speech, resistance to change, delusions, hallucinations, loosening of associations and incoherence.

Psychosis : This is the most severe and debilitating of the emotional disturbances. Psychotic children have no contact with reality. Childhood schizophrenia is quite commonly seen. In early infantile autistic children, we find extreme withdrawal, peculiar communication, and improper use of language. They only react to their own private imaginary scheme of life.

Childhood Schizophrenia (Psychosis) : Unlike autism this disorder has its onset after 30 months of age and before 12 years. The child must exhibit at least three of the following sudden anxiety, inappropriate affect, resistance to change, oddities of motor movement, abnormalities of speech, hyper or hyposensitivity to sensory stimuli, self-mutilation, impairment in social relations, absence of illusions, delusions, hallucinations and incoherence.

Psycho-physiological Disturbance : These disorders result in physical malfunctioning but without an anxiety. These children have severe eczema, asthma without emotional overlay. They also exhibit anorexia nervoa, persistent loss of appetite, and are underweight. They have painful migraine. They mostly need medical treatment.

Psychoneurosis : In this type of disorder certain functions are distorted but the child is not isolated from reality. It is said that the psychoneurotic child builds castles in the air and the psychotic child lives in them. Many children are cautions, frightened and show uncontrollable crying etc. They have phobias, manias, panic syndrome, and conversion.

Personality Disorders : These children cannot adjust to society. They are extremely shy. They have delusions of persecutions and are rigid. They lack the resilience to develop better ways of meeting emotional problems or alternatively sometimes they appear as too outgoing. The second type feel no tension or anxiety.

Transient Situational Personality Disorder : These are acute reactions to catastrophic or unpleasant incidents such as: death of a friend, relative, accidents etc. These are situational and are responsible for chronic and acute personality disturbance.

Prevalence : In a survey conducted by the National Institute of Mental Health it has been observed that nearly 1.5 per cent of population in the age group of 0-21 suffers from emotional disturbance.

THE IDENTIFICATION

Screening procedure can be more intricate and perhaps more accurate by addition of teacher rating, peer rating, self-rating, using standardised personality test and inventories. Three most widely used tests are : California, Psychological, Inventory. Very few tests are available for use at elementary level or when children are quite young. However, children's Appreciation Test, Thematic Appreciation Test, WISC and Bender Gestalt Test can be used quite effectively for identifying emotionally disturbed children.

(1) Revised Behaviour Problems Checklist from kindergarten age to grade VI with 89 items.
(2) Burk's Behaviour Rating Scales with 110 items used from grade to VII.
(3) Walker Problem Behaviour Identification checklist 50 items and from pre-school to grade six.
(4) Child Behaviour Checklist used for 4 years to 16 years.
(5) Personality inventory for children from 3 to 16 year olds 600 items broken down to 40 scales.
(6) Rorscha Ink Blot Test and
(7) Sentence Completion Test.

Behaviour assessment of children has been primarily based upon adult's judgement of children's behaviour not children's opinion of themselves or each other (peer rating). Adequate behaviour in more than one setting and requires evaluation or more than the social and emotional domains. Particularly for young children perceptual motor and language performance are more required to account for any behavioural deficit than intelligence.

There are norm referenced scale for assessing adequacy of children's performance in some areas of functioning i.e., intelligence, language, perceptual motor but in behavioural assessment norm referenced test are not readily available and assessment is a matter of subjective clinical appraisal. Similarly reciprocal influence of environment, behaviour and the person variables is a matter of clinical judgement. However, some progress has been achieved in assessment of cognitive influences on behaviour. Neuro-psychological and neuro-physiological assessments are time consuming and usually do not reveal more information than standard psychological and behavioural assessment. Behaviour rating scales, checklists and interviews with parents and children are more meaningful accompanied by direct observation of behaviour.

Identification is Easier : While there is a problem defining and classifying various types of emotional disturbance, it is much easier to identify disturbed behaviours. Most disturbed children do not typically escape notice. The most common type of disturbed children - children with conduct problem - readily attract attention with their behaviour So there is seldom any real problem in identifying them. Mature children and those with personality problems may be less abrasive, but they are not extremely difficult to recognise. Disturbed children are so readily identified by school personnel that few authorities bother to carry out systematic screening procedure. Moreover, special education services for disturbed children lag far behind the need. There is not much point in screening children for problems when the services available to treat these problems is inadequate.

Early Identification : One important point to remember is that the younger the child, the more difficult it is to judge whether or not his behaviour is disturbed. Some disturbed children go unnoticed because teachers are not sensitive to their problems or their environment. Some sensitive teachers make errors in their judgements about the disturbed behaviour of children. Some disturbed children also do not exhibit disturbed behaviours in the school. In spite of these problems, disturbed children are to be identified early so that suitable intervention programmes can be planned for them.

Identification Procedure : What technique are to be adopted for screening and identifying disturbed children ? There are two important considerations to be kept in mind while discussing about the screening and identification of disturbed children. First, there is not an adequate definition of the disturbed child. Second, there are no adequate instruments or measuring emotional disturbance. Hence identification of disturbed children depends on subjective as mentioned below:

1) Informal teacher judgement.
2) Teacher's ratings of children's behaviour.
3) Children's ratings of their peers and their own behaviour.
4) Direct observation by teachers.

The Causes

The following causes children are effective in screening emotionally disturbed children,:

Psychoanalytic Causes: There are a variety of causes for emotional disturbance. Most of them are psychoanalytic and a few of them are explained by learning. The psychoanalytic causes include : anxiety as a source of emotional disturbance, distrust of adults because of traumatic experiences, frustration of libidinal desires, parental rejection, punishment, ridicule, and insecurity deprived from lack of affection or social prestige. Emotional disorders are explained by learning psychologists using conditioning. The same disorders are also reduced by counter conditioning or reconditioning.

Environmental Conditions : There is some evidence of mental illness occurring in particular families and behaviour characteristics of twins. Schinophrenia is one such example. One the other hand, modelling explains behaviour problems. The situation is more confusing than clear. Maternal malnutrition, anoxia, head injury as well as educational school related factors explain emotional disorders.

The Problems

Emotionally disturbed children are sometimes known as problem children. Depending upon the type of problems exhibited such children are classified into three categories such as

1. Children with conduct problems.
2. Children with personality problem and
3. Children with inadequacy - Immaturity problem.

The behaviour traits and life history characteristics of such children are given below (Hallahan and

Children with Conduct Problems

Behaviour traits : Disobedience, Disruptiveness, Fighting, Destructiveness, Temper tantrums, Irresponsibility, Impertinent, Jealous, Anger, Bossy, Profanity, Attention seeking, and Boisterous.

Life History Characteristics: Assaultive, Defies authority, Inadequate guilt feelings, and Quarrelsome.

Children with Personality Problems

Behaviour Traits: Feelings of inferiority, Self-consciousness, Social withdrawal, Anxiety, Crying, Hypersensitive, Seldom, smiles, Chews finger nails, Depression, Chronic sadness and Shyness.

Life History Characteristics: Seclusive, Shy Sensitive, Worries, Timid, and has anxiety over own behaviour.

Children with Immaturity Problem

Behaviour traits : Preoccupation, Short attention, Span, Clumsiness, Passivity, Day dreaming, Sluggish Drowsiness, Prefers younger play mates, Masturbation, Giggles, Easily flustered, Chews objects, Picked on by others and plays with toys in class.

Life History Characteristics : Habitually truant from home, Unable to cope with a complex word, Incompetent, immature, and Engages in furtive stealing.

Among the family factor, Cullinan, Epstein, and Lloyd (1983) include (a) child's early separation from his parents due to desertion, death etc. (b) parents conflict, divorce (c) parent's hostility, abuse or neglect (d) parents who themselves may be incompetent or have behaviour problems

Kauffman indicated six school related factors:

(1) Insensitivity by the school to the individual.
(2) Inappropriately high or low expectation for the student.
(3) Inconsistent behaviour management procedures.

(4) Meaningless or uninteresting materials and assignments.
(5) Reinforcement of inappropriate behaviour caused by teacher attention, and
(6) Student modelling inappropriate behaviour.

Remedial Approach

It may be a worthwhile stage to combine the perceptual ability of such children with their learning ability show impulsive behaviour which is not conducive to learning. Attempt to make them more reflective and less hyperactive. Secondly, they should have less anxiety and trauma in dealing with a particular learning situation. It has been suggested that a changed model to be applied for emotionally disturbed to learn and adjust in a better way. By a changed model it is meant a set of logically derived statements of the "if and then" variety which are conditional upon the development stage or conceptual level then we can derive the specific environment most likely to produce progress for the person. The issue is not which environment is best but rather which environment is most likely to produce a desired effect for a specified person or persons that educational environment such highly organized or completely free classrooms are differentially effective with students of varying personality or abilities, is widely recognised.

Educational Provisions

How should disturbed children be educated ? There are many different answers to the question of educating disturbed children. This is natural because disturbed behaviours, range from aggressive to withdrawal and from mild to profound category. There are different approaches to the education of disturbed children such as:

(a) Psycho-analytic approach.
(b) Psycho-educational approach.
(c) Humanistic approach.
(d) Ecological approach and
(e) Behavioural approach.

A few ideas of great use in making educational provisions for the emotionally disturbed children. These are as follow:

1. Structuring limits in the classroom receives first priority. The classroom atmosphere should be more than negative restrictions. The classroom atmosphere must given support and direction to activities out of emotional chaos order will emerge among these children.
2. There is no value in concluding that emotionally disturbed children are educationally retarded. Subject matter itself should convey appropriate information for social and academic learning. These children should be given selected readings on social learning.
3. Group dynamic principles may be used for disturbed children e.g., seating arrangement, position of teachers, and pupils can be designed to encourage desired interactions between teachers and pupils, and among pupils.
4. Directed group activity can be used. This will break inhibitions. Role playing is also another technique for releasing emotional problems.
5. Involvement of the child in work as soon as he reaches the school or when is at home in any work. This way he will not get time for 'horse play' or day drawing.
6. Offer support and reward and reinforcement when they do good work; never attack the child as person; focus correction on actual task and keep relationship task centred.
7. As the child increases in responsibility and self direction, plan for more long range activities but with manageable steps.

Emotional disturbance are just like any other problem. These are not unsurmountable. Parents and teachers can help the child reach firm strong, and self directing decisions. These decisions are merely a few suggestions.

Approach of Teaching

The following are the essential points of the above approaches.

1. Emotionally disturbed is the result of some inner conflict. Hence, before any educational programme is designed for these children psychologists and psychiatrists must help to uncover the underlying inner conflict in an effort to improve the psychological functioning as well as behaviour and achievement of the child.
2. Emphasis should be placed on teacher-pupils relationship in which the child feels accepted and free to act out his impulses in a permissive environment. Initially little emphasis should be given on academic achievement or to change the 'surface behaviour' of the child. If the teacher can uncover the mental conflict half of his work is achieved.
3. Once the underlying pathology is revealed the teacher should gradually move towards managing the disturbed behaviour and academic achievement. There should be emphasis on meeting the individual needs of children and most teaching should be done through projects or the creative arts like music, art, dance, etc.
4. Educational programmes should be designed to enhance children's self-direction, self-evaluation and active involvement in the learning environment. The teachers should be non-authoritarian, open and personal in their approach towards the child.
5. The roots of emotional disturbance may in the social environment of the child in which the child lives, grows and interacts. Hence, the entire social system - the school, family, community and other social agencies must be altered as far as practicable. Hence, the teacher's concern should not be just effective teaching in the classroom but to work with the child's family, neighourhood and community agencies as well. Teacher's rapport with

parents, community members and other adults will try to achieve his goal altering the social system.

6. Educational practice must emphasize the behaviour modification strategies. School authorities must remember that every behaviour is learned. The disturbed child has failed to learn desirable behaviour and has learned inappropriate behaviours. Following the behaviour modification techniques the teacher can modify the undesirable behaviours of the child, teach him desirable behaviour through praise, reward, and recognition and develop in him the ability and confidence in learning essential academic and other skills.
7. The mildly and moderately disturbed children should be kept in the mainstream as much as possible. If it is not feasible to keep the disturbed child in regular classes all the time then he may be removed to the resource room or the special class for a part of the day with the goal of reintegration in the regular classes.
8. The curriculum for such children will be the same as for normal children with emphasis on basic academic skills (reading, writing and arithmetic), art, music dance, social skills, and affective experiences. How to manage his own feelings and behaviour and how to get along with other people are essential skills which are no less important as academic skills. Teachers are expected to adopt novel teaching methods based on their experiences for teaching these skills.
9. The basic idea in the education of disturbed children is that they can be re-educated if the social system of changed and if teachers play their role with sincerity and dedication.

Teaching Strategies

There are various methods to training emotionally disturbed children. Emotional catharsis is a psychotherapeutic which is used quite often. In this technique the causes are known, these are released through expression and acceptance and symptoms are extinguished. The other technique is interference through counter-conditioning, deconditioning, decensitization, etc. The latter method emphasises positive growth and relearning rather than the more extinction of pathological behaviour. The Rogerian method of non-directive counselling is very fruitful in such problem situations. The educational programmes should be planned quite cautiously for these children. It may be of three different types:

(a) Day school which are exclusive for these children.
(b) Special class in regular school for emotional disturbed and
(c) Integrated setting or school for emotionally disturbed.

The following three teaching strategies are employed

Behaviour Development Strategies

Drain-off of frustration acidity: When frustrations pile up to the point that the student can not continue in a pleasurable activity, sympathetic communication by the teacher may 'drain off' a surplus of the hostility-laden emotion.

Support for panic, fury, and guilt: When a student is overwhelmed by panic, fury, guilt and other emotions, adults must stay with him or her, provide ego support during the incident, and assist him or her in putting the situation back into perspective.

Communication maintenance in moments of relationship decay : When a student is so overwhelmed by frustration that or she is likely to become uncommunicative and possibly enter an autistic state of fantasy, the teacher needs to arouse any links possibly keep communication flowing.

Regulation of behavioural and social traffic : When a student fails to remember the relevant of a social rule or custom, a teacher needs to remind him or her of the basic social conditions, without moralizing.

Umpire services: When a student experiences inner conflict over choices or right and wrong or external conflict with peers, a teacher must be ready to assist decision making or even make decisions that promote an 'hygienic' (emotionally healthy) situation.

Cognitive Behaviour Strategies: The second approach is cognitive behaviour strategies meant for reducing emotional problems. The teacher models for the student desirable behaviour e.g., I am now going to do math addition aloud and the student models it by self instruction. Impulsivity is reduced by ignoring it and rewarding the alternative reflectively; use clear and definite rules to reduce uncertainty, and setting a time limit for a given behaviour to occur. If such strategies are not useful than self-instructional strategies are required to be followed by the child.

The child may be taught how to develop self-instruction to increase attention, reflection, social and academic skills. It enables to self-regulation and control. Children can be taught to monitor their own behaviour and performance.

Remediation and tutoring techniques can improve academic achievement. Academic tutoring must aim at (a) support and strengthen academic learned, (b) assist the regular teacher to provide appropriate program for the main streamed learner, (c) support the goals of regular education.

Affective skills can be developed through socio drama, role playing, play, social learning as part of normal daily routine. Social learning approach can be followed (Kauffman,) to teach the social and effective skills.

Curriculum for behavioural or emotional problems generally encompass academic skills, community link skills, vocational skills, and socially affective skills. The specific topics would include : self control, sex education, drug education, getting along with others, Walker, Mc Connel, Holmes, Todis, Walker and Golden have developed a curriculum for children's peer and Teacher Skills. Skills treaming the child studying in elementary school has been developed by MC Ginnis and Goldsteing.

Clinical Exploitation

Reality Rub-in: Making the student cognizant of the actual events that occurred.

Symptom Estrangement: Getting the student to recognize that many of his symptoms are not worth the trouble and need to be let go.

Massaging Numb Value Areas: Appealing to potential values (e.g., fairness) held by the student or peer group.

New-tool Salesmanship: Fostering through words or actions the adoption of a wider range of behavioural reactions to stress than the child currently possesses.

Manipulation of the Boundaries of the Self : Helping the student to feel greater self-worn and broadening his psychological boundaries to include a sense of affiliation with peer, adults or the setting.

The Mainstreaming

The council for exceptional children in U.S.A. has recently published in a statement, highlighting the major intentions of mainstreaming/ integration.

1. Providing the most appropriate education for each child in the least restrictive setting.
2. Looking at the educational needs of children instead of clinical or diagnostic levels.
3. Looking for creating alternatives that will help general educators serve children with learning or adjustment problems with regular setting.
4. Utilising the skills of general and special education so that all children may have equal educational opportunity.

However, the recent researches show quite disappointing consequences although the normal children in the classroom do respond quite favourable to the emotionally disturbed children. But the success of the programme depends more on facilitating different types of children. There are various interventions which aim at reducing emotional problems combining educational and psychological developments of child at appropriate stage of development. But unfortunately group treatment of these cases have not been very rewarding.

Teaching emotionally disturbed child is a challenge. There are several approaches. The Psycho-educational approach emphasize:

1. Children should develop autonomy and a positive self-image.
2. Each student has unique perception about environment and what is being taught.
3. The inner working of children minds and the forces of mental and physical development may encourage or deter their education.

The ecological approach considers the environment as problem, rather than the child. Problems among children arise because of imbalances in the social system. Parental conflicts, community disruptions maybe reflected in criminal activity. Children behaviours are not disturbed, it is more a reflection of a conflict between the individual and ecosystem in which he or she lives. Unless the ecosystem is changed improvement in behaviour will not take place. Of course, it requires simultaneous adaptation i.e., the child and environment and not necessarily the child and the school.

The behaviourist accepts that behaviour is learned and it can be treated following learning principles. There is need for over-all social change in society than mere change in the individual.

The neuropsycho-pharmacological theory assumes use of medications to treat behavioural and emotional problems. But isolated use of medication is not enough. These do not increase student achievement or relationship with peers. Drugs can radically alter behaviour but they do not teach and there fore should be accompanied by interventions.

Kauffmann stressed that "the teacher must ultimately focus on those factors that can be changed. Teachers should believe that proper classroom environment alone can make a difference in the child's life even if nothing else can be altered and hope that more than classroom can be changed."

The resource/special teacher will need regular preserves and inservice training to be capable of meeting the needs of the students with behavioural and emotional problems.

Teacher's Role

There are specially trained resource teachers for all categories of disabled children, but trained resource teacher are not available for teaching emotionally disturbed children. It is, therefore, obvious that disturbed children are to be educated in regular classrooms by regular teachers. Regular teachers are, therefore to play a very befitting role in managing such children

1. If there is an emotionally disturbed child in the regular class the regular teachers must ask the special educator or any other special education personnel for advice concerning behaviour management, behaviour modification and teaching technique.
2. The regular teacher should let the child known from the first contact that he expects a reasonable standard of conduct to be maintained. The sooner the child knows the limits of permissible conduct, the better.
3. It is essential that the teacher communicates his expectations to the child clearly and firmly. Nothing is to be gained by beating around the bush or keeping the child guessing about what the teacher has in mind regarding behaviour and goals.
4. The teacher must have realistic expectations concerning the child clearly and firmly. Nothing is to be gained by beating around the bush or keeping the child guessing about what the teacher has in mind regarding behaviour and goals.
5. It is important that the teacher empathizes with child and understands how negative aspects of his social environment (abuse at home, peers who taunt him, teachers who criticise him) may contribute to his inappropriate behaviour. If negative environmental influences can be identified should try to change them, if possible.
6. The teacher must be able to tolerate a great deal of unpleasantness and rejection. He should not be counter aggressive or withdrawing himself. Some disturbed of

the teacher. But this may not be the case always. Kind gestures, caring attitude and decent behaviour of the teacher are not always reciprocated by his pupils. Still then the teacher needs to maintain considerable patience which most teachers are not capable of.

7. There must be consistent and appropriate consequences for behaviour. The child's desirable behaviour should be immediately recognised and rewarded with praise and signs of approval. Inappropriate behaviour is to be consistently ignored or, if necessary may be handled with mild punishment. Recognition and praise for good behaviour should be given openly so that other students can see and hear the teacher. If it is necessary to reprimand the child this should be done as, quietly and privately as possible.
8. The teacher managing emotionally disturbed children should remember that good behaviour management for disturbed children has a lot in common with good behaviour management for all children. The best preventive action any teacher can take is to make sure that the classroom is a happy place where children take pride in their work and learn to treat others with respect.
9. Most behaviour problems in the classroom are noticed when children don't find interest in their education, when they fail to get any real meaning of their schooling; when the quality of teaching is poor. Good teacher do not encounter much problem behaviour in their classrooms. Good teachers are not simply teachers, they are teacher-counsellors. They impress upon the students through their qualitative teaching, effective counselling, and pleasing, personality.

"A teacher-counsellor is a decent adult, educated, well-trained able to give and receive affection, to live relax and to be firm; a professional through and through and through; a person with sense of the significance of time, of the usefulness of today and the promise of tomorrow; a person of hope, quiet confidence, and joy;

one who has committed himself to children and to the proposition that children who are emotionally disturbed can be helped by the process or re-education."

The Suggestions

The teacher can use classroom management technique consistently. He should be conversant and trained in behaviour modification techniques.

1. Positively reinforce desired behaviour among ED children. The reward may be tangible, social immediate or delayed.
2. Do not positively reinforce undesirable behaviour (i.e., given attention to misbehaviour).
3. Use negative reinforcement only, sparingly to eliminate or extinguish behaviour which is undesirable.
4. Use token reinforcement to decrease disruptive behaviour increase on take and academic behaviour. The student improves.
5. Use contingency-contract i.e., agreement in writing that specifies the desired behaviour.
6. Use Premack Principle, i.e., students with ED might get an extra minute to complete the assignment in theme. The procedure may be used to complete the assignments in time. The procedure may be used to increase the strength, frequency and duration of the less preferred response.
7. Use differential reinforcement or reduce maladaptive behaviour. Rewards desirable and do not reward undesirable behaviours.
8. Ignore disruptive behaviour, it will dissappear.
9. Do not use punishment as it has adverse side effects. This is the best behaviour modification techniques.
10. Use 'time out' procedure wherever required to eliminate behaviour while doing so the teacher must ensure that learning environment is rewarding time out refers to contigent removal of the student from a positively

reinforcing environment for some predetermined amount of time.

11. Response cost is another token economy. If the response cost is clearly defined and understood the teacher may take back the token for misbehaviour (withdrawal of positive reinforcement) which will decrease disturbing behaviours.

EXERCISE

1. Define and explain the term, Emotionally Disturbed Children. Enumerate the characteristics of Emotionally Disturbed Children.
2. Classify the emotionally disturbed children indicate behavioural disordered of such students.
3. Describe the ways and means of identifying the emotionally disturbed children. Indicate the various tests and scales used for this purpose.
4. Enumerate the problems of emotionally disturbed children and indicate the remedial approach for solving their problems.
5. Describe the educational provisions for emotionally disturbed children. Enumerate the various approaches of teaching for these children.
6. Enumerate teaching strategies for emotionally disturbed children. Indicate the mainstreaming for such children.
7. Describe the role of teachers and parents for dealing emotionally disturbed children. Give suggestions for classroom teaching.

8

ADAPTATION STRATEGIES

The nature of the adaptation depends on the nature and level of the disability. For example, most of the orthopaedically handicapped can be taught the same curriculum but they require modifications in the physical environment. The partially blind needs only large prints materials. The blind and deaf children can be integrated only after formal preparation. They also require adaptation in the curriculum for teaching the difficult concepts. If the regular teacher is aware of the educational needs of each type of the disabled, then the adaptation of the curriculums becomes easier and more meaningful. The following principles should be considered for adapting the curriculum for the disabled studying in regular schools.

The adaptation should not change the original concept of the curriculum used because the objective of adaptation is to provide the some learning experiences to both normal and disabled children.

For providing same experiences compensatory activities should be planned in such a way that the child gets wholistic picture of the concept taught in the regular classes. The objective of the instructional material should remain same for both normal and disabled children.

Modification in the instructional material should not disturbed the majority of normal children studying in IED classes. The teacher has to be alert copy the words from the blackboard. In this way, the teachers can provide a lot of feedbacks to these children.

Adapting Instructions

After ensuring that the atmosphere in the class is conducive for learning, it may be necessary to adapt instructional procedures for the students with special needs to be successful in the regular class room. Regular teachers should be familiar with typical academic problem, methods of gathering data about academic performance and strategies for adapting instructional meet special needs.

Academic Problems

Problems may, occur in any one of the three stage of learning acquisition, maintenance, generalisation. Students may require more time to learn new information and skills, have difficulty in sustaining performance overtime or fail to apply old learning to new situation.

Principles of Instruction

Despite their special learning needs, mainstreamed students have the necessary skills to participate in many regular classroom activities. Special students may be main streamed on basis of skills in subject area and usefulness or functionality of the academic subject for the student.

Now, 'what' is to be taught need not be modified if the regular education curriculum is appropriate for them. However it is often necessary to alter instructional procedures i.e., how skills and information are to be taught.

Special students and many of their peers require systematic teaching which involves stating instructional goals with precision, institution systematic institutional procedures and carefully monitoring student progress through data collection. This structured instruction is the carefully organised manipulation of environmental events designed to bring about pre-specified changes in learners' performance in skill areas of functional importance. This individualised instruction is designed to meet the needs of each student, but does not necessarily mean instruction delivered by one teacher to one student. Instruction includes the following series of five steps :

(1) Curricular choice, (2) Presentation, (3) Practice, (4) Matery and, (5) Application.

Various Factors

The student factors that influences learning are meaningfulness of take, pre-requisites acquired open communication between the teacher and student learning style, novelty in presentation, active appropriate practice, distributed practice, instructional conditions. Thus it is important to look at various factors and take following steps to make instruction effective:

1. Selecting appropriate learning task.
2. Breaking the learning task into teachable components.
3. Using systematic instructional procedure. Effective instruction following demonstration prompt practice model comprising of Demonstration, Guided Practice, and Independent Practice.
4. Considering both speed and accuracy. In selecting, and describing learning tasks, teachers should determine whether the instructional goal is rapid performance or accurate performances. This will influence both presentation and practice.
5. Deciding about maximum engaged time. Engaged time refers to the minutes and hours during which students are actively involved and participate in instruction.
6. Giving clear task directions. Directions for the learning task must be clearly stated and understandable.
7. Providing consequences for successful task performance. Successful task performance may be followed by teacher's attention, praise or awards etc. and vice versa.

8. Checking for maintenance and generalisation. Task performance should be monitored over time, and practice should be provided when necessary. Demonstration may be done to show how skills and information are used in many situations.

THE STRATEGIES

If students have difficulty acquiring skills and information, several ways for adapting instruction are available such as the following:

Modifying Materials and Activities : (1) Clarify task directions. (2) Add prompts or cues to learning tasks to assist task performance. Cues may be verbal, visual or physical e.g., underlining, signs and (3) Teaching to specific student, errors. If student makes consistent mistakes, focus on correction of these errors.

Changing Teaching Procedures: (1) Give additional presentation of skills and information. (2) Provide additional guided practice. (3) make consequences for successful performance more attractive. This includes knowledge of results and rewards supplied by the teacher and (4) Slow the pace of, instruction. The time allotted for instruction and the learning task remain the same, but less material is preserved and practised.

Altering Task Requirements: The learning task can be modified to enhance student's success for this : (1) Change the criteria for successful performances. The criteria for successful performance generally include three aspect of the taskquantity, speed and accuracy. (2) Change task characteristics. Task characteristics include the conditions under which the task is performed and the nature of behaviour itself. (3) Break task into smaller sub-tasks. If alternation of task characteristics and criteria do not produce success, the task is probably too complex and should be broken into simpler sub-tasks.

Velecting an Alternate Task : When student performance remains poor despite instructional adaptations, the teacher should consider replacing the learning task with an alternate task such as (1) substitute a similar but easier task or (2) substitute a pre-requisite task. This involves replacement of original task with a pre-requisite task.

The teacher should choose the strategy depending on the problem, nature and degree of handicap of the child.

The teacher should identify the learning difficulty of the disabled subject wise and suggest remedial exercises accordingly, but these exercises should be organized by the resource teacher outside the class, by a special arrangement of the time table within the normal school hours. For example, for developing sound discrimination, the regular teacher can give more exercises for difficult areas- for instance, if the child is unable to learn speaking the sound 'bh', I th', 'dh', etc., exercises with more than 2-3 such words should be given. The resource teacher can arrange the corrective exercise on the basis of identified areas. He should design the exercises to teach a particular sound.

The difficulty of the blind child can also be identified. For example, if the blind child, is a very poor Braille reader due to faulty movements of the finger tips the regular teacher should take the help of the resource teacher for correcting this problem. The resource teacher can help the child to overcome the faulty habit of reading Braille and teach the correct method of reading by providing regular coaching -in Braille reading in the resource room. Similarly, the teachers can identify the difficult areas for all the disabilities. This will be discussed in detail through examples. For adapting the instructional material and methodology to the needs of the disabled studying in general school according to the above stated principles, the teacher should be aware of the learning style and factors that influence learning in the general classroom. Learning is a very complex process in which a gamut of factors relating to the learning point, teaching style, and often factors related to the learning environment, play an important role. Though disabled children differ in learning styles, like normal children, they have the potential for learning academic skills. The learning process of the disabled may vary, depending on the type and degree of disability. For example, the hearing impaired will depend more on visual cues while the visually impaired need more audio aids. Likewise children with other disabilities use other sensory facilities to compensate for the deficit area of learning.

The difference between the disabled and normal child is that the normal child starts learning and exploring the environment though a natural process, whereas the disabled child learning in a restricted environment. In the case of the hard of hearing child, the input of hearing become inadequate from the time he developed the hearing impairment. This deficit impedes the natural growth of speech and language in comparison to a normal child. The environment is restricted in the sense that cannot use his hearing. Hence, his learning experience is restricted and his loss will continue to affect his academic achievement until the teacher becomes aware of the implications of the disability. The defect in vision creates problems in perceiving the whole picture of an object. This child has to struggle to get a wholistic picture of each object through other sense, mainly through the tactile and audio. If the teacher is made aware of the educational problems of each category of disabled children and is provided the guidelines to be followed for preparing adapted instructional material and methodologies to meet the needs of these children studying in the classes, it will help in academic integration.

Teaching Students

Two approaches are available for the instruction of main streamed students with learning disabilities:

Remedial Approach : Remedial techniques are used to teach basic skills and are most appropriate for elementary-age main streamed students.

Compensation Approach : Compensation techniques bypass deficiencies in basic skills in order to teach content area subject.

Basic skills include reading handwriting spelling, written expressions and maths.

The adaptations can be used for basic skills to special students in regular classroom: (1) providing prompts; (2) giving additional instruction; and (3) allowing extra guided practice.

Prompts are features added to learning tasks and are particularly helpful of L.D. students who have difficulty focusing attention on relevant .instructional cues. Prompts also structure the task and help the students know exactly what to do.

Giving additional direct instruction and allowing extra guided practice are adaptations that aid students with poor recall. To ensure successful learning the subject matter should be broken down into small steps and presented at as slow a pace as necessary. Several opportunities for practice should be available. The teacher can monitor performance during practice. A peer tutor or adult volunteer can help-Self-correcting material can be used.

Suggestions for modifications include the following: (1) Reduce the amount of reading required. (2) Substitute material written on lower reading level. (3) Present the information through another medium like lectures, class discussions visual aids such as photos, maps, slides etc. (4) Allow students with poor handwriting to use a stencil, slate or blackboard. For students, who work slowly reduce the length of the written task or extend the time limit. (5) Provide to design assignments and exams so that writing requirements are minimized. Use multiple choice and completion formats rather than essays and (6) Students may be given guidance in operating calculators wherever it is feasible.

Adjustment of Supportive Aids

Here the teacher makes use of the learning experiences of normal and disabled children for teaching the difficult concepts in the class. For example the teacher can provide recorded tapes for correcting the speech problems of the hearing impaired. The sounds should be recorded in minimum phonetic pairs so that the hearing impaired can develop adequate speech patterns. In addition, the teacher can provide materials to match the given figures on these sounds. Thus, the teacher can help the hard of hearing in learning the alphabet and the normal in learning the correct pronunciation of each sound. Similarly, the blind child can be given tactile material for learning the concept taught in the class.

For example, if the teacher is teaching about rocks and hills he can make use of tactile aids for the blind which will also help the normal children in learning about the difference between rocks and hills. The orthopaedically handicapped generally do not require any supporting aid for learning the concepts taught in the normal children in the general class. But in the case of upper limb impairment the child may face difficulty in learning basic academic skills more adequately. Supportive aids can help such children to learn more easily. For example if the child has no anus may have difficulty in developing writing skills the teacher can help the child in getting the prosthetic aids and physiotherapy for adaptation of the limbs. The teacher can also provide thick pencils or pens so as to facilitate easy holding. Similarly, the learning disabled and educatable mentaliy retarded can be given additional workbooks which will provide them enough drill for learning academic skills.

Adaptations of Mainstreaming

Academic Instruction : Academic instruction is the most common area in which adaptations must be made for main streamed students with mild retardation; they require assistance in acquisition of basic skills and work habits and in the application of these skills to daily life and career situation.

Habitation is the major approach to the eduction of main streamed students with mild retardation. The goal is not to remediate or compensate for skill deficiencies. Instead, instruction is directed toward the development of the critical skills necessary for successful adulthood.

Career Education : Career education is one way of conceptualising the habitation process for the mildly retarded. Career education can be infused into the regular, classroom curriculum in several ways like helping students by providing instruction and practice in the application of basic school and work skill; devoting a portion of regular curriculum to career awareness and explanation.

Teaching Functional Academic : Basic skills instructions must go beyond textbooks and workbook pages. It must extend into the real world if special students are to use school subjects to solve the problems of everyday life.

There are two major strategies for teaching functional academics

(1) Unit approach in which several basic skills are integrated around a central theme of interest and value to students.

(2) Functional practices activities approach in which activities promote generalisation of skills to real life problems.

Improving Work Habits: Work habits may be viewed as the behaviour a person exhibits when presented with task to perform.

Regular teacher can help their main streamed students to develop and improve their general work habits in three ways.

First, the acquisition of work habits must be accepted as a valuable educational goal. Second, students must receive instruction and practice in specific work behaviour. Third, good work-Performance must be reinforced.

Teaching Strategies

The mildly and moderately hearing impaired children can be directly integrated. They have problems in learning correct articulation and in acquiring speech and language skill at the initial stages. But given adequate training in speech correction, their speech and language acquisition and retention is like normal. The teacher should plan the instructional material in such a way that their quality of voice is developed properly. A little change in voice rhythm intensity can change the very meaning of words. The learning of these features is very important even for the severely and profoundly hearing impaired, because they have to follow lip movements which requires proper understanding of the articulation of each word used for expression.

Following suggestions are given: (1) Teacher and students should speak naturally, use natural gestures, and maintain face to face contact when speaking with hearing impaired student. (2) Encourage student with hearing loss to use their remaining hearing whenever possible. (3) Question hearing-impaired student to determine if they understand information presented in class.

Do not assume students understand material. (4) Clearly explain concepts being taught. Use visual example, whenever possible keep terminology consistent. (5) The academic problems of any student are related to their language impairment not to a lack of intelligence. Closely monitor their achievement progress. (6) Make the child sit in front and make sure that enough light falls on your face.

Modifying Instructional Procedure

Following suggestions are given for regular classroom teachers working with usually impaired children: (1) Change instructional procedures only when necessary. (2) Curriculum goals should remain the same as for regular students. (3) Provide students with instructions and experiences that will develop critical listening skills. They do not automatically have better listening skills because of their visual impairment. (4) Vigorous physical exercise is recommended for visually handicapped students. They should be encouraged to compete with sighted peers whenever possible. (5) Become familiar with the various types of special equipment used by the visually handicapped students in your class e.g. Braille writer, abacus, brailler slate, Taylor frame. (6) Write blackboard instructions on a separate piece of paper for the child with poor vision. Keep copying work for the handicapped students to a minimum. Ask parents or other students to read reference material or lengthy reading assignments to the visually handicapped student. (7) Record reading material or other assignment or the visually handicapped child. (8) Call the student by name when you speak to him. Talk directly to the student. Look at him in the face and remind classmates to do the same.

Mainstreaming Communication

The communication in main streaming refers verbal and non-verbal interaction in classroom. It generates social emotional climate of the classroom.

For students with communication disorders the major areas that need special attention are speech and language. Because of their communication difficulties, they may also require assistance in social interactions.

The regular classroom teacher should provide three things—good speech models, an accepting environment and opportunities for practising oral communication skills. Guidelines for establishing a tolerant classroom climate are as follows:

When student with speech problems speak, the teacher listen with full attention and ensure that other students listen.

Speech errors should not be criticized by the teaches or classmates and the teachers should not call attention to speech error. If the teacher accepts mistriculation and dysfluencies and attends to the content of what the special student is saying, peers are more likely to do the same.

Provides good speech and language models.

To promote acceptance while maximising communication opportunities is to seat the special student in the midst of several normal peers.

The regular classroom teacher can help mainstreamed students with language disorders in three ways. (1) by modelling appropriate grammar: (2) by helping to expand their listening and speaking vocabularies, and (c) by modifying classroom activities. It involves teaching skills.

Some suggestions in the this regard are given below: (1) Correct students' grammatical errors by demonstrating use of correct language. (2) Encourages students to ask the meanings of words they do not understand. (3) Contextualise words to teach their meanings. (4) Prepositions and action verbs are often hard to explain the words, use them in sentences to show what they mean. (5) Use of definitions, explanations and examples to teach other words e.g. define container as something that holds something else, then give examples of objects that are containers and objects that are not. (6) Includes vocabulary instruction in all curriculum areas. (7) Provides opportunities for students to practise newly acquired words and (8) Makes the directions for school task brief, to the point, and in simple language.

Many main streamed special students may leave the regular classroom for a short time each day to visit the special education teacher. When they come back they may feel lost, confused and unsure of what they should be doing.

To help special students in this regard, following suggestions are: (1) Work with the special teacher arrange the best time for each student to leave the regular classroom. Usually, it's better for special students to receive special education services when the regular class is working on activities such as independent practice rather than direct instruction, the special student's least liked rather than favourite activity. (2) Maintain a regular daily schedule so that you and the students will known what he will be missing each day (3) Arrange a communication system so that when the student returns, he will know how to find out what to do.

When students with physical and health impairment enter the regular classroom, one of the teacher's first task is to learn about their disabilities, about each students' limitations and capabilities.

The area in which modifications are usually required are arrangement of the physical environment and the format the structure of instructional activities and assignments.

The regular curriculum with its exphasis on academic skills is appropriate. However, several additional curriculum areas might be training (instruction planning for travel) may help some students to conserve their limited energy. At secondary level, other possible areas are recreation and use of leisure time and sex education.

Such students should not be automatically exempted from class room activities simply because they are disabled. However, if there are medical restrictions that prohibit their participation in some activities, then classroom standards should be changed e.g. students in wheel chairs or those with mobility problems who travel slowly may be dismissed a few minutes early from class so that they arrive at the next activity/class on time.

Allow students to take during the day if these are necessary for rest, a visit to the bathroom, medication or a special diet.

Some classroom modifications may be needed for such students but it is equally important that these students are offered opportunities to learn function independently.

Physical Environment

To ensure that the physical environment is suitably arranged to accommodate them the teacher can keep the following in mind:

1. Arrange the classroom to facilitate mobility. Make sure sufficient room is allowed for students in wheel chair or those who use crutches to move from one place to another.
2. All activities within the regular classroom should be accessible to students with mobility problems. This includes chalkboards, display boards etc. Consider the seating arrangement for special students.
3. Those in wheel chairs man need a special table or lap board to write on. Others may require special chairs that provide extra support.
4. Make sure that special equipment is kept in good working order. For Wheel-chair, check periodically for proper fit, comfort and good repair.

In addition to meeting physical health needs and modifying the classroom environment it may also be necessary to adapt instructional activities and procedures. Some of these are: (1) Fix the students paper to the desk with a string and adhesive tape/ pin applied to the top and bottom of the paper. (2) Attach/tie the pencil to the desk with a string and adhesive tape so that it may not drop down. (3) Allow students to answer questions orally or have them recorder for later evaluation as it is often laborious for some handicapped students to write their answers. (4) Ask a normal student to insert a sheet of carbon paper under his or her paper so that a duplicate set of notes may be supplied to the handicapped student. (5) When students miss school due to illness or for medical treatment, provide instruction so that they do not lag far behind and (6) Adjust assignments properly for those who work slowly in exams, more time may be allowed or the task may be modified.

Management of Special Needs of Disabled

Management of the Visually Impaired : Most visually impaired children though labelled blind, have at least slight vision called residual vision which they will lose unless they are continually encouraged to use it.

Teachers should avoid overprotecting the child. The child must be allowed to explore and experiment to bump into a wall, to fall down and to get up like any other normal child. However, teacher must make sure that the environment is safe.

With very little extra assistance, blind scholars can soon learn to manage almost all indoor and outdoor activities. Teachers can help blind children in the following ways :

(1) Make sure student tables or desk-tops are large enough for Braille writers. (2) Provide an accessible storage area with adequate space for equipment and Braille or large print books. (3) Partially sighted students should not be placed where they face the glare of a primary source of light such as near a window. (4) Scat students so that they are able to participate in activities with other class members. (5) Eliminate unnecessary obstacles. Inform students of changes in the arrangement of any temporary obstacles. (6) Keep doors completely open to eliminate the possibility of the student running into a piratically open door. (7) Allow the student to move about freely until he/she has familiarised himself/herself with the room or the route. Let them-explore and orient to the environment. (8) Light should be evenly distributed. (9) Discourage reliance upon sighted guides once the student has demonstrated the ability to travel independently. (10) Use specific words to tell the child what to do. (11) Talk to the child about everything in the environment. (12) Blind children need to learn action words. (13) Teaching blind children to listen and to sort out sounds. (14) Help a blind child learn which sounds are dangerous and, which need not be frightening. (15) Give visually impaired children many opportunities to learn through smelling, touching and tasting. (16) Teach the blind child how to go from left to right on as many tasks as possible and (17) Tell the student when you approach/level him.

Classroom Learning Environment

Classroom management elements that teacher should consider are

***Arranging the Physical Environment*:** Various considerations for arranging the physical environment are:

1. Ensure a safe and barrier-free-environment by removing objects cluttered on the floor, desks, equipment, architectural barriers.
2. Make the working condition pleasant like temperature, light, noise level, ventilation and attractive furnishings.
3. Obtain furniture and special equipment that is comfortable, attractive, durable and functional.
4. Arrange space functionally for storage working and performing activities.
5. Keep in mind the educational goals in making seating arrangements as social interactions may influence them.

***Organising the Instructional Environment*:** The instructional environment of the classroom includes the procedures, materials performance. The teacher organises the curriculum groups students.. and sets up delivery system for the presentation and practice of skills and information. This structure directly affects non-academic performance as well as student achievement. Important principles to be considered are to:

1. Organise curricular skills and information sequentially, arrange skills and information according to subjects, activities of interest.
2. Group student for instruction according to type of dislability keep it flexible.
3. Set up systems for monitoring practice. Provide instructional material which includes self-correcting material, programmed instructional and mediated instruction. These give constant feedback to the child.
4. Provide guidelines for student behaviour. Frame classroom rules and routines that are short, specific, simple clearly stated positive and enforceable by teacher, structure prompts and models.

5. Use systematic record-keeping procedures. These should be consistent and relevant.

Using Educational Technology : The current technology of education includes systematic institutional techniques, procedures for changing behaviour and technological advances in equipment, media, and learning resources. Electronic technologies such as television, radio, audio and video-tapes and computers have the capability to revolutionise the quality, productivity and availability of education.

Managing Time and Other Resources : The teacher, as manager of the total learning environment, supervises the allocation, organization and use of essential learning resources

Instruction Time: Daily schedules divide the day into time blocks and tell what activities will occur and when they will occur. Suggestions for scheduling are :

1. Move from definite to flexible schedules.
2. Proceed from short work assignments to longer ones.
3. Alternate highly preferred with less preferred activities.
4. Plan for leeway time.
5. Provide a daily schedule.
6. Schedule assignments that can be completed in a day.
7. Plan a variety of activities.

Learning Materials: For choice of material consider its validity, cost, number of students with whom it can be used, its physical robustness, probability, difficulty level, presentation sequence, input modes, to modes of response and durability and

Instructional Personnel: If teacher feel it is difficult to handle it all by themselves. They may tap two excellent sources of assistance viz. peer tutors and volunteers.

Guidance for Special Learning

Special learners are those who students as a distinct set from other students in a class and therefore require special attention. Educationally they deviate from the average students in their academic achievement.

These learners require special attention by teachers. They do not profit much from learning in average group situations.

Special learners in institutions may be classified as: (1) Gifted Children, (2) Creative Children, (3) Slow Learners and, (4) Learners with difficulty for learning.

Gifted students are those who show consistently remarkable performance in educational endeavours. They possess a superior intellectual potential and functional ability to achieve academically in the top 15 to 20 percent of the students in the institution, and/or talent of a high order.

Creative students are those who exhibit creativity. Creativity is the process of sensing gaps missing elements- forming ideas or hypothesis and testing the same. It is the ability to change ones approach to a problem to cope with ideas that are both relevant and unusual to go beyond the immediate situation to redefine the problem.

Slow learners are those students who require more time for learning than normal/average students in a class. Hence, they show marked educational deficiency. They learn at a slower rate than others.

In order to provide guidance to the above category of learners it is important to identify them. For these learners individual guidance will have to be arranged.

Identification of the special learners will have to be carried out systematically. It may be based on teacher's observation, academic records and performance in mental ability traits.

Guidance for Learners with Learning Difficulties

The following strategy is suggested for providing guidance to students who have learning difficulties.

The following are the steps for guidance for overcoming learning difficulties.

(1) Observe the interaction style of the student in the class, their assignment and other records.
(2) Administer specially designed diagnostic test.

(3) Identify the students for guidance purposes.
(4) Analyse the causes for learning difficulties.
(5) Plan alternate approaches for overcoming the difficulties.
(6) Implement the approaches.
(7) Evaluate the approaches.

Guidance for Under-achievers

Under-achievers are those students who do not achieve to the extent they can. The following steps may be followed in guiding such learners.

(1) Administration achievement test to the entire class.
(2) Identify the students who need guidance.
(3) Assist them in resting goals.
(4) Plan and implement appropriate strategies for guidance.

Guidance for Gifted Learners

The following steps are to be followed in guiding gifted students. Identify the gifted students on the basis of :

(i) Observation of student characteristics, their interaction style, quality of assignments and projects completed.
(ii) Administering tests of intelligence.

Select the most appropriate approach for catering to the gifted. The approaches are:

(i) Segregation for the gifted and arranging classes exclusively for them.
(ii) Acceleration through which students may be allowed to complete the prescribed course of study in a shorter period than normally taken by the rest of the students of the class.

Enrichment programme through prescribing enriched/ additional/depth content and suggesting additional books and journals for study by students. Evaluate each approach in relation to the constraints and restraints for implementing the approach. Implement the selected approach.

GUIDANCE FOR PROBLEM CHILDREN

Problem children as is evident from the term applied to them are children whose behaviour is not normal and it results in some or the other problem of adjustment being caused. In the words of Valentine, "Problem children are generally used to describe children whose behaviour or personality in something is seriously abnormal." In this manner the class of problem children includes all those juveniles whose character or personality shows some signs of abnormality. Some behavioural abnormalities that seem to indicate this condition are - stealing, lying, annoying children weaker and younger than themselves not doing home assignments, running away from school, or arriving late at school. They can also be called defects or abnormalities concerning character or personality because conduct of this nature indicates shortcomings in both personality as well as character.

For an understanding of the psychology of problem children it is necessary that a detailed analysis of the behaviour be made and the problematic form of behaviour distinguished from the normal forms. It must here be recalled that the problem child is not a member of a group distinct from the normal child groups. There is no distinct line that distinguishes him from his more normal counterparts as to some extent, and at varying stage in childhood the behaviour of every child becomes problematic. Almost even child, at some stage or the other and for one reason or another tells or steal something. Hence, it is not quite desirable to declare one completely problematic and another more or less completely normal. It has been seen that very often the child is prone to much naughtiness between the age of two and five, and his conduct appears somewhat problematic and strange. But as continues to grow older this naughtiness disappears and he no longer appears a problem child. It is for this reason that specialists have made very detailed studies into problem behaviour. In his book on educational psychology. Cronbach made a mention of problematic behaviour that were considered the most sure signs of problematic trouble by the best trained and particularly intelligent research workers.

The Evaluation

To discover that a child is backward is of value. To measure exactly how in much he is backward is of greater value. But to analyse precisely where and for what reason is backward constitutes a problem of the highest practical importance.

In special education, evaluation should be of both the child and programme. It should be:

Comprehensive Evaluation : To make it comprehensive it should be done by a team of experts in various fields. It should include not only intellectual development, but his physical, social development, general mental health, emotional stability, his progress in academic skills, his learning patterns, his adaptability to new situation. It should be carried out by all members of mainstreaming team i.e., teacher, psychologists, therapists etc.

Continuous Evaluation : Instructions which are useful for measuring current status may not be useful for measuring change. Continuous evaluation on progress provides the feedback that makes possible continued adjustments in methods and materials. Frequent evaluation will provide feedback for reforming of objectives and modifications according to needs of the Child.

Inclusive of Total Situation Evaluation : It should include various aspects :

1. Organisation of services for the administration and organisation of services for the handicapped.
2. Recognise the distinctive features of every child and appreciate the diversity within the group.
3. Effectiveness of curriculum, conditions under which new behaviour is acquired, conditions under which present behaviour is maintained or eliminated and conditions under which characteristics are developed and shaped.
4. Teaching-learning process, facilities, materials, methods and media.

For making integration successful., the teacher may have to extend his role beyond classroom and school such as rehabilitation, advocacy for adopting legislative measures for providing rights for the handicapped.

The Rehabilitation

For rehabilitation, an attempt is made to facilitate development of potential of child in all areas of development. This is achieved through a team of experts. Efforts of the rehabilitation team are directed towards reducing the functional limitation and ensuring maximum restoration to normal function. These efforts concentrate on promoting measures which can be taken up by family members and community level workers to help the disabled develop their potential to the maximum -find integrate them is society.

Teacher should keep in mind the achievement of certain goals. These include the following points:

1. Maximum independence in self-care activities.
2. Increased mobility.
3. Adequate communication skills.
4. Acquisition of effective strategies for learning.
5. Appropriate education.
6. Acquisition of attitudes and skills required for independent living and employment.
7. Recreation opportunities for community interaction.

Teacher as a member of the mainstreaming team works towards, the achievement of these goals. For this teacher can involve community members and parents to pool resources and to achieve long-standing and useful results.

Teacher can help citizens to develop healthy relationships with disabled persons who are trying to make their place in the community. Teachers should create a general awareness for the welfare of the disabled by familiarising people in the community with strengths and limitations of these people.

Exercise

1. Explain the term 'adaptation' and differentiate with 'modification'. Indicate the problems of adaptation.
2. Enumerate the principles of 'adapting instruction'. Indicate the steps of adaptation.
3. Describe strategies for adapting instruction and adaptation of Teaching Strategies.
4. Indicate the approaches for learning disabled children. Give suggestions for modification and adjustment of supporting aids of teaching.
5. Provide some suggestions for adapting teaching strategies for Hearing Impaired Children.

9

Learning Disability

In the years since 1963, many people have tried to define learning disabilities, but no one has yet developed a definition that is acceptable to everyone. The federal definition (U.S.A) of learning disabilities included in Public Law (94-142), the Education for All Handicapped Children Act of 1975, reads .

Specific Learning Disabilities

The term "children with specific learning disabilities" means "those children who have a disorder in one or more of the basic psychological processes involved in understanding or in using language spoken or written, which may manifest itself in a imperfect ability to listen, think, speak, read, write, spell or do mathematical calculation. The term includes such conditions as perceptual handicaps, brain injury, minimal brain dysfunction, dyslexia and developmental aphasia. The term does not include children who have learning problems which are primarily the result of visual hearing, or motor handicaps of mental retardation of emotional disturbance or of environmental, cultural or economic disadvantage".

Federal Register, 1977

Since learning disabilities could span over a variety of abilities, ten areas, each representing a basic psychological process, have been selected for the present study. A deficit in any of the area or areas or a combination of any would lead to a learning problem.

Some children who in most ways seem normal, have difficulty in learning' or remembering. They have difficulty in educational performance copying writing, listening, understanding, number speech and communication. In the present chapter their problems are discussed with a view to providing an in-depth knowledge.

The Concept

Learning disability refers to learning problems which manifest in an imperfect ability to listen, think, speak, read, write or do mathematical calculations which are not primarily due to visual impairment, hearing impairment, motor handicap, mental retardation environmental or economic disadvantages, but due to a disorder in the psychological process involved in understanding or in using language.

Kirk (1962) has defined: "Learning disability refers to a retardation disorder, or delayed development in one or more of the process of speech, language, reading, spelling, writing or arithmetic resulting from a possible cerebral dysfunction and/or emotional or behavioural disturbance and not from mental retardation, sensory deprivation, cultural or instructional factors."

The Meaning

The enigma of the youngster who has difficulty in learning is not new. But the concept of learning disability has brief and turbulent history. Some children are quite normal and yet at all times display learning problems. They write 'deb' for 'bed', was 'for' 'saw' and cannot concentrate if there is background noise. The National Advisory Committee on Handicapped Children (USA) defined learning disability as follows (1986):

"LD children exhibit disorder in one or more basic psychological process involved in understanding and in using spoken or written languages. The disorders are manifested in listening, thinking, talking, reading, writing, spelling, and arithmetic. They include conditions which are referred to as perceptual problems, brain injury, minimal brain dysfunction, dyslexia, developmental aphasia etc. They do not include learning problems which are primarily due to visual, hearing, or motor handicaps, mental retardation, emotional disturbance, or the environmental disadvantage."

There are a large number of children who have problems in learning specific subjects. Usually learning problems may occur due to any one or a —combination of the following factors:

(1) Low level of intelligence, (2) Mental retardation (3) Visual impairment, (4) Motor handicaps, (5) Economic difficulties, (6) Cultural disadvantage, (7) Poor instruction.

Learning problems caused by the above mentioned factors are not considered to be learning disability. For example, a mentally retarded child has learning problems in all the school subjects. The learning problems of a mentally retarded child are not caused by learning disability but low level of intelligence. Similarly learning problems of a blind child are due to his visual impairment and this is not learning disability.

The Definitions

The definition of learning disability adopted by National Advisory Committee on Handicapped Children (USA, 1,968) is given as under;

"Children with specific learning disabilities exhibit a disorder in one or more of the basic psychological processes involved in understanding or using spoken or written language. These may be manifested in disorders of listening, thinking, talking, reading, writing, spelling or arithmetic. They include conditions which have been referred to as perceptual handicaps, dyslexia, development aesthesia, etc. They do not include learning problems which are due primarily to visual, learning, motor handicaps, mental retardation, emotional disturbances, or environmental disadvantages.

The National Joint Committee of Learning Disabilities (USA, 1981) gave the following definition of learning disability which is unanimously accepted at international level.

"Learning disability is a generic term that refers to a heterogeneous group of disorders manifested by significant difficulties in the acquisition and use of listening, speaking, reading, writing, reasoning or mathematical abilities. These disorders are intrinsic to the individual and presumed to be due to central nervous system's dysfunction. Even though learning disability may occur concomitantly with other handicapping conditions (e.g., sensory impairment, mental retardation, social and emotional disturbance) or environmental influences (e.g., cultural differences, insufficient/inappropriate instruction, psychogenic factors) it is not the direct result of these condition or influences."

The two definitions are fairly similar. It is safe to assume that a learning disability may or may not be caused by central nervous system dysfunction. The learning disabled have significant problems in learning academic skills that are not due to other handicapping conditions. Many students with LD have a lower than average IQ, many also have high IQ and sometimes reach the gifted range.

Originally children whose achievement was far below the capability were categorised under brain,injured children, suffering from neurophrenia, minimal brain dysfunction. It was for the first time that Kirk in 1963, suggested the word "learning disabilities" top describe all the child's behavioural symptoms that arise from dysfunction of the central processing mechanisms. This term described a group of children who had disorders in the development of language, speech, reading and associated communication skills needed for social interaction. Children with sensory and emotional handicap are excluded from this category.

The term learning disability, refers to conditions which were previously called brain injury minimal brain dysfunction, sensory aphasia (the loss of the power to understand spoken words, signs, gestures or print), expressive aphasia (the loss of the ability to speak), alexia or word blindness (the loss of the ability to read a mild degree of alexia is called dyslexia), acalculia (the loss of arithmetical ability- at a lower level it is called dyscalculia) ·

agraphia (the inability to learning to write - a mild degree of agraphia is called dysgraphia).

Difference among LD, Backward and Slow Learner

In terms of degree, learning disability may be of two type - mild LD and severe LD. The mild learning disabled can be educated in regular schools. Such children are to be found in regular schools. They are, however, difficult to identify at the initial stages. They face problems in learning basic academic skills. Their problem may occur in one or more areas of learning skill in a relatively mild degree. The severe learning disabled include those who manifest an inability to master basic academic skills (reading, writing etc.). Their problems may be due to brain dysfunction or environmental deprivation. It is difficult to integrate such children in regular schools. Whatever may be the degree of disability there is always a discrepancy between achievement and ability of such children. This is the basic problem that they face.

LD and MR Children : The LD children are very often confused and misunderstood as MR children. In reality. LD children are not mentally retarded. Both LD and MR children have problems in learning academic subjects. They have their own learning styles. The achievement level of NM children may match with their intellectual functioning. Usually such children experience failure in all aspect of life and in all school subjects. Such children may learning up to the seventh standard. But in case of LD children, there is always a discrepancy between their level of intelligence (what one can do) and their actual level of achievement (what one does at present). They have problems in specific areas such as reading, speaking, writing, spelling, etc. With appropriate educational intervention LD children can rise to a level which seems unbelievable at present.

LD, Backward Children, and Slow Learner : The LD children are not the same as backward children and slow learners. The problems of backward children or slow learners may be due to low intelligence, environmental, cultural, or social disadvantages, psychological and emotional hazards, or defective instruction. But the problems of learning disabled children are not primarily caused due to these factors. But a learning disabled children are not primarily caused due to these factors. A backward child or a slow learner may perform poorly in all academic areas. But a learning disabled child has difficulty only in a specific academic area such as reading, writing, or arithmetic. The factors which cause slow learning or backwardness in learning are known to everybody. But the causes of learning disability are still a mystery.

THE CHARACTERISTICS

There have been many attempts to categories the major characteristics of learning disabled children. One of the earliest attempt was made by Clements (1966) through a Task force on LD. They observed 10 most general characteristics based on the assumption that LD is a neurological impairment:

1. Hyperactivity, 2. Emotional lability, 3. Disorders of attention, 4. Disorders in memory and thinking, 5. Equivocal neurological signs, 6. Percepush motor impairments, 7. General coordination deficits, 8. Impulsivity, and 9. Specific learning disability.

Language and Speech of LD Children : LD children have difficulty both in expressive and receptive language, and relatively more in case of the former. LD children do not have so much of phonological or articulation problems but do show problem in sentence formation i.e., syntax. They do show difficulty in comprehension of meaning and use of pronouns. They have difficulties in understanding and using passive tense, negatives contractions and past tense, adjectives and using passive tense negatives, contractions and past tense, adjectives and adverbs. They fail to maintain conversation and can not argue or ask appropriate questions. So far as written language is concerned they do problems in handwriting, spelling and punctuation. LD children have more of spelling errors than their non-learning disabled peers even when IQ were controlled.

1. They have poor receptive-auditory ability (poor understanding of spoken symbols, requests for repetition, echolaliac: confection of directions and commands).
2. They exhibit receptive—visual difficulty (sub-vocalise reading, read without understanding).

3. They have poor expressive-vocal ability (disorganised through, inadequate syntax, and dearth of ideas for expression).
4. They manifest expressive- motor difficulties (spelling disorders, drawing disorders, Omission and reversal of letters, omission and reversal of letters, omission of whole words).

Perceptual and Motor Ability of LD Children : Lerner (1985) demonstrated that LD children display problems in spatial relations, visual discrimination, figure and ground discrimination of similarities and differences, auditory sequencing auditory blending and auditory memory. Lerner (1985) further stated that LD children do display haptic and movements as well as have defects in social perception.

They do show problems in gross and fine motor skills (balance, laterality, directionality) and body and body image and imageness. They can not copy a geometric figure i.e., have visual-motor disintegration.

(1) They are unable to identify, discriminate and interpret sensation.

(2) They have poor visual decoding (unable to reproduce geometric forms accurately, figure-ground configurations letter reversals and totations).

(3) They have poor auditory decoding (inability to recognise tunes to differentiate between sounds).

(4) They cannot identify familiar objects by touch alone (cutaneous misperception).

(5) They have poor kinesthetic and vestibular perception (problems in coordination, movement, directionality, space orientation, and balance, difficulties in perception lead to difficulties in concept formation abstraction ability, cognitive ability, and language ability).

Motor Activity - These characteristics vary according to type of motor activity. These are described below:

Hyperactivity - Constantly engaged in movement, unable to sit still, too much of talking in the class, very much inattentive. (reverse of hyperactivity)-lethargic, quiet, passive.

Incoordination - Physical awkwardness, poor motor integration, poor activities in running, catching, skipping and jumping; walking is rigid and stiff, poor performance in writing, drawing; frequent falls, stubbing, and clumsy behaviour.

Preservation - Involuntary continuation of behaviour; this behaviour is witnessed in speaking, writing, drawing, pointing, and oral reading; incorrect spelling, repetition of error.

Social and Emotional Characteristics of LD. Children : They are more anxious and withdrawn, have more problems in interacting with teacher and parents, have behaviour problems and are less socially skilled. Many LD student had little insight into nature of their problem and attributed these to luck. They show lower self-concept more external locus of control and lower level of aspiration than non LD peers.

1. They are quiet and obedient but daydream and cannot read.
2. They have frequent temper outburts, sometimes for no apparent reason.
3. They are nervous.
4. They jump from one thing to another, and mind everyone's business but their own.
5. They talk of self control but cannot work with other children.
6. They are emotionally labile and unstable.

Emotional instability arises mainly due to prolonged dependency or the mother and lack of contact with the outside world which generates frustrations.

The LD children constitute a heterogenous group. Some LD children have reading problems and some others have writing problems. Some LD children have problems of comprehension whereas others may have problems in telling the time, locating a place on the map. Thus, it is difficult to mention the characteristics which are noticed in all LD children. The most frequently mentioned characteristics of LD children include the following :

Ability Level: The ability level of LD children varies from near average to average to above average.

Activity Level : The LD children may be either hyperactive of hypo-active. If they are hyperactive they show the following behaviours constant motor activity, restless, tapping of finger or foot, jumping out of seat, skipping from task to task, etc. If they are hypo-active they fail to react or seem to do everything in slow motion.

Attention Problems: The LD children have short attention span; they are easily destractible: they are unable to concentrate on any task for a very long time. They often perseverate. Their attention becomes fixed upon a single task which is repeated over and over; this may be motor or verbal activity.

Motor Problems: The LD children are generally clumsy or awkward with poor, fine and gross motor co-ordination. They demonstrate poor tactile, discrimination, excessive need to touch poor writing and drawing performance.

Visual Perceptual Problems : The LD children are unable to distinguish between visual stimuli (visual discrimination) : They are unable to perceive a figure against a background (visual figure-ground). They are unable to fill in missing parts when only part of a word or object is seen (visual closure); they are also unable to remember and revisualise images or sequences very well (visual memory).

Auditory Perceptual Problems : The LD children are unable to distinguish between sounds (auditory discrimination) they are unable to obtain meaning from the spoken word and/or environmental sounds (auditory comprehension). They are unable to attend to important auditory stimuli by pushing all other auditory stimuli into the background (auditory figure-ground). They are unable to fill in missing sounds when only parts of the word are heard (auditory closure); they are also unable to remember auditory stimuli or sequences very well (auditory memory).

Language Problems : The LD children demonstrate delayed or slow development of speech articulation, and an inability to organise words to form phrases, clauses, or sentences.

Social Emotional Behaviour Problems: The LD children are impulsive in nature. They fail to think about consequences of their behaviour. At times they exhibit explosive behaviour. They display rage reactions or throw tantrums when crossed. They lack social competence. Their social competence is often below the average for their age and ability. They are unable to adjust to changes. They exhibit rapid mood variation, even from hour.

Orientation Problems: The LD children process poorly developed concept of space, and distorted body image. They have difficulty in judging distance and size and in discriminating figure from ground, parts from the whole and left from right. They are disoriented in time and experience trouble relating to concepts like before and after, now and then, and today and tomorrow.

Work Habits: The LD children organise work poorly. They work slowly, and frequently confuse directions or rush through work carelessly.

Academic Disabilities : The LD children have problems in reading, arithmetic, writing, spelling, telling time and even locating places on the map.

In general LD children possess these characteristics. But not all LD children demonstrate these characteristics. Some LD children may have one or more such characteristics.

The Classification

The first six areas represent the process involved in visual and auditory perception, viz., (1) Eye-Hand-Co-ordination (EHC), (2) Figure Ground Perception (FGP). (3) Figure Constancy (FC), (4) Position in Space (PS), (5) Spatial Relations (SR), and (6) Auditory Perception (AP). Last four areas represent the aspect of cognitive functioning, viz; (7) Memory (M), (8) Cognitive Abilities (CA), (9) Receptive Language (RL) and (10) Expressive Language (EL). Through on line of demarcation can be drawn between the perceptual and cognitive areas for the purpose of analysis and diagnosis, the two have been separated. They should not be understood as two broad categories in which the symptoms of problem are manifested. The ten selected areas have been described in the following paras.

Eye-Hand-Co-ordination (EHC) : It is the ability to co-ordinate vision with the movements of the hands for effective use. A child having deficit in EHC would indicate some difficulty with the control of movements, required for a smooth flow of writing. Such a child may read, spell and comprehend well and may also be good at oral work. However, the visual motor production deficits due to problems in EHC, encountered by such a child, hamper his scholastic performance considerably often resulting in dire consequences.

Figure Ground Perception (FGP) : It is also called 'Selective Attention'. It is the ability to attend only to that stimuli which require one's attention at a given period and ignore the other stimuli present in order to encode the perceptual experience meaningfully.

A child poor in figure ground perception may find his perceptual world chaotic because of his inability to filter out the relevant stimuli for the irrelevant. The child would be bombarded with and array of stimuli consequently making no sense of it. His/her cognitive state is that of utter confusion. The child, therefore, fails to understand the task hand and results in either a disorganised performance or academic failures.

Figure Constancy (FC) : It is the subject's ability to identify symbols, figures, shapes despite its apparent change in size, direction and position. It involves the recognition of pictures, shapes, graphics, symbols, letters and figures.

A child having a deficit in figure constancy would indicate that his/her perception is at very concrete level. He/she can not transfer information from one situation to another and his/her perception is a matter of fact types, as it appears to him/her. He/she may fail to recognize a picture or an object if it changes its context.

Position-in-Space (PS) : It is the ability to perceive the relationship between the observer and the object in space, i.e., of it being above, behind, in front of next to etc., to the person observing.

A child having a deficiency in position-in-space may find his/her perceptual world distorted. He/she may have difficulties in doing any accurate drawing. He/she may also perceive on difference between 'b' and 'd' '9' and 'q', '14' and '4' F etc. this negatively affects his/her reading-skills consequently hampering both comprehension and content expression.

Spatial Relation (SR) : It is the ability to see a relationship between two or more objects in relation to self and in relation to each other. A child having difficulty in Spatial Relation will generally have problems in doing task involving directionality and literality in reading, writing, spelling and arithmetic.

Auditory Perception (AP) : It refers to an ability to provide meaning to auditory stimuli including reception of non-verbal information, auditory sequencing. Auditory discrimination, subject's phonemic association & his/ her verbal fluency and subject's morpheme grapheme association.

Cognitive Abilities (CA) : These include the subject's ability to manipulate the stimuli in reversed order which calls for a cognitive retracting subject's ability to categorization and the level of his/her cognitive processing, involving encoding & memory of the input from the range of his/her experimental world, the ability to recognize the subtle difference within its common category required for adequate task performance, i.e., the subject's higher level processing abilities.

Memory (M) : It is the necessary facilitator for almost all learning. It is the ability to retain what has been learnt.

Receptive Language (RL) : It includes the encoding processes of verbal visual stimuli, i.e., spontaneous semantic processing and the subjects's verbal fluency.

Expressive Language (EL) : This includes the subject's ability to use proper syntax in language, the subjects awareness of syntactical structures and metalinguistic structures and the subject's perceptual reception of the stimulus.

VARIOUS TYPES

Learning disability may occur in various forms such as reading disability writing disability; communication and comprehension disability, writing disability, communication and comprehension disability', numerical disability, etc.

Reading Disability : Children suffering from reading disability are unable to read. There are two forms of this disability. In a mild form the affected person has difficulty in reading, but in severe cases of the impairment there is a total loss of the ability to read. This is sometimes also known as 'Word Blindness' Children with the mild form of the disability are already in the general classroom. If identified early, proper help can be given and integration with their normal peers is also easier. This severely affected child will need intensive remedial exercises.

Writing Disability : The affected children are not able to write postaneously. There are two forms of this impairment—the mild and severe. Children affected by the mild form have difficulty in learning to write legibly. They study in general schools. Their problems can be corrected if identified early and provided timely help. Those affected by the severe type of impairment can copy writing without distortion but they cannot write spontaneously. They are identified by their inability to learn to write. The severely affected children need remedial exercises and are thus hard to integrate in the academic areas.

Problems in Comprehending Communication: Children with this disability have a problem in communication through writing, speaking, or reading. Those affected by the mild form of this impairment have difficulty in understanding both the spoken and written words. The child finds it difficult to understand even signs and gestures. These children can be integrated if corrective measures are given in time. Otherwise, linguistic problems of articulation and fluency may develop. The severely affected child is unable to understand speech and written material, nor can be learnt to speak, read and write. He is unable to communicate even through signs and gestures. Such children are difficult cases for integration. They need intensive remedial exercises.

Problems of Numerical Ability: The affected child has problems in calculations, even simple arithmetic, because of an inability to manipulate number relationships. Numerical inability is again of two kinds—mild and severe. Numerical problems seem difficult even if they are very simple for a normal child to do. Children with the mild form of this disability may already be studying in the general classroom. They are not easily identified at pre-primary levels. The disability becomes obvious when they start learning numbers and simple addition and substraction. If identified at pre-primary levels. The disability becomes obvious when they start learning numbers and simple addition and substraction. If identified early and with appropriate correction, they can study in the regular classes. If the problem is severe, the child will not be able to learn number symbols and their relationships. This is also termed as loss of arithmetic ability. The severe cases are difficult of integration and will require intensive remedial exercises.

The Identification

Individuals are assessed usually as learning disabled after they start having problems in school. A variety of tests are administered even after certain tell-tale signs. The three indicators of LD have to be identified: The following questions can be put to the learning disabled children:

1. Has difficulty in telling the time, remembering the order of days, months and seasons and mathematical tables.
2. Finds it difficult to organize his work and is often late in submitting his class-work.
3. Seems dull and slow in responding to others.
4. Cannot correctly recall oral instructions when asked to repeat them.
5. Does not seem to listen to or understand instructions given at home or in the classroom (asks for repetition).
6. Shows excessive inconsistency in the quality of performance; from time to time; seems to be bright in many ways, but still does poorly in school.

7. Gets easily distracted even by a slight disturbance.
8. Confuses between left and right.
9. Gets so excited that he cannot sit still in the classroom even for a short period.
10. While reading, misses outlines or reads them twice.
11. Finds difficulty in synthesising a word after spelling its component letters : Example : says b/e/g but cannot say beg, or may say bed instead.
12. Makes wild guesses at words whether they make sense or not (for example, 'huge' for 'hurt', 'turned' for 'trainer').
13. Reads word backwards (for example 'on for' 'on', 'saw' for 'was').
14. Puts letters in the wrong order (reading 'felt' as 'left', 'act' as 'cat')
15. Shortens words ('sunly' for 'suddenly', 'member' for 'remember').
16. Misreads words which look similar ('help' for 'held', 'houls' for 'horse').
17. Has difficulty in recollecting words automatically and correct sentences.
18. Misreads, number ('e' as '9', '3' as '8') writes letters in the wrong order (time for 'item').
19. Mirror writes (ram for mar).
20. Reverse letter ('b' as 'd', 'p' as 'q').
21. Mirror writes ('6' as '9', 'q' as 'e').
22. Omits letters ('limp' as 'lip', 'went' as 'wet').
23. Adds letters ('want' as 'what', 'what' as 'whart').
24. Does not write the appropriate letters when given the sound.
25. Does not pick out letter of the alphabet when the nake of the letter is called out.
26. Does not match the letters when asked to.
27. Difficulty in academic subjects. Sometimes the student is deficient in only one subject or a combination of subjects.

Guide for Teachers

The National Council of Educational Research and Training, New Delhi has developed "Functional Assessment Guide" for use by teachers. After identification and assessment, such children should be placed in an appropriate environment for their eduction and training. Mildly handicapped children can be placed in regular classroom with provision of resource room help. Severely handicapped children cannot profit from regular classroom instruction. They may be educated and trained by competent professionals in special class settings.

After identifying LD children by using the check list mentioned above the teacher should see that such children are assessed properly above the teacher should see that such children are assessed properly by the experts. Such assessment may be medical and psychological. In most cases experts such as doctors and psychologists are not available for medical and psychological assessment of LD children. In rural areas particularly, trained professionals are not available. In such cases the teacher can conduct functional assessment. Functional assessment which is not a replacement of medical or psychological assessment indicates what a child can do and what he cannot do. Based on functional assessment the teacher can plan and provide specialised service and help in the school.

Causes of LD Children

The causes of learning disability could be organised under organic, environmental and genetic.

Organic Causes : LD arises because of Minimal Brain Dysfunction (MBD). The dysfunction occurs in central nervous system which consists of the brain and the spinal cord. The malfunctioning is not due to damage, but due to dysfunction which is only minimal. Minimal brain dysfunction arises due to (a) cerebral hemorrhage, cerebral disease because of high fever, head injury; (b) intrauterine environment premature birth, anoxia, physical trauma, (c) constitutional-genetic-neuro-chemical dysfunction. It must be noted that all brain dysfunctions are not associated with learning disability and all types of learning disability do not arise due to brain dysfunction.

Hypoglycemia or low blood sugar is a cause of learning problem. Any factor that can cause neurological damage can cause learning problems.

Genetic Causes : Learning problems and hyperactivity run in families. Nearly 20% of hyperactive children had one parent hyperactive. Children with Turner's syndrome have higher incidence of learning disabilities.

Environmental Causes : Maternal factors known to have a negative effect include the use of drugs, the consumption of alcohol and contraction of rubella. Complications during pregnancy such as anoxia (loss of Oxygen), birth injury causing brain damage, and children who received neo-natal intensive care subsequently become LD. Learning disability may be caused due to insufficient early experience and stimulation. It is also caused by poor or inadequate instruction.

Problems of Learning

These children are like other children in intellectual functioning. They are not mentally retarded, nor do they have visual or hearing problems. But they have problems in spelling , reading, writing, arithmetic listening and comprehension because of difficulties in their psychological process, particularly in perception. The problem may be due to cerebral dysfunction/ emotional/behavioural disturbance, but it is not due to mental retardation, sensory deprivation or cultural instructional practices. They can be categorized into mildly and severely learning disabled.

The mild learning disabled can be educated in regular schools. Such children are to be found in regular schools. They are, however, difficult to identify at the initial stages. They face problems in learning basic academic skills. The problem may occur in one or more area of learning skill but of a relatively mild degree. The child can be helped if identified early and given proper training and practice. Since their problem is mild in nature these children can be integrated for higher classes in general schools with some adaptation and adjustment in the curriculum.

The severe learning disabled include those who manifest and inability to master basic academic skills (reading, writing etc.). Their problem may be due to brain dysfunction or environmental deprivation. It is difficult to integrate such children in general schools.

Children with learning disability differ in their behavioural characteristics. But all of them have a severe discrepancy between achievement and intellectual ability. This is the basic problem that they face. But there may also be secondary problems like emotional, and social maladjustment associated with the basic skills. A description of these problems has been given below:

Attention Disorders of LD : Attention problems go frequently hand in hand with learning disabilities. They have short attention span. Attentional problems are shown to affect students test taking abilities because attend to inappropriate distracters.

1. They cannot sustain attention for the required amount to time.
2. They are unable to attend to the relevant and ignore the irrelevant. They may be attracted to every stimulus that surrounds him.
3. They can be diverted easily from one topic to another.
4. They put excessive attention to unimportant details while, disregarding the essentials (attends to the page number than to the printed matter or the picture on the page).

Memory Problem of LD : Many LD children are passive learners and do not use strategies (rehearsal, mneumonics cues. These children are poor, ask planners and organisers. They display certain characteristics as regards remembering.

1. Disorder of memory involve difficulty in the assimilation, storage, and retrieval of information, and may be associated with visual auditory or other learning processes.
2. The LD children have difficulties in reproducing rhythm patterns, sequence of digits, words, or phrases.
3. They have difficulty in revisualising letters, words or forms.

4. Both the short-term and the long term memory of the ID child are poor.
5. They fail to see the relationship between his present and past experience.

Reading Problem of LD : Nearly 85 to 90 percent of learning disabled children have reading problems and therefore, have poor academic achievement. These include mispronunciation, skipping, adding or substituting wards as well as problem in memory, reversing letters or words and blending sounds together. They display both oral reading and comprehension problems.

In case of learning disabled children one finds visual and auditory spellers. The visual spellers write right letters in wrong orders-WTARE-Water. The auditory spellers try to sound outwards: Posishun-Position. There are also omission errors or substitution errors. These defects continue to adolescence and are responsible for learning deficits.

There are some specific problems of learning disabled children which are as follows:

(1) Eye-Hand-Co-ordination (EHC), (2) Figure Ground Perception (FGP), (3) Figure Constancy (FC), (4) Position in Space (PS), (5) Spatial Relations (SR), and (6) Auditory Perception (AP). Last four areas represent the aspect of cognitive functioning, viz. (7) Memory (M), (8) Cognitive Abilities (CA). (9) Receptive Language (RL) and (10) Expressive Language (EL).

The details have been given under the head of classifications of learning disabled children.

The Diagnosis

Assessment of pre-school level children can be made as per DIAL model (Developmental Indicators for the Assessment of Learning). It is meant for 21/2 to 51/2 year old in the areas of sensory, motor, affective, social, conceptual, language communication in less than 30 minutes. The tests consists of visual and auditory activity gross motor movements, fine motor movements, finger agility anxiety, task attention, focus and persistence, social skills, identifying objects, colours, sorting, receiving and expressing language, articulation etc.

At the elementary and secondary level identifications of learning disabilities become relatively easier because availability of instruments, teacher observations and achievement index. Each learning disabled child undergoes neurological examinations, Reading tests, Visual- motor Gestalt tests requiring them to copy various geometric forms, awareness of one's body parts (Draw a Man Test). Findings (hearing sounds) and bio-chemical screening. These medical characteristics are necessary to deal with learning disabled children besides intellectual and achievement scores.

The following tests are commonly used in diagnosis of LD.

1. Informal Graded word Recognition Test. It measures quickly reading level and errors.
2. Information reading Inventory-It measure quickly reading skills, reading levels, types of errors unknown words, related behavioural characteristics.
3. Wechsler-Intelligence Scale for Children (Revised).
4. Stanford-Binet Intelligence Scale.
5. Peadody Picture Vocabulary Test.
6. Illinois test of Psychologistic Abilities.
7. Lincoln Oseretsky Motor Development Scale.
8. Vineland Social Maturity Scale.
9. Kauffman Assessment Battery for children.
10. Kauffman Test of Educational Assessment.
11. Wide Range Achievement Test.

The Remediation

The children with learning his ability are benefited mostly from remedial instruction. Remedial instruction. Remedial instruction is nothing but good teaching with two definite and specific objectives, such as:

Eliminating ineffective habits and reteaching skills which have been incorrectly learned, This refers to remediation of defects.

Teaching for the first time those habits, skills and behaviours which have never been learned but should have been learned by the child to acquire academic skills. This refers to developmental teaching or development of increased competencies.

Remedial instruction required proper diagnosis of a child's abilities and disabilities in specific school subjects, identifying skills and process which require remediation, and then providing him just good teaching in areas of his weakness through systematic planning, individualised instruction, tutoring in one-to-one or small group situation evaluating his progress periodically and if necessary reteaching, encouraging intensive drill, practice or repetition and modifying the programme and adopting alternate materials and methods using work-books, supplementary materials and multisensory approach, most LD children improve their performance dramatically after exposure to remedial instruction in resource rooms which seemed difficult in regular classroom settings.

Remedial instruction in the resource room can vary from one hour every day to a half-days programme regularly depending upon deficiencies and the amount of training required. It is to be emphasized that the, sooner the remedial instruction starts in the elementary school the easier for the child to compensate his deficiencies and the better for his later progress in upper classes.

TREATMENT APPROACHES

There are two approaches for the care and treatment of LD children. These are: Medical-Neurological approach and Psycho-Educational approach.

Medical-Neurological Approach : The medical-neurological approach views the LD child as a patient afflicted with minimal brain dysfunction (MBD). Such a child should be treated just like any other individual afflicted with disease or injury. The most common symptom associated with MBD is hyperactivity. Thus quite logically medication associated with MBD is hyperactivity. Thus quite logically, medication of some type would be sought to alleviate the child's symptoms. The most widely prescribed drugs to alleviate the symptoms of hyperactivity are psycho-stimulants. Psychostimulants may bring about improvements in the behaviour of the LD child, but their effect on improving the learning of such children is not clearly established by research findings. Psycho-stimulant drugs can have a positive effect on a child's classroom behaviour in reducing his activity level and making him more manageable and teachable but we cannot always count on them to remediate the child's learning problems. In addition to psycho-stimulant drugs mega-vitamin therapy and diet management are inconclusive. What is needed therefore is a behaviouristic approach or a psycho-educational approach which relies on the teacher's effectiveness in working with such children, motivating them and providing appropriate instruction to them.

Psycho-educational Approach : The psycho-educational approach views the LD children not as a patient but as learner waiting to be taught. From the psycho-educational perspectives, the LD children are to be identified early, assessed medically and psychologically to arrive at a correct diagnosis of their difficulties and weaknesses and provided with appropriate instruction and training in regular schools, resource rooms, special classes or special schools depending upon their degree of disability. There are various approaches for the education and training of L.D. Children. All these approaches fall under five categories such as:

Process Training Approach : Process training is based on the contention that learning academic subjects requires understanding the underlying psychological processes. Learning disabled children have a disorder in the psychological processes which underlie in understanding or using speech, in reading, writing, arithmetic, etc. Thus it may be of value to train the LD child in the psychological process which underlay various academic subjects. For example, a LD child believed to have reading problems because of difficulties in visual perception will be trained in visual perception.

Multisensory Approach : Multisensory approach is based on the assumption that the child will be more likely to learn if more than one of his sense is involved in the learning experiences. One such method is called tile VAKT method (V stands for visual A stands for auditory, K stands for kinesthetic and T stand for tactual). For example, the teacher asks the child to tell a story. The teacher writes down the words of the child to tell a story. The teacher writes down the words of the story on the blackboard. These words serve as material as the child learns to read. In learning the words, the child first sees the word (visual). He hears the teacher say the word (auditory). He says the word (auditory). Finally the child traces the word (kinesthetic and tactual).

Environmental Approach : Learning disabled children are usually destructible and hyperactive. For such children an environmental approach is sometimes recommended by some educators. Environmental approach emphasises reducing the irrelevant stimuli in the classroom environment which might distract the child's attention from the learning task. The classroom environment may be modified in the following ways as far as possible and as per necessity to make it free from unnecessary distraction:

1. Sound-proofing of walls and ceilings.
2. Carpeting
3. Opaque windows
4. Enclosed book cases and cupboards
5. Limited use of bulletin boards
6. Use of cubicles, three-sided work areas
7. Removing the pictures, calenders and other hanging objects from the walls.
8. Ensuring a noise-free and in other ways a distraction - free environment outside the classroom.
9. Enhancing the intensity of the teaching materials in terms of colour, size, and vividness,

Cognitive Training Approach : Many learning disabled children exhibit deficient problem-solving skills. They are likely to act impulsively rather than reflectively responding quickly without considering the various alternatives. In order to reduce their impulsively and to increase their reflectivity two techniques are found successful:

Cognitive Modelling : Cognitive modelling is sometimes known as meta cognition, meta memory and cognitive behaviour modification strategy. This approach is directed towards providing LD children with an awareness of how people learn or remember.

In cognitive modelling the LD child is exposed to models (adults or peers) who tend to be more reflective so that he can imitate the model and learn the appropriate strategy. Through this technique the LD child is taught how to slow himself down before he reads a word or given an answer looks carefully at all cues and possibilities, considers his response carefully, and then responds. In remembering, he is taught to group information into small bits or clusters, rehearses these by saying them over and over to himself and even use mnemonic devices to aid in memory storage many LD children improve dramatically when they are simply made aware of the most effective way to learn and remember.

Self-instruction Training: Modelling can also be combined with self-instructional training. In self-instructional training the impulsive child is encouraged to learn to develop verbal control of his behaviour. The following is an example:

(i) The teacher (adult model) performs a task (solving an arithmetic problem) while talking out to himself loudly.

(ii) The child performs the same task under the direction of the teacher.

(iii) The child whispers the instruction to himself as he goes through the task, and finally,

(iv) The child performs the task while guiding his performance via private speech.

Through self-instructional training the LD child is helped to monitor his own performance in learning situation to be aware of his own approach to cognitive tasks.

Other Special Approaches and Techniques

The LD children have characteristics which are unique to them. Although they are not visually impaired they have difficulty in visual perception. They have difficulty in visual reception, visual discrimination., and visual memory Similarly although' they are not auditorily handicapped they have difficulty in auditory awareness, auditory discrimination, and auditory memory. They have problems in attention and retention'. These difficulties hinder their acquisition of language, their ability to read and write, listening skills, etc. Hence, special training in these areas is very useful for LD children. The resource teacher can provide such training to the LD children in the resource room. The following approaches and activities are useful for LD children.

Listening Exercise: The LD children have problems of distractibility which hinder their acquisition of listening skills and hence their ability to follow direction. Listening exercise for such children are often helpful. One exercise involves having someone who is out of sight produce various sounds for the children to identify, such as when the group goes for a walk, the children can be instructed to listen for common sound, including care running, a train chugging, or a bird singing. To improve comprehension of spoken words in children with listening problems, the teacher can give direction orally, beginning with short and simple ones and increasing the difficulty as the child progress ('stand up, turn around, and then sit down'). Riddles can also be used to develop listening power and comprehension.

Discrimination Learning: The LD children have difficulties in discriminating one letter from another, one word from another and one number from another. Discrimination learning can be encouraged among such children for the above, purpose. In discrimination learning children must be trained to attend to the similarities and difference between two letters, words, or numbers (e.g., b, d, p, q; 6, 9; 3, 8; hat, bat etc.) and then to make the correct response. In teaching such children letters, words, or numbers, these are to be written in the beginning in large sizes in crayon on news print paper. The children can trace the letters with their index fingers, while saying the letters, words, or numbers aloud. Visual and auditory attention is thus heightened in relation to these letters, words, or numbers. In order to improve their retention ability repetition or overhearing may be encouraged.

Visual Reception Training : Visual reception can be encouraged by having children identify common objects by name and tell both their proper use and to whom each object belongs. They can be asked to stand in front of a mirror each day in the resource room and comment on what they see. Children can be given pictures to interpret in terms of objects seen, colours, sizes, motion and other details.

Visual Memory Training : Visual memory can be developed by having children close their eyes and describe their clothing, a bulletin board in the room, or other children.

Spatial Training: Spatial training can be introduced by having children find the top, bottom, sides and back of an object. The concepts of up, down over, tinder, in, bigger, heavier, etc. can be demonstrated.

Auditory Awareness Training : Auditory awareness can be encouraged by having children remember various types of sounds heard during walk. The children can identify the source of each sound and give it an appropriate label. The teacher can hold a wristwatch to a child's ear at varying distances and train the child to listen and to raise a hand when the ticking is no longer audible. Directions can be whispered to the child at varying distances from each ear. Quiet periods can be held during which children are asked to listen to various sounds.

Auditory Discrimination Exercise : Auditory discrimination exercises can include hiding a ticking clock and asking a child to point to the direction of the clock. The teacher can tap several times on the desk and have the children listen count to themselves and report the number of taps. While blind folded, a child can identify a classmate by his voice.

Auditory Memory and Sequencing Training : Auditory memory and sequencing can be developed by asking children to repeat directions, phone numbers, and clapping patterns. They can listen to nursery rhymes and songs and pick out details they will be asked to repeat afterwards. The teacher can tell simple jokes and have the children repeat them.

Educational Provisions

The educational provisions for learning disabled children primarily consist of three types.

Day School : where the learning disabled children receive specialised schooling using special teachers essentially on the same curriculum but with greater care and pace. This is a segregated setting.

Special Class in a Regular School : where LD children are given special instruction in a self contained classroom by special teacher as well as regular classroom teacher do assist in teaching subject matters. These children receive instruction on academic in these classes but for social activities etc. They are with general students.

Since their number is large, and they do not pose organic problems or problems of low IQ, these children are integrated in the regular classroom with resources room facilities (main-streaming/ integration).

Teaching Approaches

The following teaching approaches are used for LD children:

1. Asal, 2. Phonices, 3. Linguistic, 4. Language Experiences, 5. Programmed Instruction, 6. Multisensory, and 7. Rebus Picture.

The details are given in the follow paras:

Asal Teaching Approach

It has the following advantages and limitations details with LD children:

Advantage : (1) Comprehensive. (2) Controlled vocabulary. (3) Sequential introduction of skills. (4) Reinforcement of skills. (5) Diagnostic and evaluative material usually provided.

Limitations: (1) Limited flexibility in teaching style. (2) Individualized instruction not encouraged. (3) Lack of depth of material necessary for skill mastery. (4) Lack of provision for processing deficits. (5) No choice of analytic or synthetic phonics instruction. (6) Subjects to repetition of the same stories and methods resulting from failure.

Phonics Teaching Approach

It has the following advantages and limitations details with LD children:

Advantage: Effective decoding techniques for pupils with good auditory abilities.

Limitations: (1) Not effective for pupils with auditory deficits. (2) May be taught in isolation. (3) Comprehension neglected. (4) Invariance in English language may cause confusion.

Linguistics Teaching Approach

It has the following advantages and limitations details with LD children:

Advantage: (1) Control for irregular spelling in initial stages. (2) Gradual introduction of phones. (3) Extensive repetition.

Limitations : (1) Little emphasis on comprehension in initial stages. (2) Vocabulary controlled for regular elements and does not utilize spoken language of pupil.

Language Experience Teaching Approach

It has the following advantages and limitations details with LD children:

Advantage : (1) Motivates with personal stories. (2) Uses pupil's oral language. (3) Can incorporate specific skill development. (4) Can include language art skills. (5) Good for pupils with good visual-motor abilities.

Limitations : (1) May be limited by pupils' language level. (2) Lacks structured systematic approach to skill development.

Programmed Instruction Teaching Approach

It has the following advantages and limitations details with LD children:

Advantage: (1) Small, sequential steps. (2) Immediate feedback. (3) May be boring.

Limitations: (1) Lacks direct instruction. (2) May be confusing format constancy.

Multisensory Teaching Approach

It has the following advantages and limitations details with LD children:

Advantage: (1) Uses more than one sensory input to get message to the brain. (2) Can use an analystic approach or a synthetic approach.

Limitations: Lack of sequential skill development in some programmes. (2) Sensory overload experienced by some pupils.

Rebus Picture Teaching Approach

It has the following advantages and limitations details with LD children:

Advantage : (1) Use a rebus (picture) instead of a word to simplify initial stages of reading. (2) Well structured materials. (3) Provides for transition to traditional print materials.

Limitations: Format appearing immature for older pupils.

General Remedial Approach for LD Children

Mildly and moderately learning disabled pupils can function satisfactory in the regular classroom with these adjustments. The regular classroom curriculum may require little modification. These are some of the general techniques of remediation but a specific theoretical model should guide the practitioner.

Cognitive Processing Approach : The cognitive processing approach provides a way of thinking about how a child learns and offers a framework for teaching. The developmental approach emphasises sequential approach for remediation. Test related approach identifies specific areas of deficiency which can be taught.

Specialised Techniques Approach : The specialised techniques indicate that the teacher would follow the prescribed order and fashion for a specified period of time. Hierarchy of skills are to be developed in the skill development approach using criterion referenced teaching. Published materials can be used for remediation of learning disability.

Behavioural Approach : The behavioural approach refers to behaviour modification approach for manipulations of environmental conditions of learning. Apply reinforcement and change behaviour. Psychotherapeutic approach should build feelings of success and establish a healthy psychodynamic relationship between teacher and student. The major cause of reading failure is dyspedagogia i.e., lack of good teaching. Inadequacy in the child's teacher and the teacher environment are the answer to remediation.

"Learning disabilities can not be corrected or cured by a specific teaching method or training technique. It is imperative that teachers have a wide range of instructional materials and techniques at their disposal and that they, are imaginative and flexible enough to adapt these to specific needs of their pupils."

Principles of Teaching

The following principles may serve as guidelines for the regular teacher teaching normal and LD children in integrated settings.

Expect the Child to Learn: Teacher's expectation is reflected in the child's performance.

Take Noting for Granted: Understand the child very patiently and carefully. The LD child may pretend to be attentive, motivated and seem to understand everything you are talking about, but in reality does not.

Bombard the Senses : Use multisensory approach to involve the child more completely in the teaching learning process.

Load up the Cues : Have the child label and describe what is happening. Use a variety of distinctive elements and changes them from time to time to bring novelty in experiences.

Make it Vivid: Increase the intensity of what is given to the child. Make it bigger, louder, more colourful, more imaginative, more exciting and more interesting. Be enthusiastic and animated.

Repeat as Often as Necessary : Assess the child's level of understanding. Be sure you have reached the child's level. Ask the child to tell you what have been presented. Repeat statements. Repeat directions. Don't be boring.

Make it Relevant: Enter the child's world, Leave the example given in (prescribed text books. Give them content that is familiar to them and part of their out-of-school life. Introduce local specific elements in your presentation.

Make it Concrete : Use pictures, recordings and spoken words. These are fine. But don't stop there. Show real objects. Let the child touch, smell, manipulate and get a direct impression and experience about concepts you are presenting.

Surprise the Child : Present novel experiences. Use different materials and methods. Excite the child with stimulating experiences.

Emphasize the Positive Achievement: Ignore the mistakes and at best make the child understand his mistakes, but in all cases recognise his positive achievements and tell it to others.

Move Sequentially : Teach step by step.

Review, Objectively : Look back. Introspect what was your expectation. Modify your strategy and get ready to move ahead again as soon as possible.

Make it Distraction-free : Remove irrelevant stimuli from the classroom. Have distraction-free physical environment in and out of the classroom.

Be a Mother : Show motherly love. Take their care. Win their heart and you will win the battle.

Be Open to your Colleagues : Cooperate with them and seek their cooperation. Share and exchange experiences and learn from other's experiences.

Teaching Method and Techniques

In spite of differential educational provisions there are certain general techniques of instruction. The following instructional techniques have been used and recommended for use with LD children.

1. Use short, brief directions, large print.
2. Use consistent language, colour cues.
3. Write directions or steps on the chalkboard i.e. underline important words etc.
4. Alternate the use of colours for each step in a series on directions.
5. Increase sound level of instruction.
6. Use diagrams or pictorial illustrations.
7. Use an overview of the lesson, ask questions, ask them to read the material, recite and review.

Since LD children lack structure and organisation, they have to be told to keep daily engaged in the activities; list all future events that need to be scheduled. Provide a hypothetical list to suggest possible events, and plan future events that must be planned, it is time to develop a weekly schedule. Pupils in the upper grades may find useful a schedule that provides for specific subject matter assignments on various types of activities.

Thinking skills can be developed by guiding students collect data by reading, listening, and observing; and discriminate differences on similarities in data. Teacher questioning can be used to prod the pupil until the ability to make these discrimination improve. Ask the pupil categories and classify the data. Labelling is important during this stage.

Have the pupil recategories and classify the data in other ways. This continuous reorganisation and restructuring is necessary to integrate new information and new experiences into the pupils, mental structures. Have the pupil make predictions based on the data. Have the pupil generate alternative predictions by comparing and contrasting possible outcomes and their effects.

Memory ability can be improved by certain specific techniques, visual and auditory messages can be recalled. Facial expressions indicative of certain materials can be retrieved. Cramming is to be avoided. Certain activities can be practiced to improve auditory, visual memories.

1. Have pupils repeat telephone numbers and street address of emergency service facilities (police, fire, etc.).
2. Have pupils learn songs by listening to the words and tunes.
3. Play games in which the first pupils makes a statement, the next pupil repeats that and adds a statements, the third pupil repeats those statements and adds one and so on.
4. Have pupils make up rhymes related to subject matter, such as, "In 1492 Columbus sailed the ocean blue".
5. Have pupils repeat oral directions.
6. Have pupils resequence cartoon strips (without words) that have been cut apart. This forces them to observe details in the pictures.
7. Have pupils describe configurations of words that are similar.
8. Have pupils repeat the sequence for a recipe that they have read.
9. Have the pupil practice attending to large units at one time. For instance, some try to copy one syllable at a time. Encourage the pupil to increase the length of the

visual stimulus that she holds in her mind as she write it down.

10. Help the pupil to practice internal auditorisation as an adjust to visual memory that is, have the pupil say the letters or words to herself while she is translating the written information.
11. Write every other item on the chalkboard with a different colour chalk. This helps the pupil to "find her place."
12. Allow the pupils to copy another pupil's work. Some of these pupils perform better with paper-to paper-copying.

Teachers must be flexible in their approach to teaching reading because of the heterogenous characteristics of learning disabled pupils. A diagnostic prescriptive approach must be used. The reading programme must be matched to pupil's need and abilities. There are several approaches having different degree of relevance.

Role of Teacher

The teacher should play the following roles in dealing with Learning Disabled Children.

Managing the Children : The child with learning disabilities needs individual tutoring in one or more of his areas of disability. Whether or not there is a resource teacher available will determine to a great extent how much of this instruction will be assumed by the regular class teacher. It is a fact that the regular classroom teacher and the resource teacher should have cooperative working relationship. The regular teacher should work the resource teacher exactly what the duties of each of them are. "Who will be responsible for what" is a basic question that is sometimes never decided. However the regular teacher has the following role to play:

The regular classroom teacher who deals with children-abled and disabled-has much opportunity to observe their behavioural characteristics, identify the LD children and refer the suspected cases to the resource teacher for taking steps for assessment and diagnosis of their difficulties and deficiencies.

He is sure of the specific deficiencies of such children should plan his instruction in a systematic and sensitive way in consultation with the resource teacher. If there is no resource teacher in his school must plan everything himself. He should remember that what LD children need is just good teaching. What is good teaching for LD children is also good teaching for normal children. There are many ways to describe good teaching for normal as well as LD children.

The LD children as a group are heterogeneous. As such they require a variety of technique approaches as well as materials to satisfy their unique educational needs at different levels of development.

At the pre-school level, the environment should be arranged to promote efficiency accessibility, independence and functionality. Safety is also a factor in the pre-school setting. Heavy breakable and dangerous materials should be out of reach of these children. At the elementary level children classrooms should not be noisy, visually distracting and sterile. The special educator and the regular classroom teaching should provide a less distracting environment for students who are overtly destructible and hence learning disabled. Such children can be placed in the centre of the classroom where more often teacher's attention is focused.

Although small group permits individualised instruction yet have demonstrated the efficacy of peer tutoring in instruction, seat work and special projects. Care should be taken to select a good regular peer.

Structure in planning the instructional programme is a must for learning disabled children. The curriculum should be organised sequential and routine based so that the LD child can attend to it carefully. For this task analysis procedure is most relevant. This enables the teacher to break the task into components and helps the student at each stage.

The teacher should also provide a summary presentation after each sub-plan of teaching so that LD children can learn well in school and this will provide as an advance organiser for learning.

The equipments and materials must be ready to be used in 'dead time' when the LD children has nothing, to do. They can not waste their times. There are a number of specific teacher procedures that have been used to remedials academic deficits or failures among LD Children. One of the general approach is learning strategies by actively involving them in the learning process mostly consisting of self-instruction and verbalisation.

LD children lack abilities for metacognition. Hence, teacher can initiate self-underline, answering questions, writing down, asking himself the purpose of reading etc., self-instructional techniques have been found quite effective for LD children.

Precision teaching is a system of evaluating and improving instruction. It is direct, continuous and precise measure of student progress where the teacher records a wide range of behaviours. They help teachers on track and make accurate instructional decisions.

As regards teaching contents and materials it should be motivating, non-complex, and appropriate for child's level of functioning, and learning style. Using student's name, talents or interest is one way a teacher can make assignments more motivating. Illustrations, too much use of colours in the students' attention and make learning exciting.

Multisensory approach also have also been applied to teach LD children. Visual Auditory. Kinaesthetic, and Tactile (VAKT) was developed by Fernald (1941) feeling seeing saving and hearing the word. Once the word is mastered the teacher helps them to write a story and then given him feedback. In this way new words are learned. Children can be taught through association of a how a latter or word looks, sounds and feels. After he learns the works sentence and story writing begin, gradually they begin to read. There are several combinations of multisensory, teaching methods.

Direct instruction which includes assessment, instruction and evaluation are used. DISTAR is one of the direct instructional system which teaching sequence are so arranged that errors are minimised, it provides ample practice, and given immediate and positive feedback, Distar includes Mathematics and reading components. DISTAR was used first with disadvantaged children and now with LD. It is a back to basics structured programme.

Learning strategies are also used for helping LD children to learn. Computer assisted instruction is also being introduced in the school system for the management of IEP.

Developing Confidence: An excellent way to help LD students who are struggling with problems of low self-esteem is to entrust them with some duties and responsibilities. Taking care of a pet or a plant makes students feel important. They will see that their presence in the class is important not only in terms of potential academic contribution but also in maintaining the life of an organism. This attitude of the teacher will bring a dramatic shift in students' self-confidence.

Classroom Management

Williams and Hounshell (1998) in their article Enabling the Learning Disabled. Teaching Strategies for challenged students say, "Many LD (learning disabled) students have the academic potential of non-disabled students but require some assistance in unveiling their potential and turning it into achievement."

Teaching Strategies: The following are the strategies for learning disabled children:

1. One of the most important things teacher should do is to provide support for risk taking and call attention to the successful work of an LD student without attaching the LD label.
2. Making use of technology is advantageous, and it is a good idea to use computers as often as possible. Computers stimulate a variety of senses for LD students and are valuable.
3. LD students are particularly receptive to television and video because they appeal to a number of sense.
4. The music sound and graphic often make learning come to life for LD students.
5. LD students feel safe when they are watching a move because there is no fear of being called on to answer a question or read aloud.

Organization of Classroom : Teacher of LD students should also structure class time so that intense, laborious activities are interspersed with relaxing, enjoyable activities that allow students to move around. The teacher should take care of the following points.

Seating Arrangement: The following are the arrangement for LD children.

1. Desks arranged in clusters, however, are more conducive to promoting children's discussion or collaboration.
2. When introducing new vocabulary words, repetition is important.
3. To avoid confusing the child, teachers should plan assignments that focus on a primary task.
4. It is better to start simply and add layers of complexity to LD students' assignments as the school year process.

Assessment Strategies : The following are the assessment strategies learning disabled children:

When assessing LD students, teachers should make assignments clear and grade using a qualitative scoring rubric. At the same time, when administering multiple choice tests, it is important that the answer choices are clear and that one choice stands out as the best answer.

A teacher in a main streamed classroom has to make the classroom personalised where individual differences are accepted and valued. Teacher lead students to value and accept personal responsibility for their own learning. They should promote independence, cooperative functioning, and problem solving among all students. Specifically they should

1. Accept the perception of learner about classroom environment.
2. Provide varieties of options to motivate each child.
3. Encourage independent and small group work.
4. Increase pupil's commitment, control and responsibility.
5. Informal and formal conferences are held.
6. Ongoing assessment and student evaluation are done to know the each student's progress.

Make these implementable in the regular classroom:

1. A structured programme has to be avoided.
2. Allow distractible student to sit in centre.
3. Use peer teaching and allow the LD child to be tutor.
4. Drive homework on the curriculum taught.
5. Keep close contact with parents.
6. Tailor the programme to student's needs.
7. Make task analysis and lead student step by step for learning.

Learning difficulties are quite pervasive and non-specific, which arise out of several factors and are achievement specific. In regular schools, learning disabled students can be handled well if regular and resource teacher become conscious and sensitive to the problems of these children. The various concerns expressed in the field are mentioned along with tips for relevant remedial measures.

The Suggestions

The following are the main suggestions for dealing with the learning disabled children :

Improving Handwriting: Poor handwriting in the learning disabled has been attributed to numerous causes : Poor fine motor control, poor visual discrimination and memory, spatial difficulties. Manipulative exercises can be used to strengthen muscles : cutting, modelling clay games. Chalkboard practice should precede pencil and paper writing. Proper position for writing habit to develop. Paper should not replaced at a slant for manuscript writing. The writing instrument is held between thumb and middle finger with index finger applying pressure. Graph paper is of valuable help to teach pupils with special difficulties. A creative teacher improves handwriting using certain techniques as detailed below:

1. Tape alphabet forms to the floor. Have them reproduce the form with coloured chalk.
2. Have pupils used a stick and their bodies to form the letters?
3. Write each letter in a paper with red marker.

4. Have pupils form letter is wet fingerprint?
5. Use coloured directional cues such as green arrows and red dots.
6. Teach manuscript letter forms that are over and slanted slightly. This will encourage left-to-right progression and will facilitate transition to cursive writing.
7. Teach pupils to start all lower case cursive letters from the line.
8. Help pupils to form an association for a letter they have difficulty in remembering.
9. Have pupils orally described their movements as the letter is being written? This provides auditory reinforcement.

The various approaches used in teaching by the resource teacher or specialist or classroom teacher have relative advantages and disadvantages.

Improving Spelling: Spelling errors are quite common among learning disabled children. Therefore a systematic work-study technique is used in the following sequence.

"Look at the word-say the word-say the word-at the word-cover the word-write the word-check your spelling-repeat". Some of the remedial techniques involve-writing the word on the, chalk and then trace it in fingers until it disappears tracing in sand, write the first letter of the word when one listens the word and them pronounce. Ask the children to spell the word properly and clap softly for each vowel sound, if possible by looking at the word.

Developing Arithmetic Ability : Ashlock (1972) made certain specific remedial instruction step for removing arithmetic errors of learning disable children. Some of the steps are as follows:

Use manipulative such as buttons and chips to teach number. Use visual material and give reinforcement. Use graph paper for alignment difficulties. Time line, coloured chalks, markings are helpful for attentions to cues. A sample problem can be given for each assignment. The size of numbers can very to indicate more or less. Reduce distractions as far as possible. Reduce number of examples in the assignment and eliminate copying. Use of display charts, abacus, playing cards, calculator, language master are quite useful.

Curricular Concerns : Learning disabled children read in the class as other children. Hence certain extra care would benefit these pupils. These concerns may relate to four areas: such as : (1) Auditory Perception development (2) Visual Perception Development (3) Sensory Motor development (4) social Skills developing among learning disabled.

EXERCISE

1. Explaln the term 'Learning Disability'. Enumerate the causes of learning problems.
2. Define the term 'Learning Disability.' Differentiate among mentally retarded children, Learning Disabled Children, Backward children and slow learners.
3. Enumerate the characteristics of Learning. Disabled Children, with reference to language, perceptual motor ability, social emotional characteristics and visual perception.
4. Classify the L.D. Children with regard to visual auditory perceptions and cognitive ability. Indicate the types of learning disability.
5. Indicate the basis of identifying learning disabled children. Enumerate the causes of learning disability.
6. Enumerate and describe the problems of learning disabled children. Indicates the basis of diagnosis of L.D. Children.
7. Describe the remediation and treatment of LD children. Suggest some training for improving and adjusting disability.
8. Enumerate the teaching approach and educational provisions for learning disabled children : Principles of teaching remedial approaches and teaching methods.
9. Describe the role of teachers and classroom management for L.D. children. Give some suggestions for improving and adapting strategies for learning disabled children.

10

BACKWARD CHILDREN

The children who fall at lower extreme, of normal distribution of educational attainment trait, are known as backward. The causes of backwardness, may be due to hereditary and environmental factors. The backward children are classified in two categories – mental retardation and educational retardation. The degree of backwardness can be understood with help of intelligence tests and achievement tests. In the classroom they deviate from their classmates in school achievement. They are not benefited by the normal teaching in school. The teacher can easily locate them on the basis of their participation in classroom activities. These children are a great liability for the society and nation as well.

Meaning and Definition: Cyril Burt has discussed the term 'Backwardness' in the book, 'The causes and treatments of backwardness.' The term 'backwardness' may be defined arbitrarily but it is difficult to define comprehensively.

According to Cyril Burt-"The backward child is one who is unable to do the work of the class next below that which is normal of his age,"

The term backwardness can be explained in terms of education quotient. (E.Q.). 'Backward child is one whose educational quotient is 95 or below. The word E.Q. or "educational quotient indicates, presumably, whether a pupil's knowledge of a group of school subjects is commensurate with his chronological age, or whether it is above or below the level to be expected to him for his age."

"Educational Age (E.A.) represents a pupil's average level of achievement in a group of school subjects, measured by means of standardized tests, and in terms of the average for various chronological ages in school" (Freeman, 1976). For example, if a student's performance on the test is at the average 8 year level, his educational age will be 8 only.

'In the Indian situation a backward child is one who being more than one year older than the average age of his class.'

-T.K.A. Menon

These children can not keep pace with the class. They are weak in class assignment, study and examinations. The backward child has backwardness either in all the subjects or in a particular subject.

"The backward child is one who is unable to do the work of the cases where their educational attainments are lower than what they are capable of."

-Berton Hart

Schonell has defined and explained the term 'Backwardness' and 'Retardation' with help of education attainment and mental age of the child.

According to Schonell Backwardness refers to educational age relative to the chronological age of a child.

Retardation refers to educational age relative to the mental age of a child.

It is evident from the above statement that backwardness and retardation are related to educational age of the children.

Dull children are those children who have intelligent quotient (I.Q.) between 70 and 85. The dullness may be one of the cause of backwardness in intelligence, but all backwardness is not the outcomes of dullness.

A child remains weak in all the school subjects, it may be known as 'general backwardness.' If a child is weak in one subject only, this may be termed specific backwardness.

The Characteristics

Cyril Burt and Schonell have statistical characterized with help of mental age and chronological age of the child:

1. The backward child's mental age is smaller than his chronological age.
2. A backward child may be retarded as well but not always.
3. The dullness of a child may be one of the causes of his backwardness.
4. A backward child has low educational attainment than what he is capable of.
5. He can not keep pace with the class even in one subject or in all subjects.
6. A backward child is unable to do the work of the class next below. Who is normal for the age, weak in class assignments and examination or class tests.

A backward child has certain general characteristics. These are classified into four main categories.

Physical Characteristics : Physically backward children are slow or inferior in physical or health development. They have certain physical defects and deficiency or deformity of eyes, nose and speech defects, their muscular coordination may be poor or slow.

Mental Characteristics : The major area of backwardness is the intelligence, their I.Q. is less than average. They lack in reasoning, abstract thinking to see the relationship abilities. They are unable to correlated their various experiences.

Social and Moral Characteristics: The social development is slow as compared with normal children. The maturity age is higher than the averages. He may be the isolate in this class. They may develop some anti-social or undesirable traits. They have poor adjustment in class as well as with his peers.

Educational Characteristics : Education attainment and participation in school programme are the basic qualities of backward children. They can not keep pace with class in academic progress. They are poor in one subject or may be poor in all subjects. They are also poor in doing the home assignments or class assignment. They have the poor interaction with teacher and poor participation in classroom activities. They are low achievers and weak in examination and class tests.

Identification of Backward Children: Backwardness may be identified by employing formal and informal methods. The observation technique is most commonly used by teachers and parents or guides, counsellors and researcher. The following are the four methods which are used for this purpose.

1. Observation method, 2. Mental tests, 3. Achievement test and 4. Personality, Adjustment inventory and Case study.

Observation Method : It is both formal and informal method of identifying backward children. Teachers and parents use this method. They observe their wards and pupils daily in home and in classroom.

Mental Tests : Its group test of intelligence, verbal and non-verbal are used to measure the mental age of the students. By comparing mental age with chronological, the backwardness can be identified. This is a statistical method.

Achievement Tests : Achievement tests in school subjects can be used to assess the level of achievement. If the child is poor in all subjects, it will be considered as general backwardness. The child is poor in one subject it will be treated as specific backwardness.

Personality Inventory and Case Study : The adjustment inventory is used for identifying the area maladjustment. The school maladjustment, indicates the backwardness. The school records or conducting case study of the child can also be used for locating the backwardness.

Etiology of Backwardness (Causes): There are several cause of backwardness, some important causes have been listed here :

1. Low intelligence
2. Physical cause
3. Poor environment of family
4. Truency
5. Poor conditions of school
6. Postural defects.

There may be other causes of backwardness, it depends on the individual conditions of living.

Physical Causes: Physical defect may be also equally important in contributing towards backwardness. Schonell how found about 75% backwardness is due to the various types of physical diseases and defects e.g. defective eyesight, hard of hearing, speech defects chronic diseases (like typhoid, tonsils, cough trouble, stomach trouble) poor nourishment and physical deformities. Burt has found the following facts through his studies: (1) 30% of backward children were poorly nourished, (2) 10% very seriously ill nourished, (3) 37% were suffering from tonsils, speech defects—stammering and stuturing. He has noted that eyesight and hard hearing was the most common cause.

Postural Defects: Postural defects may be of two types: (a) acquired, and other (b) innate. Postural defects may lead to the defects in vertibral column, which may lead to lack of concentration and sitting for long period and hence promote backwardness. Burt has found that they were very excitable and emotional. Boys were found more dominance and girls were noted with submissive timed nature. These students are either more talkative, responsive, excitable and emotionally instable or they may be slow, submissive, timid, repressed and nervous.

Poor Environment of Family : Burt has found that 12% of backward children were having poor home environment and 8% were having poor school atmosphere. If the home environment is poor, the parents cannot manage even essential reading books etc. for their children and therefore they become backward. Thus, low economic conditions of home may lead to many complexes regarding reading material, clothings (uniforms), fees etc. The backward students are also the result of broken families because they do not get love and sympathy from their parents. They feel neglected and becomes backward. Over protection and under protection both may generate backwardness. The following other factors related to home also contribute towards backwardness 1. Presences of step father and step mother, 2. Quarrels in the family, 3. Authoritarian atmosphere, 4. Mental abnormality of the parents,

5. Unhealthy sibling's competitions, 6. Low social status of the family, 7. Poverty, 8. Overcrowding in family, 9. Position of the family, 10. Bed neighbourhood, 11. Lack of appreciation from parents on success and achievements, and 12. Unfavourable comparison by parents.

Poor Conditions of School : If the teachers in the schools are not sympathetic, do not love and take care of their students, do not have willingness to work, may give rise to more backward students. Horror of teacher, lack of personnel guidance programmes, harsh treatment of teachers etc., are some other important cause of backwardness in schools. In efficient and untrained teachers, wrong and unpsychological teaching methods, defective time table, lack of interest in the subject, unhygienic conditions in schools and long absence in school due to illness etc., are also the factors which are responsible for backwardness.

Cyril Burt found that 16 percent backwardness may be due to poor school conditions.

Low Intelligence: Low intelligence or lack of general intelligence is the primary cause of backwardness. Burt has found that every three children out of five are backward children have I.Q. less than 70.

According to the findings, in every big primary school out of every 8 children 1 will have I.Q. less than 85. Therefore it is very necessary to administer and analyse intelligence test to locate such students. On the basis of these tests lack of intellectual, perceptual and visual ability can be visualized. They may help us in knowing the extent of their intelligence and to help us in perceiving the intellectual causes. Burt has recorded that 75 percent backwardness is due to low intelligence

Educational Provisions

The following methods to prevent backwardness, if it is not due to lack of intelligence. The cure for the backward students having low intelligence is very difficult and complex. They will remain always backward in studies than the average students. The following are some suggestions for the education of backward children.

1. Administrative and 2. Academic provisions.

Administrative provisions are of three types (a) Backward child in regular class or mainstream (b) The Special class for backward children, and (c) The Special schools of backward children.

Medical examinations should be arranged periodically to find out the physical status of the children. If the child suffers from some disease, the remedies should be applied for that and the education should also be arranged accordingly.

(a) It has been observed that backward children study in regular classes with the average children. The regular teaching is adequate for them because they can not pace with regular class. It is the responsibility of the teacher that he should help them to deal with them. There should be provision for tutorial classes for the backward student. Teacher should have helping and sympathetic treatment. They require sufficient individual attention in the classroom.

(b) The special class of backward children should be arranged in the school to remove their difficulties. Teacher should appropriate methods and techniques for such special class. The teacher should have special qualification and training of teaching. He should understand their needs and problems.

The class size of specially for backward students should be small 15 to 20 students. Their parents may have some objections. They should be taken in confidence that the class has been formed for their betterment.

(c) The special schools for backward children : There are separate schools for blind, deaf and dum children. Similarly, separate schools may be established for such students. The curricular, objectives methods of teaching and teachers are to be managed according to their needs and problems. The parents of such children may not like such isolation of the children from regular schools. Such school may be expensive and costly for children.

Method of Teaching

In the classroom teaching, the backward children should be treated psychologically.

1. Healthy atmosphere should be created at school and also in community. It should be conducive for learning.
2. Teaching should be arranged according to the interests of these children. Their needs and problems should be considered.
3. Backward children should not be assigned heavy load of work. They should be assigned easy school work.
4. Teacher should be serious and should take classes regularly. He should pay individual attention.
5. Use of A.V. aids should be emphasized for illustrating.
6. Parents should be informed regarding student's ability and should request to treat accordingly. They should be given progress report.
7. Practical activities should be organized for their participation. They should be assigned some practical work.
8. Teacher should not use harsh treatment for them. Their responses should be immediately reinforced.
9. Good methods of teaching be employed in class.
10. Children should be motivated properly.
11. Teacher should arrange some extra classes for these children. Tutorial classes should be organized.
12. Low intelligent children should be taught with slower speed. Teacher should pace with them.
13. Teacher should consult experts and specialists if need arise and may refer the children to them.
14. Low intelligent children should be taught with slower speed. Teacher should pace with them.
15. Programmed instructional material can be used for remedial purpose. There should be the provision for assimilation.
16. The curriculum should be according to their needs and requirements. It should be divided into smaller units.

Theoretical knowledge should imparted after the practical work.

17. The deductive method of teaching should be used by the teacher in classroom.

Significance of Creative Children

It has been established by the psychologists-Thurston (1953) Torrance (1960) the intelligence and creativity are two distinct abilities or concepts. The term 'creativity' has been explained by philosopher, sociologists, and psychometrician. There are more than fifty definitions available of the term creativity. Every child is creative to same extent in this sense. Creativity is most significant concept for the human development. The creative child is an asset to the society as well as to nation. They should identify creative children and should provide them adequate educational identity creative children and should provide them adequate educational facilities for the development of their creativity or talents. Here creative children refer to the upper extreme of normal distribution of this creativity ability.

Meaning and Definition of Creativity

The meaning and definition of creativity have been discussed in the following paragraphs :

According to Guilford creativity involves divergent thinking with regard to this trait, while intelligence involves convergent thinking with reference to number, verbal memory reasoning, perception and space. The creativity refers to originality, fluency, flexibility and elaboration. Guilford creative thought means divergent thinking and uncreative means convergent thinking. Guliford has given 120 mental abilities. The 'Structure of intellect' involves 24 creative abilities. The intelligent test do not measure creativity because these tests involve or employ convergent thinking.

Torrence's contribution is significant in this area. He has defined creativity as follows:

> "Creativity is as process of becoming sensitive to problems, deficiencies, gaps of knowledge, missing elements and so

on, identifying the difficulties , searching for solutions, formulating hypotheses about the deficiencies, testing and recasting them and finally communicating results.

"Creativity is an activity resulting in new products of a deficit social value."

All the new inventions and practices in any field are given or developed by creative persons. Creativity basically concerns with the new products or contributions in any discipline or field of study.

The Characteristics : The term Creative Children refers the case fall on upper extreme of normal distribution of this trait. Thus they are considered exceptional children. Torrence has identified the following characteristics of creative children.

1. Independent thinking, 2. Independent judgement, 3. Courageous in convictions, 4. Intuitive (intuition is his problem), 5. Curious about his environment 6. Becomes preoccupied with some task, 7. Risk taking behaviour or willing to take risk 8. unwilling to accept say so as he is not conformist 9. Visionary or future orientation or he has the vision for future problems.

Characteristics of creative children vary at different stages of development and growth.

Early Childhood: Grivin (1933) has identified the characteristics of children of 3 to 7 years age group. The children of this age group can repeat alone memory images and can organized several memory images, possess emotional realization and feeling of appreciation, can write short-stories and essay and can modify.

Elementary School Years : The creative children of this stage possess the following characteristics.

1. Keen interest drawing, 2. Creative writing and expression, 3. Manifestation of creativity in participation of games and sports, laboratory work, field work and library work. Their creative behaviours and acts are easily observable. The creativity is manifested at elementary stage.

High School Year : The purpose of teaching at this stage is to impart the knowledge of different courses or subjects but the following characteristics are noticed.

Skill of expression and writing an essay of original nature effective presentation in the debate and discussion. Expression is highly logical and unique, investigate some new technique or device.

Higher Education or Adults : At higher stage of education, reflective method of teaching should be employed which is known as creative method of teaching which provides the situation for original and independent thinking. Teaching is most thoughtful for the purpose of higher education is to develop creativity. The main emphasis on problem solving activities. Research work, essay writing and developing projects, participation in cultural activities and effective organization of educational programmes. Participation in seminar conferences and group discussion.

The Identification

The creative children are the asset to the society and for democracy. There are several methods and techniques which can be used for identifying creative children. The most commonly used methods are as follows.

1. Observation method 2. Using test of creativity 3. Achievement test and 4. participation in distinct activities.

The observation method is simple and easy method for identifying creative children. It is widely used method for this purpose.

The most scientific and objective method is the creativity tests which have already discussed. The specific areas of creativity-originally fluency, flexibility and elaborations are also located because general score of creativity has no practical utility.

Gorden and his associates have identified the psychological states of creative process. They have found the following four psychological states for developing creativity.

1. Detachment involvement 2. Deferment 3. Speculation and 4. Autonomy of the objects.

1. Detachment involvement state refers the mental state of a person to think beyond the general problem and then

shows involvement and insight into it. For example, suppose you would 'bird', how you will feel.

2. Deferment state refers to avoidance of the first solution of the problem and try to think another solution it shows the mental state of deferment.
3. Speculation state refers to the tentative solution of the problem or formulation of hypotheses.
4. Autonomy of the object: Refers to the clarity for formulated hypothesis and able to develop his own point of view related to the problem.

Other Psychological States

Elaboration : It is an important aspect of creative process "Elaboration provides an outline or skeleton of a problem and by use of his imagination completes the problem. The process of elaboration gives an opportunity to the person to develop his reasoning, thinking and problem solving abilities which are important aspect of creativity. The use of analogy, imagination expression, divergent thinking are the processes of creativity.

Approach and Methods Teaching Creative Children: There are various methods and techniques which can be used for teaching creative children. The following are some important approaches and methods of teaching creative children.

Approach of Teaching: Reflective level of teaching approach given by Hunt is most popular teaching problem-solving, most thoughtful and creative teaching.

Methods of Teaching for Creative Children

The project method can be used for smaller children at elementary schools, but the most important strategies of teaching areas follows:

1. The synectics teaching model- W. J. Gordon
2. Brain storming strategy-Fosborn.
3. Independent study, Heuristic method of teachers.
4. Conditions for creative work in school.

These have been described in the following paragraph.

SYNECTICS TEACHING MODEL FOR CREATIVITY

William J. L Gordon and his associates have designed the synectics model of teaching. The model depends upon a number of assumptions regarding the process and development of creativity.

Focus : It has the focus to develop the creativity of the students relating to the academic discipline.

Syntax : the structure of the model consists of two strategies : First exploring the unfamiliar and second one creating something new.

The first strategy involves seven phases. In first phase, teacher provides information about new topic. In second phase, the teacher suggests direct analogy and asks students to explain the analogy. In third phase, teacher gets students to be the direct analogy in the fifth phase, students re-explore the original topics on his own terms. In the last phase, students can provide their own direct analogy and identity similarities and differences.

The second strategy also includes seven phases. The teacher gets student's description of situation as they now perceive in first phase. The teacher states problems and defines task in second phase. The students suggest direct analogies, select one and explore it in third phase. The students select personal analogy in fourth phase. They take their description in fifth phase. They create and select under direct analogy based upon the conflicts. In the last phases, teacher gets to move back towards original task.

Social System :The model is moderately structured with the teacher initiating and guiding the students. The teacher introduces his activities in psychological sequence. It create the environment to develop the intellectual and emotional aspect of the students and can enjoy the learning activity. The self motivation and internal motivation is an essential for the problem-solving behaviour of the learners.

Support System : The teacher provides all types of facilities to the students to improve the creativity of the learners and groups. The students encounter the scientific problem so that they can make the problem concrete. They have to perform some activities to fined out the solution. The smaller group can work effectively for the purpose of creativity training.

Classroom Application : It is used to develop creative abilities of an individual and group. It facilitates an implicit learning. It may be used with students in all areas of curriculum both science and arts. This may be applied in the interactive teaching situation and in material for mediated learning experience. The student teachers can use this model successfully in the classroom teaching.

BRAIN STORMING STRATEGY

It is completely permission style of teaching strategy and based upon the assumption that a student can learn better in a group rather than in individual study. It is problem-oriented strategy of teaching.

Objective : The higher order of cognitive and affective objectives may be achieved by employing this strategy of teaching. Another objective is to develop creativity of the students.

Structure : It consists of a problem solving situation in which learners are assigned a problem and they are asked to discuss any ideas which come to their mind. The group is encouraged to provide and evaluate the workability of their own suggestions of the problem.

Osborn's Brain Storming Procedure : He has suggested the following steps for this strategy of teaching.

1. All phases are planned of the problem and think about sub-problems which may emerge.
2. Select sub-problems to be attached.
3. Think up about the data or evidences which may help in solving them.
4. Select the probable sources of data and collect most relevant data.
5. Decide the possible ideas through free-wheeling with suspended judgement as hints to the solution.
6. Select ideas most likely to lead to the solution.
7. Consider the possible ways to test these ideas.
8. These ideas are tested in terms of relevance, adequacy and sufficiency.

9. Imagine all possible contingencies and ways of meeting them.
10. Take decision about the final solution of the problem.

Advantage: It has the following advantages:

1. It has both psychological and educational basis of teaching.
2. It is more creative strategy of teaching and encourages for the original ideas.
3. It provides more ideas of good quality.
4. It creates the situation for more independent thinking among learners.

Independent Study

Independent study, which more usually called project work has been defined by Baskin (1961) in his book. It helps in developing student's initiative, responsibility, and understanding for what they study. This strategy is more useful for a training programme.

Objectives : The affective and cognitive objectives are achieved by this teaching strategy.

Structure: Independent work or reading is organized in small groups, but such takes place in the absence of a teacher and in view of certain regularly scheduled meetings. The programmes is defined precisely in terms of objectives and criterion test. It is a part of regular teaching and is organized for superior students. Teaching reperoire is used in this type of situation.

Principle: It is based upon the following learning principles:

(1) Freedom for work and reading, (2) Self-study, (3) Principle of individual difference and (4) Principle of involvement in the task.

Advantage: The following are the main advantages of this teaching strategy:

1. It encourages the student's participation.
2. It develops independent or original thinking among students.
3. It develops social and cognitive abilities.

4. It is definitely superior teaching strategy for traditional strategies.
5. It creates the situation for the learners to work according to their own abilities.
6. Teacher provides individual guidance to the students.
7. Conditions for creative work in schools.

School Conditions

The following school conditions are essential to develop creativity of the students.

Mental Health : The mental health of teacher and students should be sound for creative activities.

Opportunity of Expression : The teacher should provide opportunity for expressing his own ideas to other.

Self-assessment: The teacher should encourage the students for self-evaluation of his own task, performed.

Self Concept : The teacher should develop self-concept in the students.

Brain Storming: Independent study, supervised study, reflective level teacher methods and approach should be employed for teaching.

Special Programmes : It should also be organized for developing confidence and spontaneity in children.

Exercise

1. Explain the term 'Exceptional child's. Enumerate the problems and characteristics of 'Gifted' children. Describe education programmes for gifted children.
2. Explain and define the term 'Gifted' and 'Backwardness.' Indicate the main features of Backward children. Describe their problems and measures of prevention and treatment of backward children.
3. Explain the term 'Creativity. Enumerate the characteristics of creative children. Describe the approaches and methods of teaching creative children.

11

Social Backwardness

There are handicapped children of different types depending upon the nature of their handicapping conditions—mental, physical, educational. So also the superior. These children have over the years been subjected to various types of educational programmes and the cry for integration has become the order of today. What about the greater number of children who do not belong to any organic, intellectual handicap category ? These are socially disadvantaged groups who had been in the integrated system right from the beginning but were pushed back due to discrimination, neglect, poverty, caste memberships etc. There is a greater need to attend to them. The present chapter deals with delineating.

The very term 'deprivation' is multi-dimensional and seems to be a variation of 'social disadvantage.' But it is not necessarily confined to low socio-economic homes. Deprivation may be the cause of low achievement due to inadequate schooling facilities and parental indifference towards child rearing in more sophisticated homes. The ecology of both family and institution contributes a lot to educational deficiencies of the deprived. Priority has been given by psychologists in recent times for an ecological model for a better understanding of the concept of deprivation.

The Meaning

Educators categorise some what arbitrarily into one or more of the following areas of deprivation: economic, racial, geographic, social, cultural, cognitive, and/or emotional. Historically one can identify the roots of this population in terms of their educational needs, but it was not until the mid 1960s that writers such as Reissman and Havighurst and their turns at defining the characteristics that constitute this deprived, educationally deprived, underprivileged, disadvantaged, lower class, and lower social-economic group, could all be used interchangeably. This is reflected in his book. 'The culturally deprived child'. These children have some strength not only defficiencies.

There is a need to develop qualities within this population such as physical orientation, hidden verbal ability, creative potential, group cohesiveness, informality, and sense of humor.

The term 'Disadvantaged' mean children, who come from socio-economical backward section of the community who can not profit from school because of deprivation of one sort or another, and children who are seen in interior tribal and rural areas of country where educational facilities have not reached in the way we find them in a metropolitan area.

In other words, the term disadvantaged would include, children who not only belong to the above criteria but children who are exposed to disadvantaged schools in the rural and slum areas. Hence, both the ecology of the family and the ecology of the institution contribute to educational deficits of the disadvantaged.

Again, cultural deprivation refers to a complex set of conditions which create intellectual deficiency in a child. These conditions include unstimulated environment, lack of verbal interaction with adults, poor sensory experience and other deleterious environmental factors associated with poverty.

However the term 'deprived' or 'disadvantaged' or 'culturally different' was used to indicate who are marked by the following three general characteristics during their school life.

(1) Progressive decline in intellectual functioning,

(2) Cumulative Academic Achievement Deficits and
(3) Premature School termination or higher drop-out rate.

The Characteristics

- Keeping this nature of learning process aside, the gap between a culturally disadvantaged child and a normal child begins to grow with age and exposure to classroom learning. A wide gap was found between the Blacks and middle class whites when achievement tests and verbal ability were taken into account. Actually it is not stimulation but the quality of stimulation that is important. The verbal milieu in which the middle class children grow up corresponds much more closely to school learning situation. Middle class children have a superior quality of both verbal and non-verbal stimulation at home. Again the stimulation are very distinct and the reinforcement system is of a delayed kind.

The social and cultural disadvantage is not crystal clear in India. All low income group children are not necessarily at a disadvantage. The children of higher SES have culture superior to those of the low caste Harijans who are given the same low social-economic status. The distance between Brahmins and Harijans has widened due to the cumulative effects. There are empirical findings which supports the cultural effects of high castes home.

A marked difference was felt among the students of different socio-economic groups so far as intellectual capacity was concerned. It is true that better economic conditions, education and occupational status of the parents were the most significant contributory factor for the intellectual development of the children. Researchers place emphasis on stimulating environment in early life for intellectual growth of children.

The following are the main characteristics of socially disadvantaged children:

Poor Academic Performance : These children show poor academic performance of high drop-out rates, reading and other learning disabilities and have adjustment problems. Socio-economically backward children practically show every such index. They have lower grades, their health is poor and they have deficiencies in the two most skills reading and language, necessary for success in school. They have minimal training in disciplined group behaviour and educationally they are less ambitious. Children for such environments are apt to have various linguistic disabilities. They also show incapacity in cognitive processes such as: the ability to observe and stating sequences of events, perceiving cause and effect relationships, classifying concrete objects, attributing responsibility to self and in general have poor self-concrete objects, attributing responsibility to self and in general have poor self-concept. The combination of non-verbal orientation and an absence of conceptualisation very well account for their intellectual deficits and deficit in cognitive skills or in Piagetian terminology, formal logical thinking is absent in all such children or appear very late in the development.

Cognitive Deficiencies : The cognitive deficiencies are again complicated by their pattern of motivation and attitudes. Psychologists explain that these children have a feeling of alienation induced by family climate and experience combined with a debilitatingly low self concept. They tend to question their own worth, to fear being challenged, and to exhibit a desire to cling to the familiar. They have many feelings of guilt and shame. These children are wary and their trust in adults is limited. They make trigger like responses and are hyperactive.

*Apathetic, Unresponsive and Lack Initiative :*They are apathetic, unresponsive and lack initiative. It is difficult for them to form meaningful relationships. Although these characteristics are rooted in early childhood family background and social class membership of the family etc. Yet the attitudes of the teacher and the curriculum in the school increase the alienation of these children. Very often there is a communication gap between the teacher and the students, the objectives of instruction and the actual evaluation of instruction in terms of pupils performance as well as discontinuities in the meanings attached to verbal cues employed in teaching and curriculum materials and the meanings which these children have acquired in their out of school experiences.

Lower Achievement: The lower achievement of disadvantaged children could be attributed to atleast five causes: malnutrition, genetic, lack of stimulating early experience, atleast five cause : malnutrition, genetic, lack of stimulating early experience, social motivation and cultural values. In addition, the cognitive style or strategy adopted by a group may account for the lower performance of the disadvantaged children.

Basic Intelligence: Many the result supported that with exception to basic intelligence where group difference did not occur between different castes groups, the low caste children did show deficits in personality, information processing modes, and intellectual achievement. And the deficits also indicated progressive or cumulative retardation in most of the measures. Hence, in our cultural background, memberships in low caste and low income family do predispose children to an impoverished environment and the consequence of this deprivation are cumulative over time.

Socially Disadvantaged : Children from low socio-economic status (SES) and Socially disadvantaged home drop out from schools. Wastage and stagnation is a characteristic of the socially disadvantaged group. Drop out is solely due to cultural disadvantaged characteristics of low cast and rural background. The facts suggest that everything else remaining same the greater drop out rate is influenced by cultural disadvantage or deprivation. There are various causes of drop-outs but membership in low casts/low income group mostly makes on drop-out prone in school. Similar trends are seen in all states in India

Intellectual Performance : Within the deprived community the girls appeared to be comparatively better than the boys in intellectual performance. There is a curvilinear relationship between sex and arithmetic reasoning and arithmetic fundamentals across grade levels. But in reading comprehension and reading vocabulary than boys across all grade levels children girls did better having physical/orthopaedic problems did not show consistent poor performance in the cognitive tasks. The research findings permit us a general statement i.e., all groups of disadvantaged rural students are characterised by poor cognitive competence, and educational achievement. We essentially came to the same conclusion whether we analysed the result in terms of organismic variables such as : sex, race grade levels or by dichotomising the Ss on the basis of some basis of some behavioural characteristics: social emotional, physical, differentiation on physical characteristics offered some meaningful about rural disadvantaged children especially of their educational retardation. Obviously sensory impairments and general malnutritional factors do inhibit school learning.

Special Learning Characteristics

Special learning characteristics of the socially deprived or disadvantaged student might include many of the following (1) orientation towards physical and visual rather than to the oral; (2) content-centered rather than introspective; (3) problem-centered rather than abstract centered; (4) inductive rather than deductive; (5) spatial rather than temporal; (6) slow, careful, patient, and persevering rather than quick, clever, facile, and flexible; (7) inclined to communicate through actions rather than words; (8) deficient in auditory attention and interpretation skills; (9) oriented toward concrete application of what is learned; (10) short attention span; (11) characteristic gaps in knowledge and learning; (12) lacking experiences of receiving approval for success in tasks. Meeting the needs of the disadvantaged child is relatively new educational approach.

Although Riessman has made great efforts to identify some characteristics that might be construed as potentially positive qualities, he is also cognizant of the negative criteria. The disadvantage children differ from advantaged class in only six areas : self-concept, motivation, social behaviour, language intellectual functioning, and physical fitness.

The Identification

The term 'disadvantaged' is used to indicate the following observable behaviour:

1. Progressive decline in intellectual functioning in school.
2. Cumulative academic achievement deficits.
3. Premature school termination and high dropout rate.
4. Reading and learning disabilities.
5. Poor language learning.
6. In adequate social learning and observation in the absence of model.
7. Low attention span and distraction in learning.
8. Lack of proficiency in higher form of cognitive learning and transfer.
9. Lack of abstract and state sequence of events in a learning situation.
10. Inability to classify and form logical concepts, incapacity to verbalise events and solutions.
11. Lack of analytic ability which is essential for learning.
12. They show belief in external factors, e.g., luck, chance, late etc. rather than their own self and activity.
13. They cannot delay gratification. Immediate trangible and non-contigent rewards are their need.
14. They have a high sense of avoidance for failure than striving success.
15. They have poor self concept, low achievement aspiration, and low need achievement including lack of desire for self-actualisation.
16. Their general behaviour lacks intrinsic motivation. Insecurity and anxiety are very obvious.

The Causes of Social Backwardness

Cultural deprivation or disadvantaged arise due to a complex set of conditions which create intellectual deficiency in a child. Some of these conditions are attributed to unstimulating environment- lack of verbal interaction with adults, poor sensory experience, and other deleterious environmental factors generally associated with adults, poor sensory experience, and other deleterious environmental factors generally associated with poverty, low social status, malnutrition, broken homes.

It relates to the following areas of socio-cultural experiences:

(1) Housing Conditions, (2) Home Environment, (3) Economic conditions, (4) Food and Nutrition, (5) Clothing, (6) Educational Experiences, (7) Childhood Experiences, (8) Rearing Experiences, (9) Parental Characteristic, (10) Interaction with Rents, (11) Motivation Characteristics, (12) Emotional Experiences, (13) Travel and Recreation and (14) Socio-cultural Experiences.

Nutritional Deprivation or Disadvantage

Poverty may effect intellectual development through physical conditions i.e., mal-nourishment. Poverty is all pervasive in India and is responsible for social and education pathology. There is a cultural of poverty characterised by the legacy of psychological distortion which manifests itself in profound alienation from larger society and people, feeling in powerlessness and meaningless in struggles. When we live in a society of self advertisement and propagation, these people remain only conscious of their deprivation. Our attitudes further brutalises the poor and the under privileged. Psychological poverty, intellectual and effective poverty nutritional and biochemical deficiency, institutional poverty: predispose a lower SES child more than any one else for educational under achievement.

The Problems

Different studies on disadvantaged children brought another factor to the forefront. It was found that crucial handicap of socially disadvantaged children is language. Acquisition and use of language need the functioning of three psychologistic processes : (i) Receptive process, (ii) Associative process, and (iii) Expressive process. Despite controversies in this regard, all researchers agree that the socially disadvantaged child possesses a linguistic system which is different from that of the socially advantaged child.

Language Difficulties : The language difficulties may be the result of one or all or any combination of the following factors:

(a) A different linguistic environment.

(b) A different language acquisition device.

(c) A different set of psycholinguistic abilities.
(d) Economic, educational and place or residence variables.
(e) Poor and uneducated families.

Language experts felt that an inadequate linguistic environment makes a poor input into language acquisition device and hence retards language perception and production. The development of linguistic awareness and language learning are hampered in an environment where there is very little linguistic interaction.

Nutritional Deficiency: Besides language difficulties, nutritional deficiency is another potent factor for socially disadvantaged children which is considered as the greatest deterrent to physical health. Studies report that malnourishment has a serious effect on physical anomalies and deficiencies on intellectual performance of low SES children. They are inferior to advantage children in discrimination learning. According to Livingston, "Malnutrition given rise to mental apathy, a shortened span of attention, reduced mental powers and increased drowsiness, etc."

Motivational Problem : Many of the deficits observed in the socially disadvantaged are more motivational rather than intellectual and cognitive. The underprivileged children display some significant motivational problems which determine a major aspect of their behaviour patterns.

(1) The show belief in external factors i.e., luck, chance fate etc. rather than their own self and activity. This inability attribute causality to one's own behaviour accounts for poor motivation in any task.
(2) They can not delay gratification. Immediate tangible and non-contingent rewards are their need.
(3) They have high sense of avoiding failure than striving for success.
(4) They have poor self-concept, low achievement aspiration, and need achievement including lack of desire for self-actualisation.

Remedial Measures

Certain remedial measures have been recommended. It is true that deprivation does exist among the socially disadvantaged children due to predominantly.

(1) Inadequate early socialisation.
(2) Mark of opperession.
(3) Organic deficits.
(4) Inadequate social environment and
(5) Culture conflicts and educational deprivation.

Remedial Education

The following objectives should be taken into consideration for enrichment programmes on remedial education:

(1) Socially disadvantaged children must be trained to achieve three objectives, viz., Knowledge, Skill and Attitude.
(2) Self-concept, level of aspiration and achievement motivation should be accelerated.
(3) Language training and analytical thinking must be included.
(4) These children must be trained to acquaint themselves with concrete life situations.
(5) They must be aware of their various creative talents and they must be trained to develop a sense of comparative living in them, so that they can easily participate with normal students.

In order to reverse the ill effect research studies support certain measures: (1) Early modelling and imitation of desirable behaviour. (2) Language enrichment programme and stimulation at home. (3) Affective attention and acceptance. (4) Providing initial success experience to build better motivation and striving for success. (5) Removal of discrimination attitudes on the part of teachers and other significant members of society. (6) Instructional programmes may be geared to their needs and ability level. (7) Giving responsibility, recognition, tangible rewards, positive remarks etc.

(8) Exposure to sensitivity training, exposure to literature, discussion and group contracts, role playing, case conferences relating to their problems. (9) Presenting learning materials using, images, aids, and providing adequate organisers and drill. Compensatory education programmes have provide the validity of these recommendations.

EDUCATIONAL PROVISIONS

Educational provisions have been made for the socially disadvantaged by the government. In the arena of intellectual and social competence, enrichment programmes were designed to develop and enlarge children's conceptual repertoire and communicative skills. Some measures are discussed below

Establishment of Residential Schools : Steps should be taken to establish residential schools and Ashram schools for disadvantaged children like SC and ST. Of course residential type of schools are made to suit the needs of Adivasis. Measures should be taken to make these institutions more homely. Recently the government has taken the initiative to solve the economic problems existing in these types of Ashram schools. The charges for education, clothing, boarding and medical care are being met by the government. But a meticulous examination reveals that the existing number of residential schools are inadequate in this regard. So recreational centres, guidance and counselling centres should be established to meet this immediate demand.

Financial Help for Disadvantaged Children : Poverty is a pertinent factor which is found to be a barrier in the path of progress of the disadvantaged children. Of courses, the government has been giving financial aid to these students long since. On the basis of poverty-cum-merit, other backward classes are also given assistance. Pre-matric and post-matric scholarships are also being given now by the government to provide financial help. In some universities and institutions, payments for admissions and tuition fees are also exempted.

Appointment of Expert Teachers : A decision has been taken by the government to replace the un-trained teachers by trained ones and to absorb the existing hands in suitable posts. In some cases, these untrained teachers were asked to have the requisite qualification within a short space of time. Again, there is a plan to given rewards to those teachers who specialise in braille, tribal dialect and hearing aid. Residential accommodation is being provided to teacher experts and administrators who work in hilly and tribal areas. It is true that incentives in terms of additional payment, accommodation etc., reduce the truancy of the teaching experts. Also steps are being taken by the government to hold in-service training programmes and refresher courses. In some areas, teachers are also being trained in tribal dialect and tribal culture.

Craft Education : Under government instructions, some useful crafts like carpentry, weaving and tailoring were introduced to suit the needs of SCs and STs which are must for their economic development. But a proposal should be made to the government to introduce agriculture and spinning in boys' Ashram Schools and gardening in girls' Ashram Schools. Statistics reveal that the government has made craft education compulsory in some states and union territories.

Incentives to Indigent Families : It is generally found that the percentage of dropouts for SC and ST students is high during the early school years. The reason is obvious. These students come from low SES strata. Their parents are needy and impoverished. According to the parents of these children, education is not a necessity, but a luxury.

But recently government has taken steps for more enrolment of these students. Priority is being given for the education of the weaker sections of the people and children. Incentives are being provided to indigent families, so that they would be able to send their children regularly to school.

Compensatory Pre-school Education : Research works reveal that the mental development of children generally takes place between 3 and 7 years. During this period every child must be kept in a very healthy environment. Otherwise, he will face some anomalies in future. Keeping this in mind, special attention must be paid to pre-school education of every child. As a result, they will benefit from primary education in future. The disadvantaged children have poor vocabulary (which is a setback) to following the state language. Pre-school period is considered to be the formative period of a child's life. Through compensatory pre-school education, a child can improve his vocabulary and language difficulties can ultimately be surmounted. But provision should be made to supply free reading and writing materials.

Adjustment of School Hours and Vacations : Adjustment of school vacations and school hours becomes a necessity for these children to meet the socio-economic needs of the community. The percentage of dropouts and stagnation can be reduced to the minimum if school hours and vacations can be properly adjusted so that these children get ample opportunity to assist their parents. For example, in agricultural communities, the schools must have three hours duration for teaching and vacations can be adjusted keeping the sowing and harvesting periods of major crops in view. There must be holidays for local festivals and community functions.

Adult Education Programmes : Truly speaking, educated parent can get their children educated with little effort. So parents must be educated first to take care of the disadvantaged children. Reports say that in our country, a fairly good sections of people belonging to SCs and STs are not educated. So measures are being taken to educate them through adult education programmes. Through this attempt, they will be able to understand the value of education and responsibility for the future generation. Of course, the government has taken the initiative to open Anganwadis, non-formal and adult education centres to help SC and ST people.

Techniques of Evaluation : Steps may be taken to adopt new techniques of evaluation and continuous assessment of these types will be conducive. Due to the fallacious examination system and evaluation, most of the disadvantaged children fail in the promotional examinations. To bring out modern and sophisticated evaluation techniques, the teachers must be provided with item banks. Considering the stagnation and dropouts, continuous and meticulous evaluation must be introduced to help these children as far as practicable. Extra coaching after school hours may be encouraged to help the weak students.

Follow-up Action : Students coming from Ashram schools or from residential type of schools generally go for higher education or take up any job to earn their livelihood. Government has a plan to help these students by providing grants to settle down in life. But sometimes correct statistics are not available. So steps have to be taken to the names of these students from Ashram schools and adjust accordingly with the authorities.

Educational Guidance and Counselling

Education aims at bringing change which will affect the lives of students is a relevant concern for all educators. In the case of disadvantaged children, the challenge is even greater. The likelihood that these children will overcome the handicaps of poverty in rural and as well as slum areas seems to be related as to how effectively the school personnel assist them. In fact, individuality can be fostered and realised through effective guidance service and the establishment and development of these services can be enhanced by an appreciation of the ecology other the individual and ecology of the school.

Considering from all points of view, guidance activities for the disadvantaged may be organised in small groups of eight to twelve. The information giving, task orientation and counselling type of activities will be more effective in small groups for the disadvantaged because they will not be inhibited before an adult authority as is true of an individual counselling situation. Role playing as a technique is most suitable for guiding the activities of the disadvantaged. Further for helping the rural disadvantaged, guidance service, programme needs be extended through parental counselling, community resources clubs, and referral to psychologist who should be available at least in each school complex. Guidance must form a part of the entire educational programme which students should perceive as personally relevant for them.

Social disadvantage is a socio-cultural-economic deprivation combined with deficit in cognitive stimulation at home which is then carried away to school. In school, social disadvantage is characterised in terms of achievement deficits, drop out and deficit language and competence. Discrimination and isolation accelerate the deficit process. Remedial education strategies, guidance, suggested teacher behaviour would eventually contribute to reducing disparities, difference, and deficits whenever they arise.

Our schools and educational system must develop a better understanding of the implications of the social and psychological dynamics of deprivation and translate this understanding into educational programmes, into the training of teachers and administrators and into planning of curriculum and instruction. No single device will suffice to, contract or to remedy the complex factors, those are associated with the education of the under-privileged. Administratively the problem can also be taken care and by dealing with acculturation problems and school learning by providing early school experience to these children and following an unguarded sequences or multiple entry system. To unlock the hidden potential among these children, a radical change in curriculum and teaching is required. At least the new curriculums which has been introduced is constructed in such a way that it is related to the psychological realities of the psychological realities of the child, is tuned to our social and community life is geared towards achieving needs and aspirations of our people and the educational climate that is promulgated in the frame-work is more motivating in terms of teaching techniques for which orientation of teachers are conducted in a massive way by NCERT, SCERT and State Development of Education. In a nutshell it is possible to conceive of education as countervailing force to overcome the deficits accumulated in underprivileged groups or what is currently understood as the broomstick effect. It is true that it is not the educators function only to reverse the negative impact of educational deprivation, social and effective insultation, caste discrimination and economic deprivation. It involves all aspect of the community. The task surely calls for creative innovation all along the line. The crucial pedagogical problem involved is that of understanding the mechanism of learning facility and learning dysfunction and applying this knowledge to optimum development of a heterogeneous population characterised by differential backgrounds, opportunities and patterns of social and intellectual function.

For the most part, education of the disadvantaged children can be speeded up by disseminating appropriate method of child rearing systems and values among the parents much before the child comes to schools. This will definitely reduce the discontinuties in the norms of children and norms of school. In contrast to the varied, detailed and sometimes adequately designed studies and their reports, it is strange that the psychologists in this country do not take these generalisation to the reach of the common man who contribute to a great majority of the underprivileged children in school.

An important measure is to make education acceptable to the Scheduled Casts and Scheduled Tribes which /constitute a major block of the underprivileged group and make education relevant to them.

Teacher's Role

The following instructional strategies for educating the disadvantaged are suggested considering the objectives of instructions and their entering behaviour to an instructional situation. Basically there is no difference in the way in which the underprivileged children learn. Their learning processes are subject to the some general principles of learning as are the learning processes of the average or normal but with a difference the rate, the sequence, the type of materials and presentation modes. There is need of a guidelines for a teacher.

1. A continuous appraisal of progress and comprehensive measure of assessment-diagnosis via feedback should

become a part of every teaching act and basis of planning the next learning experience.

2. If instruction is to be effective these students are to be simultaneously tried to achieve the three objectives: knowledge, skills and attitudes.
3. Since the students come to the school with cognitive deficit a special hour may be kept aside for remedial teaching language, training in how to increase some of their non-intellective characteristics, i.e., self-concept, level aspiration, sense of responsibility etc.
4. Learning of concepts and ideas may be sequences before they are presented to the underprivileged group, using more of concrete and life like situations. Training for analytic thinking may also constitute a part of the instructional programme design.
5. The imposition of standardised expectation regarding performance should be replaced by individualisation in the rate of learning, exposure to varied materials. Instructions must be given how to pace performance according to their ability. The teacher has to ascertain the pre-requisites before instructing them to move to the next step and make provisions for acting initial success experiences by the group.
6. For educating the underprivileged giving recognition, responsibility, tangible rewards, positive affective remarks ,encouraged in schools. Affective interactions and developments to be supported in a schools. Affective interactions and developments to be supported in a school programme.
7. They also need to be acculturated through sensitivity training, exposure to literature, discussions and group contacts, role playing and case conferences.
8. Self-instructional materials may be used best to their advantage.
9. The curriculum should have direct bearing on their life and work especially for tribal population.

Exercise

1. Explain the term 'Socially Disadvantage Children'. Enumerate the characteristics of socially and culturally disadvantaged children.
2. Describe the procedure and basis of identifying socially disadvantaged children. Indicate the special learning characteristics of such students.
3. Enumerate the causes of socially and culturally disadvantaged children. Indicate main problems of such children.
4. Describe some remedial measures and education for improving and solving the problems of socially disadvantaged children.
5. Describe educational provisions for socially and culturally disadvantaged children. Indicate educational guidance and counselling for such children.
6. Describe the role of teachers dealing socially disadvantaged children and suggest a guideline for a teachers.
7. Differentiate between,

   (a) Socially and Culturally disadvantaged children.

   (b) Socially disadvantaged and Emotionally disturbed children.

   (c) Unachiever and Socially disadvantage children.

   (d) Socially disadvantaged and Delinquent children.

12

ANTI-SOCIAL BEHAVIOUR CHILDREN

The delinquents are anti-social behaviour children who are at the lower extreme ends of normal distribution of social tract. The problem of delinquency has posed a serious concern for persons, teachers, parents psychologists and social workers who believe in harmonious development of human personality. The teachers are responsible for shaping the personality of young students. The deteriqauents are found generally at the stage of adolescence. The children who are delinquents below the age of eighteen years are known juvenile delinquent.

Every society establishes some social and moral norms to maintain harmony and order in its structure. It persuades its members to follow them strictly by framing legal laws and codes. The behaviour which is contrary to these established norms is referred to as anti-social behaviour or crime. It involves injury either to the property or the people in the society. Society for its protection from such anti-social elements or criminals has due provision of punishment and often such people are kept behind the bars. Such anti-social behaviour or criminal tendency is not only found among the adults or grown-ups, but children and adolescents who are minor in age also suffer from such social diseases. These individuals are known as juvenile delinquents or young delinquents. Therefore, juvenile delinquents are essentially the criminals minor in age and are usually referred to as minor with major problems. They violate the law of the land and commit offences like thefts, gambling, cheating, pick-pocketing, robber, dacoity, destruction or property, violence and assault, intoxicating, vagrancy begging, kidnapping, abduction and other sexual offences etc.

Meaning and Definition

It is difficult to define the term 'delinquency' comprehensively and universally because it has wide coverage of anti-social behaviour that varies time to time, place to place, cultural, social and political conditions of particular conditions. It may be stated that the child who violates the social normal values, is called delinquent.

A child is said to be a delinquent when starts stealing, assaulting, indulging in sex offences and develops symptoms like pathological lying and truancy. These offences are said to be criminal actions when committed by a person beyond the age handled by juvenile courts. Cyril Burt, in his book revealed, "A child is said to be regarded technical as a delinquent, when his anti-social tendencies appear so grave that becomes or ought to become the subject of official action."

> "A child who deviates from the social norms of behaviour is called delinquent children."
>
> ***-Healy***

> "A delinquent is one who behaves against social norms breaks, laws, creates indiscipline in school or other institutions or disobey the rules. His immoral behaviour is considered not so serious that he should be considered a culpritry by juvenile courts look into his illegal behaviour."
>
> ***-Education Dictionary***

> "A child is technically delinquent when his anti-social tendencies appear so grave that becomes or ought to become the subject of official action."
>
> ***-Cyril Burt***

"Delinquency maybe defined as anti-social behaviour."

-Headfield

"Delinquency implies from anti-social behaviour involving personal and social disorganization."

-Neumeyer

"Delinquency, like aggressive behaviour in general, can understood as aggressive, hostile behaviour or culturally acquired way of life."

-Telford and Sawrey

"A child who breaks the law, is way ward, habitually disobedient or who behaves in away that endagests the health or moral of himself or other who attempt to enter the marriage relation without the consent of his parents, is called delinquent."

Views of Experts

The term 'delinquency' has been defined and explained by experts of different disciplines - psychologists, sociologists biologists, lawyers and experts of mental health and hygiene.

According to Biologists : The accounts for anti-social behaviour as rising from organic or pathological factors located in the nervous system of an individual. The delinquent can not adjust to social environment. Biologists emphasize the genetical basis of deliquency.

According to Mental Hygienists : The delinquency is the expression of an individual needs and his mental ailments. He can not gratify his needs by socially acceptable behaviour due to his incompetency or due to economic conditions. He tries to achieve the goal by his anti-social activities which are known as delinquent act. The delinquent behaviour is the symptom of his needs and mental ailments.

According to Sociologists : They have emphasized on social conditions which contribute to anti-social behaviour or delinquency. The political and economic stress can lead to underirable acts or behaviour. They violate the social and cultural norms. A person is compelled by the circumstances to achieve his goal by adopting antisocial methods. Thus delinquency is the result of unsuccessful efforts to achieve goals of life or society, this is the reason that a person adopts anti-social acts. It is collective reaction formation.

According to Psychologists : It is deficiency in the formation of super ego. He is unable to identify with the values of his parents and seeks pleasure at the cost of sacrificing the principles of reality and morality. The delinquency is as holes in superego. Mowrever defined delinquency as moral deficiency because of weak conscience due to improper teaching of the child in early age of life.

The delinquency is the manifestation of frustrated needs of the child which ultimately lead to aggression. The delinquent there would be a person whose misbehaviour is relatively illegal offence, which is appropriate to his level of development, is not committed as a result of extreme low intellect.

According to Travis Hirchi, "Delinquency is defined by acts, the detection of which is thought to result in punishment of the person committing them by agents of the large society."

The legal definition does not reveal any picture of the delinquent's personality or the causes of his behaviour. Law delinquent's personality or the causes of his behaviour. Law-makers are not concerned so much with delinquency as with delinquents and naturally their definition of delinquency has been mostly incomplete and misleading. Psychologists say that a delinquent is one whose attitude towards society is such that will eventually lead to a violation of the law. According to Bandura and Walter delinquency is aggression. They have tried to relate delinquency to the frustration of dependency needs which cause aggression. In many studies, psychologists came up with differences between the psychological make-up of the delinquent and non-delinquent. The difference was quantitative rather than qualitative. The consider delinquency to be an unfortunate expression of the personality and emphasis that the various indices of maladjustment shown by the delinquents have one or more personal meanings behind them.

The Characteristics

In the above definitions of delinquency indicate the following characteristics which have been enumerated as follows.

1. A delinquent child possess anti-social behaviour.
2. He breaks the laws and create indiscipline in school.
3. A delinquents, deviates from norms of social behaviour and creates problems in society.
4. A delinquent child is aggressive and hostile behaviour.
5. He behaves in such a way that it is harmful for himself and also for other.
6. His ego is bent upon immediate pleasure without obey in the norms of social behaviour.
7. His immoral behaviour is not considered so serious that may be referred to court of law.
8. His anxiety level is generally very high.
9. It is acquired behaviour by the child and not the innate.
10. The delinquents are emotional and maladjusted.
11. The economic conditions of his family is generally poor. The parents are unable to fulfil his needs.
12. Delinquency is an acquired behaviour.
13. It is unmindful of social norms and expectations.
14. Delinquency is problem for every one.
15. Delinquency is not the abnormality in its true sense.

Taking the above point into consideration, delinquency may be considered as an ego defence for the tension caused by frustration of one or several of the needs present in the individual. Due to their intrinsic nature, the nation's laws cannot be applied to every individual.

Before the age of 14, a boy is not considered capable to having sexual relations according to English law. In one case, the court had to return a verdict other than not guilty for a boy little over tens, who had raped a small girl, thereby causing her death. Considered from the psychologist's point of view, the enforcement of law by the police brings an arbitrary element into the concept of juvenile delinquency. It is realised element into the concept of juvenile delinquency. It is realised that a country with efficient police network will have a higher delinquency rate than a country where police network is fallacious. Truly speaking, the social position and influence of parents play major roles to refer a boy to a juvenile court in any country.

The foregoing discussion proves that juveniles do not fall into one simple homogeneous psychiatric or psychological category. The distinction between the delinquents and the non-delinquents is based on factors which have quantitative differences.

No one can deny the relationship that exists between delinquency and psychological or psychiatric factors. Some individuals in a group follow the rules and taboos while others do not. The latter do not form a psychologically homogeneous group. But psychology, can help to explain their behaviour. Although the majority of juvenile delinquents are found among this group, not all of them are delinquents. Again, all delinquents are not maladjusted. Delinquent behaviour can be adaptive, getting the special circumstances in which a group finds itself, although such behaviour clashes with the generally accepted laws of the society to which the group belongs. This observation is made from a psychiatrical, and thereto, to a certain extent from a psychological point of view.

The concept of delinquency is artificial in nature. This nature varies according to the laws in force or the ways in which they are applied. It becomes very difficult to establish one period and another. Research works reveal that this is a major obstacle to research and is a possible source of serious error.

The Classification

The psychologists have classified delinquency in various ways. The classification of delinquency in five categories have been done by Had Field, listed below:

Benign Delinquency : It includes such which may be termed as breach of discipline or law, or crimes from legal point of view but from mental health view, they may be normal behaviour e.g., truancy on some beautiful rainy day or for seeing some extraordinary act in the city.

Temperamental Delinquency : Temperamental delinquency of certain physiological activities. For example it is found that girls may steal the things during their m.c. days.

Simple Delinquency: Simple delinquency is the result of the conflict between the need of child and the home, school or society conditions. It is also known as anti-social behaviour. The main cause may be the poor environment, in which the child is living.

Reaction Delinquency : Reaction delinquency, as its name suggests, arise from the reactions of the children against the society when the child thinks that he is the victim of the society, he revolts and tries to break the rules and conventions of the existing society. For this type of delinquency the child should be guided very carefully and psychologically.

Psychoneurotic Delinquency : "This type of delinquency is created on account of the expression in anti-social manner of the repressed tendencies. These repressions occur on account of resentment." For example repression of sex urge or instinct may develop the tendency of truancy or telling or stealing etc. For psycho-neurotic delinquency the teachers and parents should refer their children to some clinical psychologist.

Aggressive Tendency : The mode of attack may be physical aggression damaging school property torturing, committing suicide and forgery.

The following are the other categories:

1. Aggressive and hostile basis with some person, institution, objects, elder, birds and animals and may be with self.
2. Standard basis - may be of four types (a) Institutionalized (b) Offender at large (c) Habit basis (d) Individual standard.
3. Basis of Individual standard—Individual and group.
4. Habit basis—First offender and habitual offender.
5. Truancy from school, and running from home.

Two Types of Reactions

Nowadays, psychiatry has recognised two types of reactions that are different both in terms of prognosis and management:

Dys-social Reaction: Under this type of reaction the children are brought up in a normal or immoral home or social environment. Their behaviour is in conformity with that small community although they are unacceptable to the society at large, for example, the children of gypsies, migrant or criminal tribes, Children's the children of gypsies, migrant or criminal tribes. Children's personality development is influenced by distorted values of a special sub-culture. Here the children are capable or establishing enduring emotional attachments and loyalties.

Psychopathic Reaction : The children in the second category have poor ego development and even poorer development of super ego. They are incapable or forming stable emotional relationships. They have no insight or foresight and they cannot profit from past experiences. They show poor control and seek gratification of immediate desires. Most of them are refractory to all forms of punishment. These children tend to use other human beings as 'pawns' or 'toys.'

The second group cases have constitutional or genetic defects. There are some behavioural disturbances of children that are also seen in adult psychopaths like—truancy, alcoholism, drug addiction, stealing, burglary and sexual promiscuity. In 1951, The International Union of Child Welfare especially recommended the following categories of offences (by children) for investigation. Stealing from home, persistent telling of lies, wandering from home, cruelty to animals and other children, repeated truancy, setting fire and sexual offences etc. Of these setting fire and sexual offences are not so commonly reported in India.

There may be very thin line of demarcation between deviance and delinquency because if effective interventions do not occur at appropriate stages, there is every likelihood of a deviant fuming into a delinquent. So the value system of any society, as reflected in its legal norms continues to serve as the basis for identifying juvenile delinquents. Taking this view into consideration, a juvenile delinquent is one who falls within the age group of 7-16 years (18 years in case of girls) and indulges in any act that is prohibited by the Indian Penal Code or Local or Special Acts relating to arms, gambling, explosives etc.

The Identification

The delinquent children are identified by observing their behaviours in society and school, situations.

Delinquency behaviour is a part of a dynamic process and it can be understood only in relation to the sequence of experience of which it is a part. So when we deal with juvenile delinquency, we must view it in terms of both the conditions of the individual person or the social environment in which he lives.

They violate the law of the land and commit offences like thefts, gambling, cheating, pick-pocketing, robber, dacoity, destruction or property, violence and assault, intoxicating, vagrancy begging, kidnapping abduction and other sexual offences etc.

The Causes

Delinquency is an acquired behaviour of a child which is not in accordance with social standard and norms. It is not caused by one single factor but it is an end product of several factors. Some are hereditary and other are environmental, social and psychological. There may be some physiological factors responsible for delinquency. These are as follows

Heredity Factors : In some of the studies, it has been found that the heredity also contributes for delinquency. The children may get certain delinquency tendencies from their parents (heredity) who are suffering from epilepsy etc. Certain inherited physical defects may also give rise to delinquency e.g. a ugly boy in physical aspect may wish to destroy whole society because his defect was laughed at, and therefore he may adopt anti-social behaviour.

Mental retardation and low I.Q. tendencies are also sometimes help in developing delinquency. Parents who have low. I.Q. generally have their children of lower I. Q. which may encourage anti-social behaviour.

The innate emotional unstability is also found responsible for anti-social behaviour. Aggression may lead to delinquency.

The sex of child also plays an important pail e.g. the girls show delinquent behaviour during their menses. The maladjusted parents also have maladjusted off-spring and this maladjustment may also help in getting delinquency.

Environmental Factors : The following factors play an important part in causing delinquency. (1) The poor socio-economic status of the family e.g. hunger and starvation tempt people to tread the easy devilish path of crime. (2) Unemployment for long time may lead to anti-social behaviour like stealing or getting money through using illegal acts, (3) Presence of step father or mother, (4) Quarrels among the parents, (5) Lack of parental love and affection, (6) Discriminatory on partial treatment towards children. (7) Over or under protection by parents, (8) High expectations and ambitions of parents from their children. Parents have usually high expectation, (9) Either too lenient or to harsh discipline, (10) Delinquent members of the family, (11) Immoral, gambler or drunkard parents, (12) Broken homes or delinquent home, (13) Bad friends and classmates are not good, (14) Sexual and poor films and T.V. Programmes, (15) Poor neighbourhood and bad peers, (16) Uncongenial school atmosphere, (17) Parents low character and mental abnormality, and (18) Lack of recreational facilities, or cultural programmes.

School Environment : A child enters in school after his home and family environment. The teacher is an ideal for the students. The following factors may causes for delinquency.

1. Teacher-behaviour is not impartial. He favours some of the students and his behaviour not sympathic for the students, may cause for delinquency.
2. Individual difference. In teaching process of classroom may not consider the individual difference. There is great variation among the students with regard interest needs and temperament. If the child, needs are not satisfied, it may cause great tension in home.
3. Teaching methods and techniques are appropriate for some of the students. They would like to attend the class, they may develop the habit of truancy. The high work load of assignment, lack co-curricular activities, the examination, strict discipline may cause for delinquency.

Physical Constitutional Factors : The physical deformities of a child may be one the reason for delinquency. The defects of body organs make the child sensitive and emotional. The diseases related to sex organs may cause delinquency.

Psychological Factors : Freud 'Psycho-analysis' is the significant factors for delinquency. The mental retardation development of glands, emotional unstability and mental diseases are the factors of delinquency.

Causative Factors: These are classified into two major categories:

Primary Factors: Biological and Psychological Factors

Biological Factors: (a) Inheritance and (b) Constitutional defects

Psychological Factors (a) Intellectual Weakness (b) Lack of security and affection (c) Mental disease (d) Emotional Instability (e) Weak supper ago and (f) Personality trait.

Secondary Factors: Social and Environmental Factors :

Social Factors: (a) Family (b) Society

Environmental Factors: School Environmental

Review of Causative Factors

Some eminent scholars reveal that causative factors are really hypotheses attempting to account for the deviant behaviour in the individual case. William Healy, in his research on 'delinquency,' set the pattern for this approach and discovered that, in contrast to their malty, general theories of criminal behaviour, delinquency in individual cases is a product of multiple causative factors. He has discovered 3.5 factors per case.

After a long period of time, Cryil Burt has found 9.5 factors per case using essentially similar case history methods of factor determination. But Freudians and Neo-Freudian clinicians challenged the role of multiple causative of delinquency rather they laid stress on some deep motivations.

Prevention and Treatment

Prevention and treatment both the devices are employed in delinquency. It has two phases the first phase is to treat those who have become delinquents another phase is to prevent delinquency by organizing educational programmes and other activities in such a way that children may not become delinquents.

Treatment : Generally the following methods and techniques are used in the treat of delinquents.

Psychological Method of Treatments : Psychological method involves three devices for the treatment of delinquents.

Camp Programme Approach : In this approach, a camp is made a treatment centre for the adolescent because it is generally felt that the adolescents are more difficult to handle without intensive observation. This programme has got three main themes:

(i) 'Group-counselling is keystone of the programme, which was "built around the concept of the conscious cooperation of all elements within it for the welfare and development of the inmates."

(ii) The camp programme strive to attain the cooperation of guards and to involve the inmates in their own treatment.

(iii) It has a "Probation-Recovery Camp' also if the campers do not have a desirable home to go back to. This approach has been used for prisoners in USA but now attempts are being made to use it for non-prisoners also.

Community, Planning or Sociological Method: After identifying the delinquent children efforts are made to change the environment of the children. The basic needs of child are fulfilled. Parents are also approached to have proper attitude towards the good deeds and bad habits. This method is based on good suggestion, sympathy and good instructions.

Change in the Environment: When it is found that the existing environment can not be improved, the delinquent child has to be shifted to some other good environment e.g. in nurseries or reformatories.

Psycho-analytic Method of Treatment : Though it is very time consuming and difficult method, but very pinpointed and effective one. By adopting 'Psycho-analysis' the clinical psychologists diagnose the reasons of delinquency and try to cure. "Psycho-analysis is a comprehensive approach to human behaviour whose broad outlines were laid down by Sigmund Freud. It comprises a theory of personality development and functioning, psycho-therapeutic techniques, and research techniques for the investigation of personality functions."

Treatment of delinquent children is done by psychotherapy. The counsellor or psycho-therapist may use an appropriate methods on the basis of his observation and magnitude of the problem.

Re-education : The scientific approach which is very much conducive for treating juveniles is re-education. This technique reforms the offender, re-educates him an rehabilitates him. The objectives also include the change of behaviour and attitude of the offender. By that he will look upon the world as a fully potential friend. Social adaptation under better conditions is possible through this technique.

Mental Catharsis : Catharsis means the avoidance of under repression. It provides opportunity to the child to express his pent up and suppressed emotional feelings by means of free expression. Page has rightly pointed out that catharsis consists simply in eliminating troubles, worries and conflicts. Here the therapist has to hear the delinquent's outpouring patiently and without imposing any comments of his own. Through this method, the delinquent is encouraged to realise the cause of his own problems. Play therapy, finger painting and psycho-drama are some of the important techniques which are used by the therapists to treat juveniles.

Persuasion : Through this procedure, the patient's symptoms, actions and reactions are analysed, many logical and common sense facts are suggested and the delinquents it therapists may persuade the delinquent not to get involved in delinquency in future. But this persuasion should be logical and appealing.

One major drawback of this procedure is that it is limited to the conscious level whereas the delinquents whose problems in the unconscious, cannot benefit from this technique.

Suggestion: Suggestion is nothing but the implantation of an idea and it is a successful appeal to the subliminal self. It is true that children are more suggestive than adults. Positive suggestions may strengthen the superego of juveniles. Basically this technique implies the influence of one person upon the other and it is a process of communication from one personality to another. It is one of the oldest techniques of mental treatment and is used to supplement other methods of cure.

Change in Environment: Different studies on delinquency reveal that changes in human and material environment of the delinquent can help in removing many of the symptoms of the delinquency in him. Nobody is a born delinquent. Rather delinquents are the products of environmental influences. Psychotherapists suggest that the delinquents may be shifted to better environments like foster homes.

Prevention : The purpose of prevention is to develop attitudes, moral value and other competencies among the children so that they may not acquire anti-social behaviour. The prevention measures have a very wide field and requires the cooperation of home, school society and other social agencies. The causes of delinquency have been discussed that parents behaviour and home conditions are responsible for delinquency There is an urgent need is to educate parents. The method of prevention of delinquency are as follows:

Family System and Well-adjusted Homes : Rapid urbanisation and scientific advancement have resulted in weakening the family affecting vitally the important husband-wife and parent-child relationships. The consequential social change has an adverse effect on unified life in a family. In our tradition-loving society, the family is the sole agency for handing down the cultural heritage. The behaviour of the individual is regulated by social control groups to which he belongs. In big cities, people keep oneself to oneself. They have no group security. Though physical health is good, many reactive depression, attributed to boredom, social isolation and a false set values.

Parents should not quarrel in front of their children and they must observe the norms of good conduct. They should be impartial and just to all the children. Besides that the parents must be aware of the interests of their children. The children should be made to realise that the parents are always there to help them whenever they face any problem.

Home Conditions : The following preventive measured should be used for improving the home conditions:

1. Proper atmosphere should be provided in the home.
2. Have sympathetic and affectionate attitude towards children. Parents behaviour should be encouraging.
3. Parents should be given the knowledge of child psychology and child guidance. They should understand the needs of the children.
4. No over or under protection be given by the parents.
5. Keep conscious watch on the friends of your children.
6. Population-education' should be given to parents.
7. Adequate amount of pocket money be given to the children.
8. Parents should provide good examples themselves, show good or ideal behaviour.
9. Parents should know about the progress of their children in school. They should know their company in which they move.

State and Social Agencies : May be helpful or preventing delinquency in the following ways.

1. Should establish good schools with good staff equipments and atmosphere.
2. Should make provisions for educating the poor students by giving concessions and financial assistance.
3. Should try to eliminate evil influences in the society e.g. drinking and gambling.
4. Should open some 'Children homes', to provide homely atmosphere to illegitimate children.
5. Should open reformative agencies like Child Guidance Clinics, Juvenile courts, Children-gardens, and Children societies and clubs.
6. Should sterilize persons having serious mental disorders to save our new generation.
7. Strict film censor policy should be there.
8. Anti-social persons should be adequately dealt with the law.
9. Should establish welfare councils like Bharat Scouts and Guides. National Youth Services, Red Cross Societies etc.

10. Slums area should be improved.
11. Students should not be allowed to participate in political activities.
12. Proper books and library facilities should be provided.
13. Should have provision for daily assemblies and for moral and religious education.
14. Should pay attention to improve the curriculum of the school for each class more pertaining to practical life.
15. Proper records should be maintained about children.

Legal Provisions

The 1860 Indian Penal Code which was the first modified law of the country under British rule had sections 82 and 83 which related to juvenile offienders which also defined the lower age limit for criminal responsibility and in the modified 1884 and 1898 Code. Sections 29 (b) 199 and 362 relate to the treatment of juvenile delinquents. These sections had the suggestion for socialised treatment of young offenders. The later Reformatory School Act of 1876 and its modified version of 1897 provided on all India basis that young offender might at the discretion of the sentencing court, be detained in reformatory schools for period of three to seven years instead of undergoing a sentence of imprisonment.

The report of the Indian Jail Committee (1919-20) emphasised the treatment of the youthful offenders for their reformation. In pursuance of the recommendation of this committee, Madras, Bengal, and Bombay enacted their Children Acts in 1920, 1922 and 1924 respectively. (The Bombay Children Act was revised in 1948). The main purpose of these Acts, in general, was to provide for the custody treatment and training of the children who fall foul with laws. The Punjab Borstal Act of 1926 was also enacted to provide for Borstal Institutes for the young. 1948 Bombay Children Act was applied in Delhi and in 1960 Government of India enacted the Children's Act 1960, for Union Territories and so also Haryana a new state, enacted the Haryana Children Act 1974, which deals with the juvenile delinquents and neglected children and aims at their rehabilitation.

The effects of programmes of rehabilitation in some institutions, though very few, are found to be good in social and emotional adjustment and even the hardened boys were won over by affectionate and human touch in some institution.

Practical Aspects

In practice, however, the conditions for the education, training and rehabiliation of these unfortunate children in various states are not what these should be. There should be special schools for these criminal children like Approved Schools in U.K. and the institution of juvenile police, Juvenile courts, remand or observation homes for their residence during trial, helped by proabtionary officers and psychiatric social workers, have to be properly organised. A more humane approach is called for the these deviants have to be kept busy when they are young otherwise they will keep the society busy when they are grown up.

Juvenile Court

The Juvenile court was first instituted by the Bombay Act of 1924. Generally it is the court for young criminals. The main idea behind it is that the delinquent is not allowed to mix with other criminals. In this court, hearings are not conducted openly. Even the court is presided over by a juvenile judge.

A juvenile finds himself in the remand home before his trial. Sometimes even after his trial. A remand home is a sort of waiting room for the young criminals. Keeping the juvenile in remand homes serves two purposes:

(1) He is segregated from other criminals and

(2) He is available for trial, whenever is wanted.

Before the hearing is held, some proabtionary officers are appointed to study the young criminals and their environment. They study the situations before the case comes for hearing or after the case has been disposed off. A probationary officer is a counsellor as well as a friend to the young offender who also' is placed on probation. Then the young criminal remains in a certified school till he completes 18 years of age. If he behaves well, he may be let off earlier.

Since the approach to delinquency is mostly penal and administrative every local authority of the country has to provide "Remand Homes" within its area to receive children waiting for their trial.

Educational Provisions

The following are the main educational provisions in main streaming for delinquent children.

Adequate Schooling : Adequate schooling can contribute, a great deal towards the prevention and control of delinquency by playing a more responsible role. Personality development of children is largely influenced by the schooling. That is why, in many affluent societies, attempts are being made to make the school an extension of home with the same atmosphere of informality and freedom.

First, the school needs trained teachers with high moral character. They must be prepared to solve the problems of the students psychologically.. In the school edutation must be imparted according to the child's interests and abilities. Besides this, the school must have library and recreational facilities. Children must be encouraged to read. They are to be motivated by the teachers. Further, a coordination between homes and schools should be maintained. Teachers and parents should inform each other about the problems of the child.

Recreational Activities : Research reports show that the recreational activities play an important role in preventing delinquency. In rural areas, the lack of healthy recreation and of a community centre may induce youths to make their gathering place with gamblers, prostitutes and other dubious acquaintances. Poor children living in slums do not have facilities for any healthy recreation. In most cases, it is necessary to take the child away from its unhealthy surroundings. It is wise to institute active guidance, allowing the child to establish new emotional bonds with healthy people. Improper use of leisure time is another sole cause of delinquency in children. Properly organised and supervised play and recreation can not only prevent delinquency among children but also improve their physical and mental health. Organised recreation has therapeutic values the provision of adequate broad-based recreation services may make a substantial measurable contribution to the dimension of the problem of juvenile delinquency.

SCHOOL ENVIRONMENT

School environment can be made conducive for learning with the help of the following measures:

1. Only good and trained teacher should be appointed.
2. Individual attention should be paid to children.
3. Healthy recreational and co-curricular activities should be provided.
4. Teacher should teach according to the age, ability and level of the students. He should pace with students.
5. A. V. aids and library facilities should be used to make lesson more interesting.
6. Teacher should select right teaching strategies.
7. Educational, personal and vocational guidance programmes should be started, counselling facility should be available.
8. Teacher should try to maintain democratic environment of class and school. The school climate should be more open of class and school.
9. There should be good coordination between homes and school through proper 'teacher-parent associations etc.
10. Medical check up should be arranged periodically for diagnosing physical defects, deformities and disease, among students.

The delinquents are found at stage of adolescence or secondary and higher secondary level. The child enters into the school with set pattern of his behaviour and attitudes. Even then education can play crucial role in both treatment and preventing delinquencing.

Crow and Crow, formulated four objectives of education (1) Self-realization, (2) Human relationship, (3) Economic efficiency and (4) Civic responsibility. The education so designed to achieve these objectives. It will prevent the delinquency.

Education is creature and creator of the society. The school is secondary social institutions and class as social phenomenon. Thus, education and school has an important role to play, to control and prevent delinquency. The parents cooperation is also essential in this context.

Exercise

1. Explain and define the term, 'Delinquency'. Enumerate the main characteristics of delinquent children. Indicate the legal definitions of delinquency
2. Classify the delinquent children or delinquency. Indicate the behavioural symptoms of different type of delinquent children.
3. Describe the procedure of identifying the delinquent children. Enumerate the causes of delinquency.
4. Enumerate the causative factors. Describe the ways and means for prevention and treatment of delinquency. Indicate methods of treatment for delinquents.
5. Describe the legal provisions for delinquent children in our country and other countries.
6. Describe the educational provisions for delinquent children. Indicate the objectives of education and methods of teaching such children.
7. Write notes on the following:
   (a) Juvenile court for delinquents.
   (b) Delinquents and criminals.
   (c) Socially disadvantaged and delinquents.
   (d) Delinquents and emotionally disturbed children.

13

Slow Learners

Historically, the slow learning child has been described in numerous ways. Ingrain (1960) considered them as educable mentally retarded, child. Johnson (1963) stated that "slow learning comprise the largest group of mentally retarded persons". Today the term 'slow learner' most accurately describes children and adolescents who learn or underachieve, in one or more academic areas, at a rate that is below average yet not at the level considered comparable to that of an educable mentally retarded student. Intellectually, sow learners, score most often between 75 and 90 IQ-between the borderline and low-average classifications of intelligence.

Slow learner children represent a group who underachieve in the classroom. While no special educational provisions are required for them, special instructional techniques are a must. The present chapter brings into the knowledge of students.

Meaning and Definition

Slow learners constitute an appreciable fraction of our population. As Burt (1973) has rightly pointed out the term 'backward' or 'slow learner' is reserved for those children who are unable to cope with the work normally expected of their age group. Kirk (1962) took 'rate of learner' as the basis for identifying slow learners. According to him, the slow learners, gifted and the average children can be classified according to their 'rate of learning'. He also strictly refused to equate slow learners with mentally retarded because the former is capable of achieving a moderate degree of academic success even though at a slower rate than the average child. As an adult, a slow learner usually becomes self-supporting, independent and socially adjusted; but in the early stage, adapts himself to regular class programme which fit in with his slower learning ability.

The term 'slow learner' is frequently used to cover various groups of children otherwise referred to 'dull' 'retarded' or 'educationally subnormal. In the present circumstances it is used more widely to indicate the fairly large group of children whose learning is slowed down by one or more factors of which limited ability may be one. The common factor with all pupils seen was some measure of educational retardation, the contributing factors being manifold e.g., culturcal and poverty, family inadequacies, and parental disharmony. Pupils from such homes as these may well function as 'slow learner' even though their intellectual potential may be considerable higher.

Previously psychologists held that slow learning is directly related to intellectual ability. But recent studies in this regard revealed that heredity alone is not responsible for the backwardness of the child; but environment contributes significantly to the scholastic achievement of the child. The backward child is a slow learner and he finds it difficult to keep pace with the normal child in his school work. Taking only I.Q. into consideration, we cannot call a child who is a slow learner, mentally retarded. On the whole the only difference between a slow learner and the average child is his slower rate.

Slow learner is not discussed in the standard special education textbook. In fact, slow learners are not special education students. Slow learners receive additional supportive services, in the regular classroom, curricula and learning. Some slow learners are not special education classroom or because they would otherwise fail in the regular classroom even though they do not have special education needs.

There is no diagnostic or descriptive profile that characterises the slow learner. Slow learners are described by their specific academic weakness.

During the last several years there has been increased interest in the education of slow learners, otherwise known as backward pupils in schools. These groups as has been said does not come under special education categorisation, yet because of their incidence in the classroom there is a need for prevention and treatment of backwardness whether they are in ordinary schools or in special education classes. The word 'slow learning children' is a broad generic term as stated by Tansley and Guilford, 1971).

The Characteristics

One of the most frequent complaints about backward children is the weakness of the memory. Burt (1946) remarked or all special mental disabilities that hamper educational progress, the most frequent is a weakness in what may be termed as long distance memory. Dull children need to go over material more times before it is fixed in their minds, and more frequent revision is required to prevent forgetting. There is no doubt the ESN or slow learning children have poorer powers of retention than average children but it would be a mistake to assume that remedy lies in repetition. The quality of imparting initial learning is important.

(1) Slow learners have limited cognitive capacity. They fail to cope with learning situations and to reason abstractly. Rational thinking become practically impossible. They have the capacity to succeed in rote-learning. These children show interest in learning where relationships are clearly demonstrated. With regard to retentive memories they require more practice and revision in comparison with normal children.

(2) One of the pertinent characteristics of slow learners is poor memory. It occurs due to lack of concentration. It is impossible to say how much a child can learn and retain although he is motivated externally and internally. Experimental evidences reveal that very often the full children can recall facts about their local cricket team as well as its players.

(3) Classroom situations include distraction and lack of concentration of slow learners. This typical behaviour is also associated with poor motivation. Again different

studies also report that when the learning material are presented through concrete situations, the slow learner's concentration and attention do not differ significantly from that of a normal child.

(4) Inability to express his ideas through language is another significant characteristic of a slow learner. A slow learner also lacks imagination and foresight. He faces difficulty to foresee consequences in the future.

(5) In developing societies, has slow learners invite social as well as educational problems. Of course, some dull children are very poor in scholastic achievements in the school. Their performance is not satisfactory. But some children who come from sophisticated homes show good performance because they get help and encouragement from home. This is only possible at the primary stage of education. But at the secondary stage, the frustrations and failures come from different sources. The children develop an attitude of resentment towards the authorities and create problems. This kind of attitude may lead to anti-social behaviour in the future.

Three Major Areas

The above characteristics of slow learner are related to three major areas:

Physical Characteristics : There are three groups of children who are show to develop both mentally and physically and three appears to be a slow growth potential resulting in all round immaturity. (1) The ENS/slow learning children are poor in dressing, using drawing and writing materials and tools. They need large practice in climbing, jumping, skipping, dancing, games etc. They also need feelings of success and confidence and improved social development. (2) Many ESN children have better physical development than mental development. (3) Children whose capacity to learn is reduced because of sickness, minor ailments, malnutrition etc. The children can be screened for sensory defects if any which are not easily observed but affect the learning and adjustment of children. Regular physical and motor development activities can be introduced to benefit these slow learners.

Weakens of Attention : One cause of poor memory is weakness in attention. These children are restless and destructible. There are evidences of avoidance resulting from previous failure and consequent dislike of a subject. They often glance at words than read them carefully. Attention may be poor because of mismatched or irrelevant materials. The method of presenting learning materials may not facilitate accurate perception of it.

One of the says in which memory of slow learners can be improved is by ensuring that as many associations are made as possible. These children are weak in this regard. The teacher must therefore pay special attention to getting children to see links which brighter children would probably see for themselves various sensory modalities can be used to present the links and associations. For example the word 'night' can be first sequence, of letters n-i-g-h-t. Then visual displaying, speaking, asking him to write down linking it with light, sight, pight. What is important-presenting the material in a way that facilitates the making of generalisations. Meaningful associations are of great importance. Words can be taught by appropriate actions here, there, down, up, over, under. The slow learner can learn by understanding and then they need more repetition, revision, and practice to retain.

A Feeling of Insecurity : Slow learning children have a feeling of insecurity which arise out of personal inadequacy physical or mental. They are unable to control feelings of aggression or outbursts. The ESN children continuously seek attention and approval of the teacher. They do experience the need for acceptance from the peer groups. The isolated child may withdraw still further. School should provide means for successful achievement which will enhance the sense of self-esteem. These children are more dependent and have limited capacity for taking responsibilities. Opportunities for becoming independence and responsible are to be provided in the school. They are as such not curious. If school can offer security and affection it can go a long way in the education of slow learners.

On the other hand, children whose basic needs have been inadequately satisfied they may be difficult to motivate to learn. They instead are upset by feelings of hostility and jealousy or riddled with anger for their own failures. They use several defenses

. immaturity, regression., compensatory activity, withdrawal, fantasy.

The characteristics are not directly related to low intelligence so much as to the educational consequences of low intelligence. Educational and social failures are to be avoided in planning activities in the school.

The teacher in trying to promote social and emotional development must try to recognise the where the child is and start from that point. The child has to learn how to control socially unacceptable expressions of temper, jealousy, egocentricity.

Duty of Family

The family is of first importance in creating a sense of security. The child besides other family conditions (disharmony, separation) feels insufficient share or affection or is disappointed then there is an emotional problem. School can provide experience of success but attitude of the family is more important. Parents are not prepared to accept the child's backwardness. Sometimes they are over anxious which contributes the education backwardness.

The Classification

These 'slow learners' can be placed under three categories : Those who show signs of brain damage or neurological deficit like Aphasias (can see and read the words but cannot say what it means-can bear words but cannot be given their meaning-can hear and see words but cannot write). The use of unaffected sensory apparatus (Vision or Hearing) and hands in building up proper meaningful associations yield positive result in these case. Reports reveal the some children have either been forced to change from their left handedness to right-handedness or have a 'Split-literality' (Crossed-Eve-Hand Dominance), i.e., they have a dominant right-handedness with a left eyeness or difference in the perception and shape of the object through their left and right eyes. This is popularly known as 'Primary Reading Disability.'

Research has shown that specific reading disabilities (dyslexia) are seen in about 10-12 percent of school-sense children who are intellectually normal. They have a poor sense of self-esteem and some children show signs of mild depression. They have adequate vision but their reading ability is retarded. Usually this disability is more pronounced in the boy than in girls. Very often, these children show signs of tension in habitual manipulation of body parts, and aggressive behaviour. These children can memorise will, often spell words or numbers without working what they are spelling or having a 'numbers-sense."

The Identification

The defects of children who are blind, deaf or physically handicapped are readily apparent to the observers. The handicaps of educationally subnormal or slow learners are not always so obvious. They are less able than most children to meet the normal demands of education and life in modern community or society. Culturally it is relative. In a less advanced society, even they do not draw attention.

The period at which their limitations arise are most obvious is that of school years. The normal living demands certain intelligence, capacity for abstract conceptual thinking., intellectual skills, mininum attainment in reading, writing, simple calculation. A proportion of students are so limited in their capacity to learn that they are handicapped to meet the demands of the normal school learning. Others are learning difficulties and therefore are slow learners. If teaching is not suitably geared to their slow rate of progress and are not modified to use the most effective ways of learning these children fail to achieve success. Hence, there is a need for special educational measure to ensure for these children the maximum progress of which they are capable in the traditional three R's and in practical, social and personal life. These are quite apparent in the context of universal education in the closing educates of the present century and which started in the closing depable of 19th century. The application of psychology to education and to the study of child development began to have increasing influence. Binet's contribution to mental testing contributed to a large extent to the realisation of differential treatment for children as per their ability and needs. Burt's forty years of research provided a foundation of knowledge about the extent of backwardness, its causes and the broad lines of treatment for the slow learning children.

Slow learning and /or educationally subnormal children have limited intellectual development. Many of these children grow up in circumstances which limit rather than foster the development of intelligence. Very poor homes rarely provided as good opportunities for the incidental learning as average or good homes do. Skeels and Day (1939) and Skodak and Skeels (1949) studies showed that removing children from extremely unfavourable environment to one which is very much more favourable would seem to result in quicker mental development during pre-school years. Nursery school experiences accelerate mental growth. Unfavourable school and home conditions and responsible for decline of intelligence.

There is every possibility that in a classroom there must be some slow learners. These children consist of a group with mild handicaps. They come to school regularly; but they are likely to become dropouts if their needs are not met. From the psychological point of view, it would be conducive for these children to be identified earlier. Then necessary steps can be taken to help them in their learning. Survey works reveal that it is somehow easier to identify more severely handicapped children than the mildly handicapped ones. A teaching expert is easily able to identify and deviation in classroom behaviour pertaining to learning difficulties of children. He has primary knowledge about the fact which spells out clearly that the slow learners require more time and more help to acquire the skills in comparison with the average children. These children also rely more on concrete learning rather than abstract learning. Psychologists and experts use various tools and techniques to identify slow learners. These are as follow:

Observation Technique: Observation of children's behaviour by the teacher as well as experts may help in identifying slow learners. This observation may be done under simple as well as controllable conditions. While observing children's behaviour, a strict watch can be kept for their reaction to various situations. A child's behaviour is not only observed in the classroom, but also on the playground, home and in the group etc. Observation may be done by just watching the child's behaviour directly and by moving along with the child. It should be kept in mind that for this technique, the observer should have the capacity for analysing and interpreting the information gets from his observation. Observation technique is conducive for ascertaining the recreational, occupational and extra-curricular interest of children.

Case Study Method: As we know by this technique, the history of the child, his family, his early life and home environment are revealed. Through this method, psychologists also try to study the learning difficulties, adjustment problems and behavioural problems of a child. By finding out the causes of such abnormalities of children, psychologists as well as teaching experts are abale to suggest the best possible remedial measures. Of course, this is a long drawn process and psychologists undergo a strain in interviewing such children, their relatives and parents at short or long intervals.

Other Tests

Medical Examination : Before confirmation, the developmental history from early childhood should be meticulously verified by a qualified medical expert or medical practitioner. Under strict physical and medical examination, the anomalies, disabilities and handicaps can be highlighted.

Scholastic Tests : Evaluation or deficiencies in school achievement can be possible through scholastic tests. These tests can throw light on areas like arithmetic, reading, spelling, composition, writing, language and comprehension. General and specific problems of children are singled out by the psychologists and educationists through scholastic tests, and causes of anomalies can also be evaluated properly.

Personality Test: Through personality tests, attempts can be made by psychologists to throw light on the emotional characteristics of children as well as temperamental traits. Evidence shows that there are certain personality traits which have direct relationship with specific backwardness. Persistence, sensitiveness, concentration, emotional stability, assertiveness etc., are some of these traits. Thematic Apperception Tests (TAT), Rorschach Ink Blot Test (RIBT), Word Association Test (WAT), Free Association Test and some psychoanalytical procedures are very much helpful to the psychologists here. Research analysis by WIP. Alexander has also revealed that teacher's assessment of children's traits for personality can be every profitable used for diagnostic and productive purposes.

Intelligence Test: Through the use of any standardised intelligence tests the intellectual level of children can be assessed. Both verbal intelligence tests and non-verbal tests can be used for this purpose. But psychologists prefer individual verbal tests to group verbal tests. An expert can get a true picture of the mental capacities of backward children by giving many intelligence tests. A single test is not sufficient to bring out the full picture of the mental capacities of a child. Psychologists use more than one standardised test to ascertain a particular anomaly.

Psychometric and Psychological Tests: For diagnostic purposes, psychologists use psychometric tests which are of a sensory nature. For better appraisal, analysis and evaluation of specific skills of backward children, these tests are primarily used. By these tests, psychologists try to discover the exact nature of errors made by the backward children. Again some other psychological tests may also be used to assess span of attention, auditory perception, steadiness, memory and reasoning powers.

The Causes

Educationally subnormal children or slow learning children were pupils who by reasons of limited ability or other conditions resulting in educational retardation, required some specialised form of eduction, wholly or partly in substitution for the education normally given in ordinary schools.

These terminologies have less stigmatised effect. They are not based on medical or psychological categorisation but purely on educational needs. The causes of the educational backwardness are: school absence, ill health., unfavourable school and home conditions, and emotional barriers to learning. The cause is not so much of limited ability. Therefore, these children need suitable arrangements in ordinary school. The forms that special educational treatment should take will need to vary according to local circumstances.

The causes of slow learning are many. Some important ones are discussed below :

Poverty : In a developing country like India, poverty is considered to be the primary cause of slow learning. Poverty affects children in two ways-(i) by impairing children's health, and (ii) by reducing their learning capacity. Again it brings rare opportunities to acquire general knowledge through enriched experience. In other words a child from a sophisticated family has a variety of avenues to explore and gets plenty of materials to meet his requirements. He gets educational toys and books which are conducive to acquire general knowledge to improve his educational background. On the contrary, a child from an impoverished family does not get enough opportunities to live a full life. However poverty is not the sole cause of slow learning. We have to investigate into other causes to gain first hand knowledge about slow learners.

Intelligence of Family Members : Another potent factor of learning is the level of intelligence of parents as well as family members. It indirectly affects the slow learning of children. It is true that educated and intelligent parents can provide educational experiences and materials to their children according to their own intellectual level. But if the parents are not intelligent or sophisticated, they cannot take positive steps towards the upliftment of their children. Again, the economic condition of the family also plays a major role to permit the parents to spend a little amount of money on the their children regularly, If their purse permits, then they become interested to purchase for their children some materials which have educational value. A sophisticated family which is economically sound can provide better opportunities for their children. Children coming from affluent families which have high socio-economic status are not usually slow learners. Research evidences also confirm this fact.

Emotional Factors : Emotional factors contribute a lot towards the slow learning of children. Psychologists confirmed this through their research analysis. When a child comes to the school, he brings his emotional world with him. Experiments have already established the fact that tensions and conflicts exercise a negative effect on learning of the child. So the tensions at home, the relationships between the siblings and parents themselves have an adverse effect on the child, not to mention the frustrations, which he sustains from his family and form the external world. Research data revealed that in the democratic homes, children get less frustration than the autocratic home. So, in a way, we can conclude that children from autocratic homes are usually slow learners.

Personal Factors: Besides all these above factors, there are some personal factors which are more or less responsible for slow learning. Personal factors include long illness or long absence from school and lack of confidence in self. It was found that children who lack self-confidence are usually slow learners.

Slow learners or backward children may be of three types:

(i) Very backward because of retarded mental development accompanied by psycho-social deficiencies. They need special educational treatment outside the ordinary school-special school or special class.

(ii) Ability is not quite limited but have difficulty in learning than average children due to school and family or personal factors.

(iii) They can be dealt with in ordinary schools although they may derive benefits from special classes not limited in intelligence but have problems in reading and writing where as arithmetic and other subjects are high. Their cause may range from specific perceptual difficulties to emotional maladjustments. For them some form of remedial teaching is required.

The slow learning children have IQ as high as 90s but are within 75-90 points. Remedial education benefits these children although in some regular school there are many slow learning children and hence, a special class for them is sometimes necessary. The children receive education in special class or school but move to regular school after backwardness is removed.

There has been growing interest in placing slow learning children in regular school. But there is a need to allot enthusiastic and experienced teachers to remedial classes dealing with slow learners. In addition all teachers during training should have some instruction in methods of teaching, the early stages of reading and number and to be made aware of the methods of helping children who cannot keep up with their age group.

A crucial time for getting to groups with backwardness in the last year of the primary school and beginning of junior schoot (upper primary). Remedial assistance should continue the secondary school. Because the gap between the average pupil and the slow learner widening with age.

Hence, the special class for the slow learning children should have 1:20 TP ratio and a little lower standard curriculum. Usually in our school system they are placed in section C or a special section of the same class.

It is not possible to clearly find out who are backward because of limited potentially for development and those whose emotional disturbance has retarded development. The latter group can not be placed in the classes for ESN or slow learners. Many infant school arrange for extra attention to be given to these children either by holding reading groups in the head of teacher's room by running a small remedial class. Such arrangements can be most valuable as a first step in the prevention of backwardness. From here one can know how are to be lead to a drit, and the foundations give in special school would be lost.

Slow learning or backward children do well in lower Primary School if they follow the infant school approach or if there is a special class'. A proper diagnostic procedure is followed by using medical examination, psychological evaluation, educational assessment, social history of family and cultural setting.

The Problems

A checklist containing 69 behaviour symptoms arranged under five problem patterns was primarily aimed at identifying specific problems of mild retardates who constitute a significant group of slow learners. A single problems provides a clue to analyse certain learning problems of child.

Cognitive Learning Problems : (1) The slow learners learn at a slower rate and they face difficulty in retaining what they have learned. (2) The slow learners prefer concrete learning to abstract learning. (3) Transfer of learning becomes impossible for slow learners. (4) They lack judgement and common sense and they are highly destructible. (5) They gain from direct teaching and do not acquire skills incidentally and (6) A slow learning is an underachiever and has a very short span of attention.

Language or Speech Problems : (1) Verbal expressions for slow learners are difficult. (2) Oral reading is more difficult than silent reading. (3) slow learners face articulation problems. (4) Proper expression of thoughts becomes difficult for them.

Auditory Perceptual Problems : (1) Slow learners face trouble in writing from dictation. They usually leave common prefixes and suffixes while writing. (2) slow learners fail to understand verbal directions. So They are unable to give proper reply, when a question is asked. (3) They prefer visually presented materials to orally presented materials. (4) Identification of different sounds becomes different for them. They also find difficulty in distinguishing between similar sounding words. (e.g.; Tap-Tap-Tap, Pen-Pin etc.). (5) Slow learners usually given inappropriate answers to verbal questions. They also fail to learn the art of counting by memory.

Visual-Motor Problems: (1) Slow learners are easily distracted by visual stimuli. They have awkward movements. (2) They find it difficulty to discriminate between colour, size and shape relationship and are unable to recall to memory the objects that they see. (3) They have a very poor handwriting and face difficulties in motor work. Very often they complain about physical problems. Recognition of common objects becomes a problems for them. (5) Slow learners prefer part learning to whole learning and find oral learning tasks easier.

Social and Emotional Problems : (1) Slow learners do not have the stamina to sit in a class for long periods. (2) They are lovers of solitude and are not gregarious. They fail to make friends and are not at all sociable. (3) Slow learners become aggressive towards their friends and peers on trivial matters and they are afraid and self-conscious. They daydream in excess compared to normal children. (4) Nail-biting is another interesting characteristics of slow learners. Sometimes they also engage themselves in anti-social activities. (5) Their mood changes frequently and their achievements is below expectancy. (6) They prefer not to work in a group and have inappropriate and excessive verbalisation.

REMEDIAL PROCEDURE

The following are the three major procedures for slow learners children:

Remedial Instruction : Generally, teaching experts provide remedial instruction for slow learners. Studies have shown that the remedial instruction proved profitable in case of special slowness in a specific subject area. First, the deficiencies are determined and confirmed by the experts given these children some diagnostic tests. The cooperation of specialists is sought to deal with special slowness. The following points are taken into consideration for smooth working of a remedial programme.

1. Gradation of teacher materials may be carefully done taking the capacity and requirements of children into consideration.
2. Short frequent lessons should be introduced instead of long lessons every seek.
3. Experts should be aware of the fact that a friendly approach in remedial teaching is highly conducive.
4. To generate interest, social skills and confidence in slow learners, priority should be given to art, music and drama.
5. Practice, drill and review should be given importance by teachers while dealing with slow learners. Repetition and direction should also be emphasised.

Health Environment : An important aspects of remedial measures for slow learners is rich environment. The school atmosphere of children should be healthy and reasonably free. Sometimes poor environmental factors contribute a lot towards the slowness. These should be removed as early as possible. Again, there must be provision made for a variety of approaches to the various subjects. Very often, the slow learners, suffer from emotional problems. So care must be taken to place them in protected environment.

Periodical Medical Check-up : Physical anomalies are important contributory factors for slow learning. Poor health and other malfunctions also have similar effects. If a particular anomaly is detected and correctly recognised, then a slow learners may become a normal learner after treatment. So special medical check-up should be arranged for every slow learner.

DEVELOPMENT OF SLOW LEARNERS

This can be looked from two points of view.

Personal Development: The personal development of the slow learning children should ensure development of personal hygienic, capacity to organise leisure time activities and capable of understanding limitations and of matching the aspirations to the abilities. Social qualities would include getting along with others, listening to and learning from others, as well as avoiding over compensatory behaviour such as showing off, boasting and lying. These can be cultivate during the school years by training mentioned earlier under the social and emotional characteristic heading.

Social Development: Social education must be viewed as an integral part of the whole educational process in play, in school work, at home. The special/ school special class teacher must have some understanding of the child's family and community setting. The regular classroom teacher where the slow learners are found at the early stages of education must be sensitive to these needs and provide directions. The following some of the cardinal principles.

1. Children can not become socially competent and mentally well if they do not have feelings of success. In school only curricular success is assessed rightly or wrongly.
2. All learning situations and procedures should be so planned as to encourage independent work habits and self-direction. Pupils anticipation in learning is a must.
3. Some aspect of social education must be developed step by step procedure, demonstration and daily practice, (feeding, dressing, cleanliness).
4. The way school and class are run as communities can make a contribution to the development of social responsibility. The discipline system should therefore be consistent and fair and imposition of authority may be kept at a minimum.

Only then development of independence, self-reliance and an ability to adapt the changes by the slow learners would be possible. The "regular class teacher" should have all these competencies outlook and experience to handle slow learners in the classroom integrated or otherwise.

Educational Provisions

One of the pertinent characteristics of slow learners is that they learn slowly and unevenly. Again, they are unable to cope satisfactory with the usual educational standards of the ordinary school. However, with proper guidance and care they are capable of being educated. In adulthood, they become self-supporting, independent and socially adjusted. One defect, however, which is worth noting is that most of the slow learners are not properly identified till they attend school.

Conscious efforts are being made to help the children after being identified. Psychologists specify that the remedy for slow learners lies mainly in their nature and the extent of the causes which produce it. Of course, each case is unique and requires specific remedial measures. Psychologists recommend the following remedial measures which may prove conducive to slow learners.

Organisation of Curriculum

In case, the slow learning children are placed in the special class or special school, the curriculum has to be based on logical, physical and social aspects. The contents however, may vary according to the age and need of the child. The curriculum, must be specially designed to assist the total growth as well as to develop basic skills and knowledge. It should not be mere watering down of the curriculum designed for a normal school. To segregate children and given such a curriculum would be a travesty of special educational treatment. On rare occasions they should be placed in a special class.

However, it must involve (1) central core language and number (b) periphery subjects e.g., environment, creative and aesthetic activities, and practical interests. Both should be related. Time table must keep a balance between core and periphery subjects as well as social and group activities. The organisation should take the following consideration into account.

1. The smaller the school, the more generous should be teacher-pupil ratio. The class size should 20. The school is all age and mixed.
2. The younger the age the smaller should be the class if the teacher is to provide stimulating environment.
3. Some provisions should be made for extra remedial work.

Flexible Curriculum : Educationists may take care in preparing the curriculum for slow learners which should be as flexible as possible to suit the requirements and needs of the individual students. Slow learners are generally interested in concrete perceptual experiences. So attention must be paid towards concrete aspects of work. Educationists should lay less emphasis on abstract and theoretical studies. Because slow learners do not grasp abstract things easily. Again emphasis must be placed on the use of visual and concrete aspects of work. Experiments on slow learners revealed that the learning of generalisation abstractions and concept is difficult for theses children. So teaching experts should strictly avoid these concepts. The crafts which are found to be conducive the these children include mental work, wood work, leather work, cane work, knitting, tailoring and other subjects of household economy.

Special Methods of Teaching

Educationists as well as psychologists have conducted many experiments to devise special methods of teaching for slow learners. Their results indicate that the slow learners require short and simple methods of instruction based on concrete experiences. Verbal instructions should be limited. Educational excursions to places of historical, geographical, scientific and cultural interest may be conducted. The use of pictures, models, charts, films and other audio-visual aids will also be profitable. Employment of project methods is helpful in imparting education. As the slow learner needs security, an atmosphere of assurance and love should be created. Direct experiences and concrete example are great help for children.

Home Visits by the Teacher : To make family environments sophisticated and healthy, the teachers should take an interest in visiting the homes of the parents and advise them accordingly.

An unfavourable home environment and autarchic homes are important factors for slow learning. Teachers may suggest some remedial measures for slow learners to the parents relating to home environment.

Maintenance of Progress Record: Assessment of children's progress is essential for recommending their entry into a higher group. There should be a well planned regular evaluation of the progress of the children in all curricular or co-curricular aspects. Records of evaluation should be preserved properly. Progress charts and cumulative record cards may be of great help for them. These records are essential for individualised treatment. Condensed case history with assessments helps the teachers to provide better educational treatment for slow learners.

Programmed Instruction : The programmed instruction material can be prepared for slow learners.

Teaching Techniques

Individualisation of treatment should be adopted to teacher slow learners children according to the needs of a particular type of mental ability.

User of appropriate methods of learning. The various aspects of growth physical emotional and intellectual should not be considered in isolation but as parts of a dynamic integrated process.

Providing Motivation : The slow learners are to be motivated. It can be done through a sense of satisfaction through a sense of accomplishment. He can learn if the situation given him security and confidence. Good teacher pupil relationship is vital at all times.

Learning Readiness : Activities should be planned to provide readiness for learning for pre-school stage of all kinds intellectual, emotional social and physical. The teacher has to recognise whether the child is ready for the next stage by systematic observation of his performances.

A Practical Approach : Practical approach based on meaning and usefulness. The slow learning children would be more at home if they can hear, see, and touch and which are within this experience. Teaching which is related to practical human experience is more successful than teaching which involves abstractness, symbols and delayed gratification.

Concept Formation: Slow learners children are capable of making simple generalisations but they must be given ample opportunities to experiment, explore and discuss. The child can be shown or let to discover relationships, similarities, his curiosity is aroused, his interests can be expanded and enriched. In a nurturing classroom he will be willing to experiment and learn by doing. His concepts are to be developed.

Grading of Work : In case of SL children the materials are to be graded to ensure continuous progress and feelings of success. This is real difficulty for the teacher as textbooks are written by others. The teacher can make his own material or analyse the task and make a graded presentation to ensure learning by the slow learning pupil.

Assessment of Progress : It is recommended that of the SL child a cumulative record be kept of his achievements over a period so that individualized treatment is ensured. The child here can compete against himself.

Consolidation : Frequent repetition, adequate revisions are to be encouraged for better consolidation of the learned material.

Activity Methods: The child must do things with his body, his head and his brain. He must be given freedom to learn and experience. He must experiment and experience.

Cooperation among Various Professionals

In diagnosis, treatment and research cooperation between teachers, doctors, psychologists, administrator and social workers is vital. The psychologist can make a contribution by providing a detailed picture of the child's personality, by discovering any anomalies in development, perceptual and conceptual difficulties, intellectual strength and weaknesses emotional abnormalities and by investigating learning difficulties generally, including treatment procedures. The importance of social workers is greatly felt but it has not taken off.

Parent Education

There are many difficulties that can arise because of wrong attitude in home. The improvements brought by teachers of SL children are often nullified by bad home conditions and parental neglect or ignorance. Parents therefore need advice on how to promote development of their handicapped children. The parents therefore are to be guided and in this context a social worker would be of great assistance.

Developing Skills and Abilities

The measure task of a teacher to develop the following skills and abilities among slow children:

Teaching for Verbal Ability and Skills : In school verbal instructions and explanations are quite important. Many of the slow learners have retarded speech: articulation, vocabulary, brief sentence, grammatical errors. Emotional reluctance is the chief reason for their backwardness of expression. They need a great deal of speech stimulation through play, and through talking to adults, listening to them. Expression is often lacking in order, sequence and selectivity. Error in usage are quite frequent i.e., he runned, the catched etc. These children are also poor in remembering messages and listening to instructions, stories and other forms of spoken words. Attention therefore, should be given to listening and reproduction skills.

Poor language may be due to several factors: poor background of speech and language at home, a limited background of experience, emotional and social factors and the limitation of the slow learner's thinking capacity.

These children can develop their language by talking about what they have seen or done, by discussing what they are going to do and how they are going to do it. These are most effective for they evoke stronger feelings of enthusiasm and interest and therefore expression.

The teacher should guide and stimulate the child's thinking about his experiences e.g., what they noticed while going to school, climbing tree, making and explaining scrap books, explaining what they learned in television, role playing in a drama in school, listening to stories, puppetry allowing the puppets to speak to each other conversation among peer groups. The fact that many children do acquire a better form of speech for use in school does suggest that progress can be made.

Developing Reading Skills and Competency : Reading similarly is not an isolated skill. It is an aspect of the integrated language development programme which includes speaking, writing and spelling. For slow learning or backward children a sound reading programme is necessary. It should consist of :

Development of Reading Readiness : In the early stages visual method should be used. Teacher should concentrate on the acquisition of slight vocabulary of meaningful words. The classroom should contain plentiful materials to allow activities at different levels of maturity: sand, water, paint, clay., toys, colour, picture books, scrap books, group models. These increase knowledge and interests, vocabulary, powerful expression, improved work habits, social relationships, interest in reading, classification, labelling, visual discrimination by looking at pictures, jigraw puzzles, matching games, drawing and tracing pictures, personal and social development through play.

Acquisition of Sight Vocabulary of Meaningful Words: The teacher gives written sentences and words and ask the child to draw a picture on the opposite page about what she/he read. The child was asked to trace over the words and sentence. The teacher makes independent sentence cards and word cards independent of the book. In this way, the child recognises the words. Each child learns comprehensions and it becomes an ego involved activity. In this way the slow learning children learned, consolidated their learning, learned vocabulary. The child gradually learns through supplementary materials.

Development of Independent Reading : Backward children are usually deficient in these abilities and require a systematic programme of word recognition exercises of reading progress is to be maintained. It should be a rigid, isolated, elaborate course of phonic drills or word form, and an interesting, integrated controlled attack on the analysis and synthesis of sound units which will lead to continuing improvements in reading for content and ideas.

Development of Speedy, Relaxed and Silent Reading : The choice of books is important at this stage to cater for the children's individual interests and reading levels Backward/SL boys should be little less difficult than their level or understanding SL girls like family situation books, fairy stories and books on animals. With these children particular attention has to be paid for word meaning, comprehension and development of ideas.

Writing plays an important part in reading process and programme. It assists visual discrimination and memory and the relation between visual and auditory patterns.

Some fundamental cognitive incapacity underly reading problems of slow learner. In fact, it requires a significant change in the attitudes. The anxiety which is likely to control the slow learner should be reduced by giving continuous encouragement and initial success. The crux of the matter is motivation. The non-reader is to be persuaded that reading is interesting, it can be useful to him and he can master it.

Remedial teaching must take into account the child's weakness noticed at reading. Silent reading and refreshing are quite significant. Silent reading can be brought by work sheets with instructions. The other method is Kinaesthetic method i.e., tracing and writing words. Systematic work in spelling and a technique of learning would be important in doing so.

Developing Number Ability and Skills : Arithmetic is a way of thinking about number. Arithmetic teaching therefore is concerned with application of number system to the arrangement, manipulation, and the development of the ability to deal with member relationship symbolically and by abstraction in the absence of concrete objects. They should be taught through concrete- pictorial symbolic models in addition to general pedagogical concerns being kept in mind. Piagetian approach to teaching number system and arithmetic is quite effective i.e., conservation and formal logical operations.

The Piagetian approach to teaching of concept of number and arithmetic through conservation exercises have been exemplary, e.g., more less, same or less, long and short, heavy and light, fast and slow, middle and end, before and after. The readers are here referred to a book written by the author on this approach. The examples of mass, quantity number area, volume, movement are all found in the text.

Developing Creative Arts : It has been said earlier that most slow learners enter into school with needs of achievement and success to counteract their loss of confidence and sense of inadequacy. Many children are able to achieve success or have it contrived for them in one or other creative activities. On the this foundation academic achievement can be based. Apart from this there is a valuable relief and relaxation obtained through touching and handling of materials of moving about and doing. It is as if saying X is frustrated and fatigued in his school work then let him do his painting. There is much to be said in favour of formal work being closely and genuinely linked with creative work. Pent up feelings and hostility or frustration finds a safe outlet in a free drama. The fact that such outlets are achieved in a situation watched and controlled by a tolerant teacher seems to make emotional release all the more effective. Art has therapeutic value.

One of the outstanding characteristics of slow learner is poor concentration. They are often destructible and lacking is persistence. Within limits the ability to concentration is learnt in the repeated experience of absorbing and satisfying activity. Plan and creative work offer conditions for the development of concentration and persistence.

Teacher's Role

More specifically, Tanseley and Guilford (1971) suggested that the teacher of slow learners should:

1. Organise the class in small, carefully, selected group.
2. Have wide range of supply of activities e.g. readers, free access to arts and craft materials.
3. Pay particular attention to preparation of materials.
4. Allow brighter children to help duller ones.
5. Encourage children to participate in planning activities.
6. Allow as much as freedom as possible within the well established limits.
7. Avoid rigidity and accept student's suggestion.
8. Be sensitive to children's suggestion.
9. Have several periods each week when the class is engaged as a whole on one activity, story; drama, music.
10. Try to obtain parental cooperation.
11. Do not be reluctant to admit failure with an individual child.

THE SUGGESTIONS

Slow learning children can not advance much but their intellectual limitations, often reinforced by social and cultural ones, restrict the range of his experience as well as the depth of his understanding. The child's activities in relation to his environment nourishes his mental growth and language development. Their experience and knowledge can be increased at the initial stage by understanding of the natural environment, why and how things happen exploration, talking and questioning, nature study.

It is said by Seguin—

1. Teach nothing indoors that can be learned outdoors.
2. Teach nothing with dead things when you can make observations on living things.
3. Nature should be classroom and the school book in case of difficulties.

Of course, the metropolis/urban schools may apply these principles by appropriately having pets and acquarium and by arranging field trips occasionally.

Non-promotion : Experimental facts of a group of psychologists are in favour of non-promotion of slow learners. These psychologists follow a policy of promotion of slow learners. These psychologists follow a policy that permits retention of a child in a class for the second year. But very often it is found that when a child is not promoted and retained in the same class, he resorts to self punitive measures. For this reason, many educationists object to this idea of non-promotion. Rather, they lay emphasis on remedial instructions and understanding.

Reinforcement: Slow learners lack the experience of reinforcement in the home environment. Fear of failure and disinterest are pertinent in their daily school activities. So adequate and appropriate measures should be taken to improve their academic status. When a slight improvement is noticed some motivational techniques may be used to stimulate. Use of illustration, examples and aids may also be conducive for creating motivational atmosphere inside the class. A teaching expert should try to instill confidence in children and he must also make constant efforts to remove fear of failure.

Individual Attention : Treatment of slow learners should be given individual attention. The teaching experts may place emphasis on recognition of individual differences among students. They must also respect the individuality of the child through helpful environment. Again, teaching experts should be very kinds and sympathetic towards their students. The teachers should allow the students to proceed at their own rate of learning. One of the best advantages of this method is that there is no failure since the children are assessed against their own success. Complete freedom is given to children to budget their own time to bring out their assignment forte.

Schedule of Reinforcement : The research studies have revealed that continues schedule of reinforcement is effective for slow learners. The positive reinforcement works well for dealing slow learner in classroom teaching. The teachers should be sympathetic and helpful to them.

Exercise

1. Define and explain the term 'slow learner' Differentiates with under achiever and backward children.
2. Enumerate the characteristics of slow learners and classify the slow learners.
3. Describe the behavioural aspects of slow learners and indicate the causes of slow learning.
4. Enumerate the problems of slow learners and suggest remedial measures for the improving slow learners.
5. Describe the educational provisions for slow learners with reference to the following points.
   (a) Flexible curriculum
   (b) Method of teaching and
   (c) Techniques of teaching.
6. Indicate the role of teacher for developing abilities and skills among slow learners. Give some suggestions for the teacher dealing slow learners.

14

Health Problems

Some children have health problems that interfere with their education. Notable among these are rheumatic heart disease, and tuberculosis. There are cases of kidney ailments and infections such as asthma, eczema, hay fever, chronic health disorders such as: epilepsy, diabetes, migrane headache. But children with chronic illnesses are likely to be enrolled in any classroom.

Meaning and Definition

The term physically handicapped has been used in literature in various ways: Physically disabled, crippled, orthopaedically impaired, or otherwise health impaired. Physical handicaps and divided into two types : Orthopaedically impaired and health impairments for the purpose of special education. The legal definition of the term orthopaedically handicapped is a severe, orthopaedic impairment that adversely affects a child's educational performance. The term includes impairments caused by a congenital anomaly e.g., dub foot, absence of somebody organs, impairments caused by disease, e.g., cerebral palsy, amputations, and fractures or burns that cause contractures. A similar definition has also been adopted by Department of Social Welfare, Government of India.

A physically disabled child be defined as one whose physical or health problems result in an impairment of normal interaction with society to the extent that specialised services and programmes are required. This group is extremely heterogeneous group and includes varied disabilities and conditions out of which the commonly encountered are:

Cerebral Palsy (CP) : is a non-progressive disorder that affects gross and fine motor co-ordination. It is often associated with convulsions, speech disorders, hearing defects, vision problems, deficits in measured intelligence or combination of these problems. Main types of cerebral palsy are Spasticity, Ataxia, Athetosis, Rigidity and Floppiness.

Myopic Dystrophy : is a disease in which the muscles progressively weaken and degenerate until they can no longer function.

Policmyelitis (infantile paralysis) : is viral infection that affects or destroys some cells in the spinal cord leading to paralysis of part or parts of body or entire body.

Spina Biflida : is a congenital defect that result when the bones or a part of the spine fail to grow together resulting in gap in the spine. The area affected and symptoms very depending on the location of spine affected and the extent or disorder.

Amputation : it is the absence of some limb.

Physical and health problems may have grave, little or no effect upon the school performance of the student.

The legal definition for other health impairments is having an acute condition that is manifested by severe communication and other developmental and educational problems, or having limited strength, vitality or alertness because of acute health problems e.g., heart condition, tuberculosis, rheumatic fever, nephritis, asthma, hemophilia, epilepsy, lead poisoning, leukemia, or diabetes that adversely affect a child's educational performance.

Certain crippling and chronic health disorders in children are seen as a result of infection after they are born. Some of the common examples are poliomyelitis, estomyelitis, tuberculosis, cerebral palsy. Although, the first three do not invariably lead to brain injury, perception, vision and audition deficiencies yet these children demand special educational treatments.

However, there are certain neurological disorders which are not categorised as either crippling or a special health problem e.g., aphasia- language disorder due to brain injury. Hence, from an educational point of view crippling and neurological impairments would include all children with non-sensory physical impairments whether they are accompanied by a neurological damage or not, and whether they resulted in chronic health condition of not.

Basically non-sensory physical impairments may be classified as crippling and chronic health ailments. The cripples have muscular and skeletal deformities which are obvious. They may wear braces, prosthetic devices such as artificial limbs or may be moving with crutches or wheel chairs.

The second category of children are confined to bed for relatively long periods of time and just do nothing. The crippled children are known as orthopaedically handicapped or motor impaired whereas the second category were known as special health problem cases.

Some students with physical and health disorders begin their school careers with an identified handicap. With others the problem is first noted after they have entered the school, or it may result from an accident or disease that occurs during the school years. Because of heterogeneity in this group, a single list of signs to identify them is not possible. However, all of them have a common problem of posture, mobility, difficulty in performance of physical activities.

Almost all children with locomotor handicaps, sensory impairments, speech impairments and with mild and even moderate intellectual disabilities can be conveniently placed in ordinary schools. However children with more moderate and severe intellectual deficits and multiple handicaps will still have to be placed in special schools or classes depending on the nature and degree of disability. Thus special education will be provided in (i) Integrated; and (ii) Special Schools.

The Characteristics

Some children with epilepsy are intelligent. Others are mentally slow. Ocassionally fits that are very frequent and severe can injure the brain and cause of increase retardation. Treatment to control fits is important.

Some children may have both minor and big fits or they may have first minor ones and later develop high one's. There is a sign of warning or aura. They may suddenly cry and then are finds suddenly jerks or are thrown immediately. These fits vary in duration.

After the fit is over the child may be very sleepy and confused. He/she may feel body-ache and feel weak.

Children with severe problems, like heart problem, diabetic, epilepsy, need to rest after 10-15 minutes of studying. It is difficult to accommodate them in general classroom since they require constant medical care and the full attention of the teacher.

Epilepsy is the most common neurological disease. In 1870, Jackson defined epilepsy as a group of disorders with paroxysmal and excessive neurocal discharge that cause a sudden discharge in neurological function. There is a sudden change in intellectual, sensory, motor, autonomic, or emotional activity, limited in length and presumably associated with neuronal over-activity.

The Classification

Those who have poor physical condition, make them inactive and who require special health precautions in school. Such children can be categorized into the following groups.

Children With Mild Health Problems: It Comes under the educable IED group. Their health problems do not interfere with educational learning. But precautions need to be taken in terms of getting adequate medical check-ups and support.

There are children with severe health problems who cannot be integrated in regular schools. The severity of their health problem interferes with educational planning. They will need constant medical care and are therefore not be able to participate in the academic and non-academic activities of general classrooms. Children with severe problem, like heart problem, diabetic, epilepsy, need to rest after 10- 15 minutes of studying. It is difficult to accommodate them in general classroom since they require constant medical care and the full attention of the teacher. Such children need to be educated either at home/hospital or in special classes in general schools. Some health problems are discussed below:

The problem may occur in disabled children hence the knowledge of the symptoms and their implications can help the teacher in minimising these problems and helping the disabled to develop their talents like others.

Different Problems

Epilepsy (Neurological Disease) : This is one of the special health problems which is generally faced by children. The symptoms of this problem are : (i) the child shakes violently as if in the grip of hysteria, (ii) there is constant recurrence of fits, (iii) the child loses consciousness, (iv) he falls and moves arm and legs violently, (v) the child may become pale. (vi) he falls and moves arms and legs violently, (vii) purposeless activities such as rubbing of arms and body parts, (viii) the child starts taking off his clothes. The problem is due to brain injury or an extra growth in the brain. Some drugs are available to control the fits, and the extra growth can be removed by surgery. Epilepsy is treated as a special health problems.

Since the fits are painless to the victim, it is important that the teacher should remain calm and not attempt to restrain the child's movements. All sharp objects that may injure the child should be removed from around him, but the movements must not be interrupted. If the mouth is open some soft objects such as a handkerchief should be placed to prevent the tongue from being bitten. The child should be allowed to rest after the fit and the parents and doctor should boycott among peers and to protect the child from such treatment, the teacher can use this opportunity to explain the problem to the entire class. The teacher should also explain to the other staff- members and the community that the cause of epilepsy is not evil spirits but injury of the brain. The child is normal in his/her intellectual functioning. This will help in better social, emotional and academic integration of such children.

Diabetic Problem : Children with the problems show the following symptoms: Frequent urination, abnormal thirst, extreme hunger, frequent change in weight, generally rapid loss sleepiness, weakness, usual disturbances are felt more acutely and frequent skin infections such as boils and itching.

This problem can occur in both normal and disabled children studying in your school. As a teacher you are expected to identify these symptoms at an early stage. The problem is because the body not producing sufficient amount of the hormone called insulin and can be controlled by given insulin in the proper dose at the proper time. The teacher's role is to help the child to get medical examination and to take medicine and diet according to the doctors' prescription.

Asthma (Bronchial Problem) : Generally, the problem of asthma is overlooked in our classrooms but since it creates some social and emotional problems for the child so it is better if the teacher is made aware of it. The child suffers from breathing trouble due to allergy. The commonly seen symptoms are: difficulty in breathing. The child takes large gulps of air becomes pale, breathes noisily and perspires too much. Asthma is caused by allergens such as dust and the pollen of some plants. It may also occur due to excessive physical activity or emotional reaction. Drugs can be given orally or by injection, which help to control the problem, but it is not completely curable. Teachers who have such children in their class should help these children by keeping them away from dust and pollen. They should not be asked to do strenuous exercises. The teacher is also required to help the affected child to adjust to the problem and to involve in social activities that are not too rigorous.

Juvenile Rheumatoid: Pain in the joint which occurs in younger children is known as juvenile rheumatoid. Such children have a skin rash and swelling and redness of the eyes. There could be some retardation in growth since it is a disease that attacks the joints. It may cause stunted growth. Swelling and pain occur in the fingers, wrists, elbows, knees, hips and feet. In severe cases, it left untreated the joints become stiff, making movements difficult and painful. Juvenile rheumatoid is a chronic infection of the connective tissue of the body. Drugs and special exercises can prevent the disease from becoming too severe. In the case of such children the role of teacher is very important. The teacher must be understanding and at the same time, not overprotective. Such children require more time to finish their assignments. Various adjustments such children require more time to finish their assignments. Various adjustments such as writing aids and special paper and pencils can be provided to the children who have stiffened upper limbs. Since such children are physically weak, the teacher should not insist on their participating in all the activities.

Anaemia health problem is a condition in which the child suffers from severe loss of blood. Children who suffers from anaemia have periodic attacks of acute pain, may be weak and prone to jaundice and leg ulcers. They have pain in the abdomen, knees, elbows and other joints in the body. They suffer from constant headaches and may occasionally faint, feel ringing in the ears and see spots before the eyes. The major cause of this loss of blood is the loss of the red pigment of blood cells known as haemoglobin. The shape of the red blood cells change to sickle-shaped. A complete cure is not possible in server cases of the disease. Children afflicted with the disease need to rest frequently and be protected from further infection. The teacher should allow them more time to finish their assignments. Since it also leads to lack of oxygen, frequent hospital treatment is required. Teacher should get the children medically examined if he suspects any such problems in them. The children with mild type of anaemia need only periodic medical check ups and medicines according to doctors' prescription. They can be integrated without any problems.

The Areas

The following are the main areas health problem impaired children:

Psychomotor : There are several type of epilepsy: psycho-motor, petitmal, grandmal. In psychomotor epilepsy the individual is violent, vigorous and is doing some automatic action, which appear to other as meaningful but are meaningless. During the seizure the child's behaviour is inconsistent. The makes sucking noises with his mouth, move his hand aimlessly, strikes a child, tears up paper, move about the room. But the individual does not remember what he has done. Such behaviours include temper tantrums also.

Petitmal : In petitmal, the child loses consciousness for a few seconds but does not fall. His eyes may roll up or there may be a rhythmic blinking of eyelids. He drops things, appears to be staring straight ahead, or stands still, unaware of what is going on around him. The teacher often thinks that he is not paying attention. He quickly recovers and goes on what he was doing not inconvenience him or to any one to great extent. But if such seizures occur quite frequently the child is apt to lose the thread of a lesson and be handicapped by gaps in continuity. The teacher should watch for sign that indicate a child is having a seizure and repeat directions. He may have missed or checked to see that he has understood what was going on in the class.

Grandmall : A child who has grandmal seizures has less consciousness and fall rigidly on the floor. This is preceded by strange sensation known as aura (warning) and by a shrill cry. His muscles first tighten, then accompanied by salivation, twitching and tremors may follow. Then comes a deep sleep, come or stuper. The seizure may last for a minute or two and when he recovers he may be dull or disoriented. He may want to sleep for some more time and consequently his school programme may be impaired.

The Identification

The following are main symptoms of health problem impaired children:

1. Shortness of breath
2. Frequent cough
3. Blue appearance of skin
4. Increased appetite
5. Gets easily tired
6. Restless inattentive
7. Slow and inactive
8. Irritable
9. Temper tantrums
10. Abnormal thirst, frequent irritation
11. Itching
12. Perspires often

13. Dust allergy
14. Loss of weight.
15. Very easily tired.
16. Excessively restless.
17. Extremely slow and inactive.
18. Unusually breathless after exercise.
19. Subject to frequent dry coughs or complains of chest pain after physical exertion.
20. Cheeks, lips of finger tips have a slightly bluish colour.
21. Has slight temperature most of the time.
22. Extremely inattentive.
23. Faints frequently.
24. Complains of pains in the arms, legs, or joints.
25. Easily irritated-gest angry easily, loses temper, may exhibit destructive, aggressive tendencies without proper reason.

A teacher in the integrated classroom teaching can identify the children of health problems by observing their behaviours, of special health problem. He can deal with such children according to their individual special needs.

Causes of Health Problems

Michael (1994) summarised the causes of epilepsy as follows:

1. Ideopathic-causes not known-(30-50) percent
2. Genetic -(10-20) percent by inheritance.
3. Metabolic errors—PKU, Maple syrup wine
4. Congenital and peri-natal infections.
5. Encephalitis and meningitis (brain fever) and severe dehydration.
6. Brain tumors—Intra Cranial space occurring lessions.
7. Brain injury before birth at last among 1/3 of epileptics.
8. Cerebral haemorrhage and
9. Drugs and lead poisoning.
10. Cerebral palsy and epilepsy often occur together.

Brain damage can be prevented during pregnancy. Avoid marriages between close relatives. Anti fits medicines are to be taken for 3 to 4 years to prevent epilepsy occur further.

The Treatment

There are no medicines that can cure epilepsy. There are no vaccinations that can prevent epilepsy. However, medicines can prevent occurrence of fits if these are taken regularly. Sometimes preventing fits for a long time seems to help stop epilepsy permanently.

Treatment for epilepsy generally consists of four parts (1) identification and eliminating of factors that cause or precipitate attacks (2) sustaining of general mental and physical health and social integration (3) pharmacological therapy that raise the convulsive threshold to prevent attacks (4) surgical therapy for carefully selected patients with seizure of focal origin or for those for whom medication has proven completely ineffective.

The commonly used anti-convulsant medications in pharmacological therapy are Diantin, Mysoline. Sarontin, Tegretoe, Clonopin, Depakene for different types of seizures. The most significant treatment in epilepsy is the growth of good physical and mental health. A nutritious balanced diet and adequate muscular activity will be paralleled by the relief of emotional stress, and the creation of an atmosphere of productive and normalcy.

Educational Provisions

Since the new policy of education (1986) advocates placement of these disabled children in a integrated setting, so far as it is possible and it is a relatively new concept with which our classroom teachers will have to be familiar, it is important for all teachers in the school to understand what integration means; what are the models of placement of such children; what impact it has on the role and responsibilities of school personnel.

As used in special education, integration refers to the education or pupils with special needs in ordinary schools. Integration provides a natural environment where these pupils are along side their peers and are free from the isolation that is characteristics of special school placement.

The concept of integration is a complex and dynamic one. It has evolved from a simple opposition to placement in a special school to encompassing a variety of arrangements in ordinary schools. This diversity is commonly described in Warnock Reprot (1978) wherein distinction has been made amongst different forms of integration—locational, social and functional.

The 'locational' integration relates to the physical location of special education provision. It includes special units or classes in ordinary schools. The special and the ordinary school share the same site. 'Social' integration relates to its social aspect, where children attending a special class or unit eat, play and interact with other children, and possible share organised lot of classroom activities with them. The third and the fullest form of integration is 'functional' integration. This is achieved where the locational and social association of disabled children with their peers leads to joint participation in educational programmes. Where children with special needs join, part-time or full-time, the regular classes of the school, and make full contribution to the activity of the school. Another form of integration suggested by some authors is 'societal' integration.

The best environment for mainstreaming is a classroom that is appropriate to the needs of the handicapped students. A programme continuum provides full spectrum of services that may be tailored to the individual needs of each student at any given time during his educational career.

To meet the broad and many faceted changes occurring in schools in response to POA (1986) and (1992) envisaging integration, corresponding changes in teacher education are both necessary and inevitable. These may include the following programmes :

1. De-institutionalisation of many seriously handicapped children.
2. Rapid return of many handicapped students from special day class and school to regular classroom
3. Decreasing direct service of special education teacher and emphasising indirect service such as consultative and support function.
4. Participation of regular classroom teacher in determining and writing individualised education plans (IEPs) for students with special needs.

5. Determination of education'goals and programmes for exceptional students, based on specific individuals' learning needs rather than gross categories of exceptionality.
6. Formal involvement of parents of exceptional students in assessment, placement and planning activities.
7. Involvement of other school personnel.

Fundamental changes are being made in the governance of schools as well as in the role of most school personnel. Inevitably, there is gap between theory and practice and many pupils still go to special schools even if they do not need to. To bridge this gap, educational programmes must change to meet new school policies and to prepare school personnel for new roles.

Teacher's Role

A teacher has to play the following roles for dealing H. I. Children:

(1) Ease the child to the floor.
(2) See that is not apt to injure himself by striking furniture or sharp comers while convulsions.
(3) Turning the child's head to one side and carefully placing but never forcing a folded handkerchief of a soft object between back teeth is sometimes advised.
(4) Do not use a pencil or other solid object for the teeth.
(5) The teacher should help other children in the classroom to accept this seizure calmly and to understand that there nothing contagious or harmful about in convulsion.

Children with epilepsy do not have necessarily low intelligence due to seizures. They show some signs of maladjustment because social stigma and frustrating environment. Majority of the children with this condition can attend regular school. Nonnal acfivity and exercise may actually reduce the frequency of seizures. Incidence is reduced by following ketogenic diet (high fact and carbohydrate) and anticotivulsive therapy.

The Mainstreaming

The regular classroom will provide most children with chronic medical problems with maximum educational opportunity. These who present physical problems present little limitation of activity and therefore should not be deprived of such opportunity. This of course, requires extra teacher training, planning and ingenuity. This of course, requires extra teacher training, planning and ingenuity. Children are very sensitive to their teacher and her attitudes and it should be remembered that teacher's attitude have a contagions effect on the feeling of the total group.

In his environment children will have to face their difference recognise their limits, be assured of their acceptance as they are, and then be given opportunity for participation and enjoyment of class projects. In each they need support and understanding of the teachers.

The human-centred schooling approach should be followed for those children. The child's self concept his adjustment with others should receive primary focus. The teacher has to participate in overall planning for the pupil.

Special attention has to be paid towards the social and emotional adjustment of the child who because of his disability might feel different, unaccepted, and some what insecure. He may fear the physical and social consequence of such efforts.

The teacher should be aware of their specific health problems, the therapeutic measures to be taken and the necessary programme alteration. A comprehensive remedial programme is necessary for this group. These factors should be kept in mind while developing programmes for the health impaired.

For helping these children particularly with health impairment standard of achievement expected should be kept at par with the needs of the group and remedical education must compensate the difference of the classroom attainments. Some interesting low level reading books should be on their hand or in library. Teacher clan help parents in planning home and community participation for the children.

The 'Buddy' system already referred in case of hearing impaired, visually impaired may also find a place in case of chronic health disorder cases. The buddy will be responsible to the teacher who will make the necessary adjustments and medical referrals.

No specific prescription can be offered for educating children with chronic illness. Their problems vary, according to diagnosis, degree of involvement or limitation and supplementary care.

Children do move from one facility to the other. Need for programme continuity, teacher sensitivity, and support as children are transferred can not be over emphasized.

Special Schools and Special Classes

Special schools and special classes for health impaired children are midway between home and hospitalised instruction.

Most special class accommodate physically limited children by offering a comprehensive remedial health programme. Not all children need health programme i.e., health habits, dietary adjustments, rest etc. In a few other cases, special classes prepare them for regular class, placement by raising their educational achievement and adjustment. Comparative efforts will be exerted towards developing poise in social relationships by participation in both independent and group activity. Fostering self respect and confidence through achievement in a semi-sheltered classroom setting will do much towards alleviating fear of inadequacy in regular programme.

No child should be placed in a special school or special class without complete physical evaluation. Normally Health Impaired children are placed in special class according to their types and degree of illness. Teachers should introduce the children to as many aspects of the school programme as possible and encourage them to explore all the ways in which they can prepare for participation with their own class and with other children in school. The school curriculum should also take into consideration the child's need for adjusting to the pace of non-handicapped. Curriculum roads to maturity and self understanding should be explored.

National Provisions and Assistance

Since the advent of independence, the Government of India have taken a number of initiatives in the field of special education, vocational training, rehabilitation, manpower development and technology upgradation. Important schemes of the Ministry of Welfare are as follows:

Assistance to Voluntary Organisations for the Disabled: The Ministry of Welfare Government of India gives upto 90 per cent assistance to voluntary organisation for the education, training and rehabilitation of the disabled. For rural areas, assistance is given upto 95 per cent. In 1993-94 about 315 voluntary organisations were provided with assistance to the tune of Rs. 10.40 crores. A component to rehabilitate mentally ill persons has been added in the scheme.

Assistance for Aids and Appliances : The Government of India under this scheme provides free aids and appliance to those persons with disability whose monthly income does not exceed Rs. 1200 while 50 per cent subsidy is provided to those whose income is between Rs. 1201-2500 per month. This scheme is being implemented through both governmental and non-governmental agencies.

Assistance to Voluntary Organisations for Rehabilitation of Leprosy-cured Persons : This scheme envisages providing financial assistance to voluntary organisations working for leprosy-cured persons. Assistance is given upto 90 per cent such voluntary organisations who develop programmers for a awareness generation. Early intervention, educational and vocational training, economic rehabilitation and social integration of the leprosy-cured persons.

Assistance to Voluntary Organisations for Persons with Cerebral Palsy & Mental Retardation: This scheme aims at developing organisational and infrastructural facilities for manpower training and professionals, hostels and other assistance required for imparting training of various categories of workers, trainers such as vocational teachers, rehabilitation wardens etc. in the field of Cerebral Palsy and Mental Retardation. Assistance is given upto 100 per cent of expenditure for recurring and non-recurring items.

National Trust for the Social Welfare of Persons with Mental and Cerebral Palsy : A National Trust for the Welfare of Persons with Mental Retardation and Cerebral Palsy is proposed to be set-up. An amount of Rs. 1.25 crores has been earmarked for this purpose.

The objectives of the proposed National Trust would be as follows:

(1) To arrange, to provide care and rehabilitation to the mentally retarded and the cerebral palsied as a step

towards social security who are under the guardianship of the Trust.

(2) To lay down guidelines for the improvement of the existing organisations which are engaged in taking care of mentally retarded and cerebral palsied depending upon the availability of finances.

(3) To set up homes and services institutions for providing residential care to persons with mental retardation and cerebral palsy.

(4) To provide financial and technical assistance to the organisation providing care and rehabilitations services to persons with mental retardation and cerebral palsy.

(5) To provide guardianship and foster care and to take over the guardianship rights of the persons with mental retardation and cerebral palsy after the death of the parents, if so, desired by the family or in absence of family support.

(6) To extent and support the welfare programmes of families/foster families/parent associations and voluntary organisations.

(7) To provide legal aid to the mentally retarded persons and their families.

(8) To receive, own and manager properties bequeathed by the parents to maintain their child with mental Retardation or Cerebral Palsy after their death.

Exercise

1. Define and explain the term 'Health Impaired Children'. Enumerate various disabilities and conditions of such children.
2. Classify and enumerate the characteristics of Health Impaired Children and indicate main disease of such children.
3. Enumerate the areas of health problems impaired children. Indicate the basis for identifying such children.
4. Indicate the etiology of heath impaired children describe remediation and treatment of such children.

15

HEALTH OF THE MIND

The development of child's personality and his general adjustment can not be ascribed by the influence of parents and family, of the community and the school practices but mainly depends on the mental health of the learners and the teacher. It is said that mother is first teacher or equal to the several teacher. It is said that mother is first teacher or equal to the several teacher. The home is the principal environmental factor contributing to his personality development and his adjustment, mid there after, during his school years, he is still subject to the influences of home and community. Especially his home should have provided for his basic organic needs and should have furnished an environment well suited to meet his needs for security and adequacy. The pleasant and satisfactory experiences should be provided for the personality development and adjustment of the student.

The knowledge and understanding of learning, intelligence, personality and motivation is sufficient for a teacher but the must understand the mental health of the students. Mental health influences the functioning of students and also their physical health. The mental health and physical health are very closely related to one another. A teacher has to deal with normal students in the class room as well as in the school. Mental and physical illness have the adverse effect on their performance and learning, outcomes. It is essential to understand the concept of mental health of students.

Meaning and Definition

Health is as freedom from ailments, it is the general notion about health. Mental health is like physical healths, consists of the absence of serious defects or mental ailments. It is the approach of physician who gives you a physical test. He has a checklist of defects or ailments considered to be serious. If a person is free from these ailments considered to be serious. If a person is free from these ailments or symptoms is considered healthy. In considering either physical or mental health, such a checklist of ailments would emphasize defects which produce distress or interfere with the large functions of the individual.

Another approach to mental health is a number of feelings, attitudes or ways of behaving which lead to distress or interfere with larger goals and which are unusual or inevitable. These conditions are abnormal in the sense that there is departure from normal behaviour. This departure from normal is said to be ill mental health.

The concept of norm comes to act as an adaptation level. People to this norm are considered healthy but those are below the norm, it would draw our attention and are known unhealthy. In matters of health, mental or physical, this adaptation level or reference norm is not always a simple mathematical average. It is sometimes based on what would be expected if nothing unusual had occurred.

Health is also considered as positive attainment. Mental health should not be measured by the evils we avoid but by positive steps we take towards our true potential. In this view, descriptions of the healthy person are almost descriptions of the ideal person.

1. Minimal concept of mental health is considered as the absence of illness. It is the freedom from ailments, absence of mental disorder. He has the good resistance to stress.
2. Enlarged concept of mental health is considered as attainment of positive values and attitudes. He has enjoyable experiences, happy, zestful and creative person.

He has the potentialities for effective functioning day to day life.

The positive view mental health emphasize on effectiveness and competence. It is said that 'health mind in healthy body'.

The Concept

During the present days mental ailments have increased tremendously and have involved serious problems at the national level in industrial development, social and economic changes. The problems of mental health has acquired importance in the national developmental programmes.

It is difficult to define the term Mental Health comprehensively. The definitions of mental health have great variations but the fundamental elements are more or less the same, inspite of workings used in their definitions.

Norma E. Cutts and Nicholas Moseley have defined the term Mental Health comprehensively-

> "Mental health is the ability to adjust satisfactorily to the various strains of the environment, we meet in life and mental hygiene as the means we take to assure this adjustment."

In the process of education mental health plays a significant role. The sound mental health is the first condition for the education. Mental health is most important condition for effective teaching and learning. It is, said that sound mind in sound body.

Thus, mental health and education are closely related to each other. The students learning or achievement depends on their sound mental health. It is essential to the learning process as intelligence. It is a crucial condition for education.

The following criteria have been identified of mentally healthy students or persons. It is also known as positive mental health signs

1. Possesses socially adaptable behaviours.
2. He is emotionally satisfied.
3. He possesses adaptability and resilient mind.
4. His desires are in harmony with socially approved norms.

5. He is enthusiastic and reasonable.
6. He possesses good habits and constructive attitude.
7. He has insight into his own conduct.
8. He has own philosophy and values of life.

It is a fact that healthy person is in conscious control of his life. There is consistency in his behaviour and conduct. A healthy person is aware about his own strength and weakness. Psychological healthy person does not live in the past but he always plans and thinks for future and acts according into the present. His future orientation is very realistic according to his own capacities and resources.

Mental Ailments

There are many positive aspects of mental health, the avoidance of specific ailments may not be the objective of mental health but it is one of important objective. There are several types of ailments of mental health.

(1) Distortion of Reality or Denial
(2) Unusual difficulties with anxiety.
(3) Difficulties with Self-control and
(4) Inadequate relation with other persons.

Distortion of Reality or Denial : An important feature of mental ailment is a distorted view of important facets of the world. The person may refuse to face his own hates, or fears or off beat desires. Some such moderate denials or distortion are of course quite typical. As a matter of fact, there may even be some advantage in temporarily turning our backs on some of the more unbearable pressures.

Unusual Difficulties with Anxiety : Anxiety is no mark of mental ill health. The lack of anxiety situation. Under these circumstances, reality anxiety as it is termed would be normal. It is only when such anxiety seems out of proportion to the menace that would consider that something is wrong. Such neurotic anxiety is unhealthful in and of itself. It brings serious distress.

Difficulties with Self-control : Lack of self-control has long been identified with poor adjustment. The self-control is regarded as the key test of emotional adjustment. Mental ill health may be associated with both the amount of control maintained and the type of the control that is used The self-control can not eliminate the basic urges or drives. On the contrary, the wholesome personality is endowed with strong urges or drives. The happy, admirable persons is well equipped with vigorous appetites and a full quota of needs. In a proper balance between drive and control there should be evidence of a happy and spontaneous energy. The balance maintains joyfully and zestfully to his task.

Inadequate Relations with other People : Social relations are related to mental health in at least two ways. First of all, to avoid ill health, we must have make some kind of adjustment to other people. Second, our must have made some kind of adjustment to other people. Second, our relations with other people often cast some light on other aspect of adjustment. They serve as an index by which other facts of mental health may be observed.

Positive Indications

In describing some of the mental conditions are to be avoided and our attention should be on positive attributes which are as follow:

(1) A Positive view of the self.

(2) Striving toward a Confident mastery.

(3) Specific. Positive goal.

(4) Self-concept and

(5) Mental health, Character and Morality.

A Positive View of the Self : The feeling about himself should be based on a view of himself that is reasonably, free about, himself should be based on a view of himself that is reasonably free from distortion. He should have some general notion and the notion he should not be too far from the objective truth or reality of life. He must also recognize the significant traits that given him some concern, his poor eyesight, his fear of rough and tumble games, his tendency to stammer. Self-acceptance has an intimate relation to freedom from distortion.

Striving toward a Confident Mastery : One of the attributes of positive mental health is that of commitment and striving. The healthy person does not merely avoid evils and handicaps, nor does he deal with them by simple retreat. As he gains success in these enterprises, he gains confidence in this ability to master other problems.

Specific Positive Goals : The several Psychologists who put forward the goals of positive mental health have, in total proposed a long list of desirable attributes.

Mental Health, Character and Morality : Mentally healthy child is the good child. The positive mental health called for a reasonable degree of socialization and, sensitivity to the needs of others. Mentally healthy child generally possess good character and morality

Indication of Superior Mental Health

The following are main indications of superior mental health:

Adaptiveness and Flexibility : It includes ability to deal with the world, to specific objectives and to carry them out, being guided by the results of the efforts.

Capacity to Gratify One's Needs: It means spontaneous actions in the relaxed enjoyment of life has sexual capacity. Ability to work for one's own interests.

Competence and Goodwill in Dealing with Other: He takes part in productive work and meets responsibility in a manner approved by other and fulfils the commitments to others ability to accept help. Trust and liking for people. He is capable of intimacy and warmness.

Intellectual Ability: He is accurate in his perception of reality and of self ability to solve problems in rational much common sense. He has broad comprehensive view of life.

Emotional Control : He is capable to handle anxiety and frustration, moral and conscientious. He is courageous and high morale.

Autonomy, Productivity and a Sense of Worth : He takes initiative, self-reliant in making contributions, Emotionally independent, detached, strong sense of identity and feeling of self-determination, He seeks self-actualization, sense of achievement and self respect.

Integration and Equilibration : He maintains balance and consistency in dealing with opposing forces, mature unifying view of life and given impression of maturity.

Theoretical Basis of Mental Health

There are various theories of psychology which deal with the concept of mental health. Theories related to the needs provide the basis of mental health.

1. Maslow's Hierarchy of needs.
2. Murrays Need Theory, and
3. The Hygiene Theory of motivation.

Maslow's Hierarchy of Needs : Maslow (1948) developed hierarchy of needs with the primitive needs at the base and deferrable needs superimposed. There are five levels of needs psychological safety needs, love and belonging needs, esteem needs and self actualization needs. Next to physiological-needs involved in avoiding danger or securing safety. One step beyond this is the need for esteem. Esteem need includes both the good opinion of other people and self approval. When pressure from these other needs is partially relaxed that the individual can get on with self-actualization.

Throughout the hierarchy, any second order need will be at a disadvantage in competing with first order need. A fairly strong urge toward artistic creating, for instance, might be ruled out by weaker but more primitive need to avoid the contempt of others. When the basic needs are satisfied to some degree that the student can hopefully address himself to the more ambitious goals of competences and achievements.

Contribution to 'Education': The teacher of course, can not be the key person in helping the student meet the basic needs in such a way that he will be free to go on to higher level achievement. The teacher can, however, do much toward providing the student with some of the esteem and affectionate regard so important to his well-being. The teacher's warm emotional support can help make the classroom a less stressful place and enable him to take the risks necessary for self-actualization.

Theory of Motivation : Fredrick HerzBerg (1966) formulated a new theory of motivation. He has explained the 'Need of theory' and classifies human needs into two factors:

Hygiene Factors : These hygiene factors are involved in the learning environment. These factors refer to the following components of learning situation. (a) Working conditions (b) Administrative norms of schools. (c) The form of supervision of school and (d) the safety and standard of school.

These factors provide the encouragement to the students to work hard. These factors are related to the environment or working conditions. These factors are pre-requisite for higher order of learning.

Motivators: The factors are related to the activities and behaviour of the learners rather than the environment of learning. These are organized in teaching-learning situations such as reward, verbal praise, recognition, success, knowledge, of result and novelty. These factors are of four types

(a) Achievement and performance (b) Recognition and Responsibility (c) Advancement and freedom and (d) Personal growth.

The factors have the permanent influence on the change of behaviour of the students whereas hygiene factors have temporary effect. The internal motivation is more effective than external one which is helpful in satisfying higher needs of esteem and self actualization. A teacher's responsibility is in both factors hygiene and motivators. The hygiene factors are related to the school environment and organizational climate. The teachers and principal have to manage and organize hygiene factors in the school campus and in the classroom. The students are encouraged and praised by the leachers for their good performance and desirable behaviour in the class and school by establishing rapport with them. These factors contribute to their mental health.

Influencing Factors

There are several factors which influence the mental health of child.

The influence of parents and family life of the community and of school practices upon the personality or mental health of the child. The following are the main factors and areas of these influences:

Influences of the Parents and Family life

The influence of Poverty on the child's personality.

A feeling of insecurity and

A feeling of inferiority.

The parents who reject the child.

Effect of Rejection on the child.

Expression of Rejection by the parents.

Origin of Rejection in the parents.

Unattractive children.

Relationship between husband and wife.

Immature parents.

Parents who over protect the child.

Expression of over protection by the mother.

Effects of over protection on the child.

The influence of the community on mental health.

Effects of school practices on mental health of children and their personality

(a) The effect of over competition in school.

(b) Over restriction in the classroom.

(c) Unsuitable curriculum.

(d) Teachers method of handling the, class

(e) The effect of the teachers personality on the class

(f) Teachers report of behaviour problem in the class room

(g) Treatment of behaviour problem in the classroom.

The influences of parents, and family life, community and school practices have been enumerated. There are four major factors of parents and family life and sex factors of school practices are listed here. The details of these influences have been given in the following paragraphs

INFLUENCE OF THE PARENTS AND FAMILY LIFE

The following are the main major for influence of the Parents and Family Life. The details have been given as follow :

Influence of Poverty on the Child's Personality: An excellent description of the effect of poverty on the personality of the child has been made by Plant. He points out that 'hardening' of the personality results from constant financial strain. He feels that "this is not a mechanisms of resignation, but the development of patterns of response. That prevents each experience of want (it matters little how drastic) from resulting in the emotional reverberations which accompanied the first such experience." This is similar to reaction which Lewin calls 'encysting' in which the child attempts to make himself unassailable, in effect, by erecting a wall between himself and the environment.

A Feeling of Insecurity : Feeling of insecurity is a second resultant, according to Plant. Children who have suffered, repeated and serious blows to their sense of adequacy from a long-continued real fear of cold and hunger are likely to show a picture of anxiety and panic. This feeling becomes so firmly bound up with the personality structure that late acquisition of a sufficient income will not remove it.

A Feeling of Inferiority : According to Plant a third resultant is a feeling of inferiority. This may be found in children above the lowest economic levels; it occurs whenever there is a marked discrepancy between the economic status, reflected in type of home, clothes, belongings etc. of the child and that of other children with whom, he is in contact, This feeling is likely to become heightened during adolescence when material and social problems are more in the focus of a child's interest.

Parents who Reject the Child

A child is said to be rejected when he is disliked or not wanted by one or both parents, a situation which inevitably result in insufficient meeting off the child's needs for affection and belongingness. Children whose parents strongly dislike them at times; but love them most of the time are not considered to be rejected, consequently the following discussion is not applicable to them.

There are still many gaps in our knowledge of rejection. It cannot be distinguished as yet the supposedly different effects on the child of (1) rejection by both parents as opposed to rejection by one, (2) the sex of the rejecting parent in relation to the sex of the child, and (3) the degree of affection shown by the non-rejecting parents. There have been however, a series of excellent studies which throw light on the problem, and we will draw freely from these in the course of our discussion.

Effect of Rejection on the Child: The pattern of behaviour of the rejected child is reported to depend primarily on, one or more of these factors: (1) a desire to win affection or at least attention, (2) a, wish to retaliate against people for the hostility shown him by the parents, or (3): feelings of worthlessness and anxiety. It is, of course, incorrect to attribute his behaviour entirely to one or another of these categories since, for example, one for of behaviour (that is activity calculated to annoy) maybe based on a desire for attention plus a wish to retaliate.

It is a very difficult to diagnose rejection from the behaviour of the child alone because children who are not rejected may show some of the same symptoms.

Expression of Rejection by the Parents : The sign of rejection exhibited by the parents vary from those which are obviously unequivocal to those which might possible indicate dislike for the child. Rejection is easily diagnosed when the parent's feeling is fully conscious and when there is no attempt to conceal it; not so easily diagnosed otherwise.

Some parents will frankly acknowledge that they heartily dislike their children and wish they had never been born. The majority of rejecting parents are not so outspoken, but express their feelings in the way they treat the child. Getting rid of the child is one of the most obvious signs of rejection. Desertion of the child or placement in an institution, boarding home or boarding school (for the higher income groups) is a common device among rejecting parents. Harsh treatment, being very strict with the child, using severe physical punishment, are all too frequent practices.

Some of the more subtle methods of expressing rejection are (1) expecting the child to live up to standards that i.e. much too high for him. (2) never saying anything favourable about the child, (3) comparing him unfavourable with sibling or children in the neighbourhood, (4) responding with surprise to favourable statements made by other about the child, (5) taking conscientious care of the child needs but with an air of martyrdom.

Origin of Rejection in the Parents: The soil from which rejection grows is likely to be an unsatisfactory marital adjustment. The mother's feeling toward a disliked husband may be extended to the child. The husband may dislike the child of his unloved wife. Interference with the sources of satisfaction of the parents is an important cause. In homes of low economic level, the birth of a child means cutting down on necessities of life for the family in order to meet the baby's needs; on a somewhat higher level, parenthood often means giving up the possibility of further education, or drastic reduction in accustomed comforts. When the wife is employed in a job in which she takes a great deal of pleasure, childbirth means at least temporary and often permanent separation from the position.

Immature Fathers and Mothers who are still dependent on their own parents and who tend to take more interest in dancing, entertaining, and having a good time than in child-rearing are likely to continue to resent the presence of a son or daughter.

Unattractive Children are likely to be rejected. Unattractiveness need not be as obvious to an observer as lack of beauty, a malformed body or mental deficiency. A special quality or lack of it may maketh child seem unattractive to his particular parents—a boy to parents who keenly hoped for a girl; a frail child, even though charming, to parents who emphasize strength and agility; a slow child to parents who think quickness is the sumum bonum; even minor matters such as lack of interest in music when the parents put a high premium on this art-these traits and others may constitute special kinds of unattractiveness.

The relations between the husband and wife : for example when one parent becomes so occupied with the child that the previous degree of affection for the spouse seems to be lacking or to be greatly reduced the child may be rejected by the offended parent. The situation may be even, more critical when a step parent enters the home. It is normal for step parents to feel insecure in the new role at first, but one in whom this feeling is intense and persistent may easily begin to believe that the child is preventing a happy relationship between husband and wife.

Parents Who Overprotect the Child: A child is said to be overprotected when he is excessively cared for, shielded, and loved. As very little is known about overprotection by the fattier, probably because he assumes the responsibility for the child's care so rarely, this discussion will deal only with the overprotective mother. Much is still unknown about the causes and the effects of overprotection on the child, in spite of a number of excellent investigations in this field.

Expression of Overprotection by the Mother : overprotection may result from either domination or indulgence, or vacillation between the two. In any type of overprotection, however the mother characteristically spends a great deal of time with the child, takes excessive care of him, and as a result succeeds in preventing the development of this independence. Specifically, she is likely to sleep with the child for years, amuse, play with, and found him for hours at a time.

Effects of Overprotection on the Child : children of both dominating and overindulgent mothers often lack self-reliance. In both cases they have been for so long dependent on their mothers that they are unlikely to be able to assume responsibility for tasks or for minor life-problems. They continue to fine their security in the presence of their mothers, in whose absence they find it difficult to cope with the world.

Parents who Show Favouritism: When a strong preference is shown by the parents for one child the effect on both the favoured and the unfavoured child (for simplicity of discussion, only two-child families will be considered) is likely to be unfortunate. The favoured child may reflect, though in a mild form, the characteristics of the over indulged child. The unfavoured child is practically certain to show some form of jealousy. Young children often make bodily attacks on the sibling, although direct aggression against the sibling is not always shown in their behaviour. Because of the feeling of injustice and lack of sufficient affection, they may exhibit negativism, restlessness, fighting, and attention-demanding activities especially in relation to their parents but also in relation to other adults and children. The behaviour of all unfavoured children does not show aggressive characteristics. Some will become despondent and withdraw. Others will throw great energy into competing with the sibling in socially approved activities, and still others will try to behave as differently as possible from their rival.

Parents who Have High Moral Standards : Children from homes with moral standards much more rigid than those of the rest of the community may be taught that sex is evil, that one thousand and one normal activities are sinful, e.g., smoking, card-playing, going to the movies or the theater, dancing, and reading modern novels. This makes it inevitable that the child will meet numerous situations which would never have been a problem for him if it had not been for his rigid moral training. The most serious result is that children who accept this teaching acquire such severe consciences that they believe they are continually failing to live a proper life. Normal social relations are almost impossible for them in an average community and, all to frequently, they develop neurotic tendencies.

The child has as patterns parents who are dissolute, deliquent and of ten drunk one can not expect the child to the admirable personality traits. The effects of the home broken by divorce or separation are too familiar to relate. The poverty, rejection, over protection, favouritism and other specific condition cause for the ailment of mental health.

Influence of the Community

Community influences on child personality adjustment are so multiform and the literature dealing with them is so indefinite that it is impossible to treat the topic adequately in a short space. Some community conditions obviously important to children are

(1) the extent to which recreational facilities, social centres, and social agencies exist, (2) the degree of freedom allowed children by community-folk ways, (3) the disparity in economic levels, (4) the extent of race prejudice, (5) the extent of tolerance or intolerance of religious sects. These are only a few of many community factors which indirectly affect the favourable or unfavourable development of children's personalities. A more general factor which should be mentioned is that the organisation of the community.

School Practices on Children's Behaviour

The school practices have significant influence on the children behaviour and their personality development. The important practices have been discussed in the following paragraphs:

The Effect of Over Competition and Examination in School : Authorities feel that the whole system of grades, examinations, and marks tends to place and undue emphasis on competition. The result in many cases is to discourage the slow learners and even many average pupils. The relatively fast learners are likely to get inflated notions of their own abilities. Excessive competition tends to breed an indifference to the welfare of others and to enhance self-interest.

Examinations, especially long ones, when used as even a partial basis for marks in a highly competitive atmosphere are likely to cause an undue strain and fatigue in many children..

The attendant strain may be increased in schools in which the results of examination are used as the primary criterion for rating the effectiveness of the teacher without taking into account the level of ability of the class. When examinations are used primarily for diagnostic purposes to detect areas of weakness in the children's knowledge and skill so that subsequent work may be better directed-then they are serving a worthy purpose.

Unsuitable Curriculum : If as too frequently occurs, the curriculum has little relation to the life. Problem of the children makes on contribution to their present needs, many unfortunate effects are produced. Antagonism to the school accompanied by misbehaviour may be expected, and a desire to "quit school" at the earliest legal age is likely to be born and nourished. Inquiries into the cause of delinquency have shown that some bright delinquents were first attracted to the questionable thrills of stealing as a result of their intense boredom with the curriculum of their school. Equally unfortunate is the plight of youngsters in many schools who are expected to master material beyond their ability.

Over Restriction in the Classroom : Many elementary and secondary schools unduly restrict the behaviour of their pupils. The ideal of many schools is pin-drop quietness and a place for every child and in the place. The traditional recess periods and the occasional working at the board are far from sufficient for most elementary school children's need for movement and activity. In the primary school the needs for movement and activity. In the primary school, the needs for both activity and rest are usually handled satisfactorily, but despite the difficulties adults themselves have in going for long periods without large-muscle activity the expectations that older children and adolescents can do so is seldom challenged in practice. Pupils not only suffer from over restriction in activity but also from lack of freedom to direct their own behaviour.

Teacher's Methods of Handling the Class : The teacher's methods of handling pupils can be considered primarily a function of his personality and his personality and his knowledge. His skill is dependent not only upon knowledge of children in general, but also upon knowledge of the individual children in his class and knowledge of how to meet the personality needs of children and control their behaviour in ways beneficial to them. There is likely to be a close relationship between the teacher's personality and the methods of controls he naturally tends to use.

The Effect of the Teacher's Personality on the Class : It may be surmised that the best liked teachers provide a warm, friendly and relaxed classroom atmosphere in which the children could not only do their best work and have the most enjoyable time, but also would have opportunity for wholesome personality development. The least liked teachers probably had the opposite effect.

Some teacher really enjoy teaching and they have devotion to their job of teaching. They have high aptitude of teaching and high favourable attitude towards teaching have the positive effect on the class. The involvement in teaching according to Morrisan also contributes in the involvement of the class in their teaching activities.

Teacher's Report of Behaviour Problems in the Classroom : The Wickman study which demonstrated that teachers tended to consider violations of classroom order, dishonesties, and immoralities as more serious than recessive and withdrawing personality traits, while the opposite was true of mental hygienists, has had wide publicity. Although this study has been justly criticized as being unfair to the teachers because they were asked to rate the items on the basis of their seriousness in class. Other investigations not subject to this defect have shown substantially similar results.

Treatment of Behaviour Problems in the Classroom : These kinds of treatment technique used are even more revealing of the lack of appreciation of mental hygiene principles. A combination of categories I, II and III, all essentially punishment, totals 56 percent of the techniques used. Constructive or non-punishment techniques comprise approximately 25 percent. Deprivation—a method of meeting the immediate situation which may or may not have beneficent effects, depending upon the circumstances and type of deprivation-was employed 19 percent of the time. Campbell comes to the following conclusions:

(1) The teacher apply direct measures as punishment or reward for treating undesirable classroom behaviour of children. Skinner is of the view that undesirable behaviour should be ignored and desirable behaviour should be immediately rewarded or reinforced. This treatment avoids the adverse effect of punishment.

(2) The teachers are rated highly successful in classroom control use rewards or reinforcement and provide direct help more frequently than the other teachers. The results the Skinner's thesis of ignoring undesirable behaviour, he is not in favour of the punishment for kind to the students in the classroom.

Special Problems of Adjustment

There are some special problems or adjustment of children which cause the aliment of mental health. These have been listed as follow:

1. Physically handicapped child
2. Schooly child
3. Child with sensory defects
4. Intellectually gifted child
5. Dull child
6. Isolated child, and
7. Inferior child

The above mentioned children have special problems which may cause their ailments or maladjustment. Wise handling may do much for such type of children. Their problems and treatments have been discussed there.

Physical Handicapped Child: Physically handicapped children because of their condition suffer more frustrations than the average child. The usual play and social activities are usually slower in their school work. Besides having fewer immediate opportunities for social recognition, most of them must look forward to a vocational future that is far from satisfying. As a result of their physical condition, also, unwise parents and teachers are likely to overprotect them.

It is not unusual, therefore, to find self-consciousness, sensitivity, timidity, self-pity, and a feeling of inferiority among their personality traits, and withdrawal as a favoured means of meeting difficult situations. Wise handing may do much for the physically handicapped child. To avoid in a natural manner, calling attention to his defect while at the same time arranging for special ways for him to receive merited recognition usually and markedly in this adjustment.

Sickly Child : The sickly child, is in many respects subject to the same restrictions as the physically handicapped child. He too cannot play as vigorously or do his school work as efficiently as the average child. He is likely to be considered lazy because he tires easily. Either as a reaction to the specific nature of his, discomfort or because of the pampering; he receives at home, may be easily irritated. When a server illness kept him out of school for a considerable length of time, he is likely to be unusually worried and tense about the work has missed. The child who has been sickly but has since become healthy, has special problems too. Often it is harder to convince the parents than the child that he is really well. Occasionally, however, the child who has acquired the habit of non-participation in many play and social activities and bow feels inadequate in them is likely to continue his previous pattern of behaviour.

Child with Sensory Defects : Of the possible visual defects in childhood the most common are near-sightedness (myopia) and farsightedness (hyperopia). The effect on the personality is likely to be more serious for unsuspected hyperopics than for myopics because in addition to the inferiority feeling likely to result from repeated failures in schoolwork and in sports, farsighted children are plagued with headaches and often with nausea.. These conditions can make their school experience so unpleasant that truancy may result. The child with unsuspected defective hearing is likewise handicapped in those phases of school work which depend upon the auditory sense and in games and social relations with his peers. He may appear to be inattentive and stupid. The most frequent reaction to defective hearing is excessive shyness and a tendency to withdraw.

Gifted Child : Louttit has very aptly enumerated the most frequent sources of difficulty in the adjustment of the superior child:

(1) Lack of teacher's recognition of superiority leading to an antagonism toward the school as an institution.

(2) Lack of parental recognition of superiority with resulting lack of stimulation or positive discouragement.

(3) Superiority over available associates so marked that social adjustment is extremely difficult.

(4) Development of poor study or work habits because of lack of stimulation of classroom work.

(5) Development of inferiority feelings because the child's interests and activities are not socially recognized by his group.

(6) Development of a boastful, conceited personality because of unwise emphasis by adults.

(7) One-sided personality development because of lack of normal social activities resulting from parental intervention.

Dull Child: Dull children sometimes called 'low-normal' or dull normal, those with I.Q's roughly from 75 to 90, are confronted with unusually severe hazards in the ordinary public school. Few schools have a program which meets their needs. Usually they are left to sink or swim (usually sink) in classes too, large to be handled satisfactorily even for the average child. The difficulty of the academic work, the speed expected of him as well as the frequent inability, because of lack of facilities, to demonstrate what talents he has, constitute the major sources of frustration in the school life of the dull child. When to his, as sources of frustration in the school life of the dull child. When to this, as occasionally happens, is added the antagonism of the frequent humiliation he suffers at the hands of his classmates, it is little wonder that damaged personalities and annoying behaviour result.

Isolated Child: The excessive mobility of the family due to his father or mother job is transferable. When the family moves, the child friendships in school and neighbourhood are interrupted, and it is not easy to form new friendship in a neighbourhood or in school. The child feels isolated. The broken home also make him isolated child.

Isolated children often feel their plight keenly. They lack the status. Conferred by valued membership in a group and are likely to give up attempts at friendships and retire into a world of unreality. In addition, they feel that something is wrong with them, They in some way are inferior and different from the rest of the children.

Delinquent Child: 'Typical' delinquent is a boy who lies in a 'blighted area' of a city in home of low economic level with low moral standards as well. His parents are either not living together or are antagonistic to each other. They either utilize psychologically poor methods of discipline or reject the child altogether. His I.Q. is between 80 and 90 and he is retarded in school. Delinquency, however, may be found in children, in whom not one of these factors is present. Nevertheless, the environmental mass, approach to the prevention of deliquency is still the most feasible and rewarding.

Inferior Child: Children with a persistent feeling of inferiority are by no means rare in our school system. Ninety-two percent of the men and 98 percent of the women reported that they had an inferiority complex. Ninety percent of the men and 91 percent of the women reported a persistent feeling of inferiority during the current year.

The inferiority complex stems from large discrepancies between a child's level of achievement and his level of aspiration. Any factor which depress the first or raise the send enhance the suffering of the child. Some of the most important facts which tend primarily to lower the achievement level are (1) real or imagined physical defects (2) poor health, below average mentality (3) low organizing above programmes. They should know the basic principles of social or economic status, and (4) continued failure. Factors which tend primarily to raise the level of aspiration are: an undue emphasis on the child's natural inability to do things as well as older children or his parents; excessive competition in school or sports and insistence by parents or teachers on too high standards.

The school, then has the responsibility of providing a hygienic, friendly environment with understanding teachers, of aiding the continuation of sound personality growth in well adjusted children; and of assisting the children whose personalities are already wrapped. Over competition, unsuitable curriculum over restriction, and poor methods of handling children are some of the factors which tend to retard personality development in any child.

Mental Health in Schools

The role of parents and family is significant in the personality development of children. The teacher and school assume great responsibility in the process of development of children. They spend day time in school and the main focus of the school to develop the potentialities by satisfying their needs. The school provides the proper climate for their physical, social, emotional and intellectual development. The following are the situations and activities are organized in a good school.

1. School environment or climate
2. Democratic environment or freedom of expression
3. Provision for co-curricular activities
4. Social emotional climate of classroom
5. Guidance and counselling services in school
6. Supervised study or provision for assimilation
7. Tutorial system in school and remedial teaching
8. Educational Excursion or field trips
9. Organisation of debates and group discussion
10. Scouting and girls guiding, N.C. C. programme and
11. Teacher taught relation or rapport with students.

The above programmes and activities are helpful for generating conducive climate in the school. The students develop the positive attitude towards school and teachers. It should provide feelings of security irrespective cast, religion and socio-economic status. The environment should be free from fear and tensions.

Teachers must have the knowledge, understanding and skill for organizing above programmes. They should know the basic principles of human behaviour problems and ailments of mental health. He must be emotionally stable and have positive attitude towards teaching and students. It is also essential that the teacher's mental health should be normal. The mental health of teacher and students are the significant ingredient for teaching learning process.

The understanding of ailment of mental health is enough for the teacher, but he should be capable of providing guidance and counselling for the problems of the students. The educational guidance is essential for the students. They should be given remedial teaching for their difficulties of learning. They should be provided recreational facilities in the school by organising the co-curricular activities and educational trips etc.

Mental Health of Teacher

Mental health of teacher is much more important than the mental health of student. If a teacher is not sound in his mental health can not do justice to his students and can not provide guidance in their problems. His maladjustment may have the adverse effect on children. Therefore it is also essential to understand the cause of maladjustment or ailment of mental health as teachers or well as remedial measures.

Sources of Ailments of Mental Health of Teacher: The dissatisfaction in teaching arises from the following important sources:

1. The heavy pressure of work load on teacher.
2. Inadequate salaries to the teacher.
3. Occupational insecurity.
4. Restriction on outside activities.
5. The lack of acceptance by the society.
6. Autocratic administration and supervision and
7. The lack orientation courses or refresher courses.

The mental health of the teacher is necessary to improve by improving conditions of teaching and conditions of services. This can best be effected by means of strong professional organization. The teacher can improve his own mental health, if he is able to increase his understanding of himself, accept himself largely as he is and take an active part in directing his life rather than being content with responding to pressures.

Sources of Satisfaction in Teaching Procession: The following are the sources which arise satisfaction in teaching profession :

1. The socially useful character of the work.
2. The creative expression involve.
3. The stimulation of broad interest.
4. Personal growth and development in teaching.

5. The opportunity for association with youth.
6. The opportunity to influence social and national policy.
7. The merging of one's interests with those of the group.
8. The partial satisfaction of the needs for affection, respect, independence, freedom for expression and for maintaining the self-esteem.
9. The teaching is a naval profession and
10. Teaching involves a variety of activities physical, social, emotional and mental development.

Ways for Improving Mental Health of Teachers: There are various factors in school and outside the school which influence mental health of teachers. The listed factors help in maintaining mental health of teachers.

1. Improving teacher-principal relationship
   (a) Democratic administration.
   (b) Impartial behaviour of principal.
   (c) Planning in advance.
   (d) Seniority should be considered in assigning responsibilities.
   (e) Proper distribution of work load.
   (f) Principal should have helping attitude towards teachers.
   (g) Teachers problems should be given due weightage.
2. Improving teachers relationship, should have co-operative spirit among teachers.
3. Organizing refresher and orientation courses for the teachers.
4. Teachers should be allowed to attend seminars workshops and conference for their personal growth.
5. They should be encouraged for academic excellence.
6. Improving teacher community relations and community serve by teacher.
7. Improving teacher-taught relations, teacher should receive due regard and respect from the students.

8. Teachers should be rewarded or reinforced for better results or effective teaching or providing remedial teaching and guidance to the students by the principal and school management.

There is a tendency to criticise the teacher by principal, students and other colleagues in our school system. The principal should have the leadership qualities to encourage or praise the teachers for their good work and performance.

There is rapid development and advancement in every field of study and also in teaching methods and techniques. They should be encouraged to attend refresher courses, orientation programmes and workshops organized by different agencies for the excellence in jobs. In school library and reading facilities should be maintained having up-to-data literature. Teachers should also be encouraged for experimental projects and innovative ideas in teaching learning situation. Teachers should be well informed with new trends and technology in the field of education.

A Great Deal

In the pre-service teachers training more and better courses should be offered in mental health and hygiene. The teachers trainees like such courses and many gain a great deal of insight through them. If in addition, enough psychological counsellors and psycho-therapists and medical services could be provide to all teacher training institutions, great efforts could be made in increasing the mental health of the profession.

The reading habit of books, provide guidance to the teacher related to his life

1. Develop the habit of success in life.
2. Prepare teachers to face reality or hard facts of life.
3. He learns to react normally to emotional situation.
4. He begins to avoid worries of day-to-day working.

These are the realities of life, these may cause some sort of ailments, tension or anxiety. The above guidance is very realistic approach for avoiding causes of ailments and he may be able to maintain his sound mental health.

Exercise

1. Explain the term 'Mental health'. Describe the need for a teacher to have the knowledge and understanding of mental health of the students.
2. Enumerate the types of mental ailments and point out the indications of positive mental health or sound mental health of an individual.
3. Describe the theoretical basis of mental health. Indicate the Maslow Hierarchy needs theory which provides the basis of mental health.
4. Enumerate the factors influencing mental health of child and suggest some remedial measures for these causes.
5. Describe the effect of school practices on children's behaviour and personality development of students.
6. Enumerate the special problems of adjustment of children.
7. Describe the role of teacher and school programmes in maintaining the mental health of students in school.
8. Indicate the importance of sound mental health of a teacher in school and classroom. Describe the sources of ailments and satisfaction in teaching professions.
9. Describe the ways and means for improving mental health of teachers.
10. Comment and illustrate the statement 'Sound Mind in Sound Body' or 'Sound body possesses sound mind.'

Additional Reading

Bhaskara Rao, Digumarti (1994). *Scientific Aptitude,* New Delhi: Ashish Publishing House. ISBN 81-7024-658-X.

Bhaskara Rao, Digumarti (1995). *Animal Kingdom.* New Delhi: Discovery Publishing House. ISBN 81-7141-274-2.

Bhaskara Rao, Digumarti (1995). *Batracology.* New Delhi: Discovery Publishing House. ISBN 81-7141-279-3.

Bhaskara Rao, Digumarti (1997), *Scientific Attitude.* New Delhi: Discovery Publishing House. ISBN 81-7141-308-0.

Bhaskara Rao, Digumarti (1996). *Scientific Attitude vis-à-viş Scientific Aptitude.* New Delhi: Discovery Publishing House. ISBN 81-7141-308-0.

Bhaskara Rao, Digumarti, Editor (1996). *Encyclopaedia of Education for All,* 5 Volumes. New Delhi: APH Publishing Corporation. ISBN 81-7024-759-4 (set).

Vol. I *Education for All: The World Conference.* ISBN 81-7024-760-8.

Vol. II *Education for All: The EPA-9 Summit.* ISBN 81-7024-761-6.

Vol. III *Education for All: Quality Education for All.* ISBN 81-7024-762-6.

Vol. IV *Education for All: Planning and Monitoring.* ISBN 81-7024-763-4.

Vol. V *Education for All: The Indian Scenario.* ISBN 81-7024-764-0.

Bhaskara Rao, Digumarti, Editor (1996). *Global Perceptions on Peace Education,* 3 Volumes. New Delhi: Discovery Publishing House. ISBN 81-7141-319-6.

Bhaskara Rao, Digumarti, Editor (1996). *National Policy on Education*. 2 Volumes. New Delhi: Anmol Publications Pvt. Ltd. ISBN 81-7488-323-1.

Bhaskara Rao, Digumarti, Editor (1997). *Care the Child*, 2 Volumes. New Delhi: Discovery Publishing House. ISBN 81-7141-394-3.

Bhaskara Rao, Digumarti, Editor (1997). *Education for the 21st Century*. New Delhi: Discovery Publishing House. ISBN 81-7141-389-7.

Bhaskara Rao, Digumarti, Editor (1997). *Reflections on Scientific Attitude*. New Delhi: Discovery Publishing House, ISBN 81-7141-319-6.

Bhaskara Rao, Digumarti, Editor (1997). *Success Story of a Primary Education Project*. New Delhi: APH Publishing Corporation. ISBN 81-7024-850-7.

Bhaskara Rao, Digumarti, Editor (1997). *World Food Summit*. New Delhi: Discovery Publishing House. ISBN 81-7141-386-2.

Bhaskara Rao, Digumarti, Editor (1998). *Adolescence Education*. New Delhi: Discovery Publishing House. ISBN 81-7141-432-X.

Bhaskara Rao, Digumarti, Editor (1998). *Community and School Nutrition Education*. New Delhi: Discovery Publishing House. ISBN 81-7141-435-4.

Bhaskara Rao, Digumarti, Editor (1998). *District Primary Education Programme*. New Delhi: Discovery Publishing House. ISBN 81-7141-396-X.

Bhaskara Rao, Digumarti, Editor (1998). *Earth Summit*, 2 Volumes. New Delhi: Discovery Publishing House. ISBN 81-7141-435-4.

Bhaskara Rao, Digumarti, Editor (1998). *National Policy on Education: Towards an Enlightened and Humane Society*, New Delhi: Discovery Publishing House. ISBN 81-7141-426-5.

Bhaskara Rao, Digumarti, Editor (1998). *Reforming School Education*. New Delhi: Discovery Publishing House. ISBN 81-7141-403-6.

Bhaskara Rao, Digumarti, Editor (1998). *Teacher Education in India*. New Delhi: Discovery Publishing House. ISBN 81-7141-406-0.

Bhaskara Rao, Digumarti, Editor (1998). *World Summit for Social Development*. New Delhi: Discovery Publishing House. ISBN 81-7141-420-6.

Bhaskara Rao, Digumarti, Editor (2000). *Education for All: Achieving the Goal*, 3 Volumes, New Delhi: APH Publishing Corporation. ISBN 81-7648-152-1.

Vol. I *The Global Consensus*. ISBN 81-7648-155-6.

Vol. II *Mid-Decade Review Reports of Regional Seminars*. ISBN 81-7648-154-8.

Vol. III *Issues and Trends*. ISBN 81-7648-155-6.

Bhaskara Rao, Digumarti, Editor (2000), *International Encyclopaedia of AIDS*, 11 Volumes in 13 Parts. New Delhi: Discovery Publishing House. ISBN 81-7141-6 (Set).

Vol. 1 *Introduction to HIV/AIDS*. ISBN 81-7141-523-7.

Vol. 2 *HIV/AIDS—Issues and Challenges*, 2 Parts. ISBN 81-7141-524-5.

Vol. 3 *HIV/AIDS—Socio Economic Realities*. ISBN 81-7141-524-3.

Vol. 4 *HIV/AIDS—Law Ethics and Human Rights*, 2 Parts. ISBN 81-7141-526-1.

Vol. 5 *AIDS and NGOs*. ISBN 81-7141-527-X.

Vol. 6 *AIDS and Home Care*. ISBN 81-7141-528-8.

Vol. 7 *STD Case Management*. ISBN 81-7141-529-6.

Vol. 8 *HIV/AIDS Prevention and Care—Teaching Modules for Nurses and Midwives*. ISBN 81-7141-530-X.

Vol. 9 *HIV Prevention Education for Education for Educational Institutions*. ISBN 81-7141-531-8.

Vol. 10 *Instructional Modules for AIDS Education*. ISBN 81-7141-532-6.

Vol. 11 *School Health Education to Prevent AIDS and STD—A Package for Curriculum Plannèrs*. ISBN 81-7141-5338-4.

Bhaskara Rao, Digumarti, Editor (2000). *International Encyclopaedia of Science and Technology Education*, 11 Volumes. New Delhi: Discovery Publishing House. ISBN 81-7141-548-2 (Set).

Vol. 1 *Science and Technology Education*. ISBN 81-7141-568-7.

Vol. 2 *Science Education in Developing Countries*. ISBN 81-7141-570-9.

Vol. 3 *Organisational Structure of Science*. ISBN 81-7141-570-9.

Vol. 4 *Science Education in Asia and the Pacific*. ISBN 81-7141-571-7.

Vol. 5 *Science and Technology Education for All*. ISBN 81-7141-572-5.

Vol. 6 *Values, Ethics, Talent and Girls in Science and Technology Education*. ISBN 81-7141-573-3.

Vol. 7 *Popularization of Science and Technology Education*. ISBN 81-7141-574-1.

Vol. 8 *Science, Power and Society*. ISBN 81-7141-575-X.

Vol. 9 *Information Technology*. ISBN 81-7141-576-8.

Vol. 10 *Teacher Training in Science and Technology Education*. ISBN 81-7141-577-6.

Vol. 11 *Teacher Training in Science and Technology: A Curriculum Framework*. ISBN 81-7141-578-4.

Bhaskara Rao, Digumarti, Editor (2001). *Distance Education in Different Countries*. New Delhi: APH Publishing Corporation. ISBN 81-7648-229-3.

Bhaskara Rao, Digumarti, Editor (2001). *Decentralised Management of Education (Management of Education in Panchayati Raj and Municipal Bodies)*. New Delhi: Discovery Publishing House. ISBN 81-7141-617-9.

Bhaskara Rao, Digumarti, Editor (2001). *Electrochemistry for Environmental Protection*. New Delhi: Discovery Publishing House. ISBN 81-7141-619-5.

Bhaskara Rao, Digumarti, Editor (2001). *Global Educational Studies*. New Delhi: Discovery Publishing House. ISBN 81-7141-616-0.

Bhaskara Rao, Digumarti, Editor (2001). *Global Synthesis of Educational Assessment*. New Delhi: Discovery Publishing House. ISBN 81-7141-613-6.

Bhaskara Rao, Digumarti, Editor (2000). *International Encyclopaedia of Human Rights*. 7 Volumes in 13 Parts. New Delhi: Discovery Publishing House. (Royal Size). ISBN 81-7141-567-9 (Set).

Vol. 1 *International Instruments of Human Rights*, 2 Parts. ISBN 81-7141-595-4.

Vol. 2 *Regional Instruments of Human Rights*. ISBN 81-7141-604-7.

Vol. 3 *Human Rights and the United Nations*, 2 Parts. ISBN 81-7141-605-5.

Vol. 4 *Fact Files of Human Rights*, 3 Parts. ISBN 81-7141-605-3.

Vol. 5 *Study Stories of Human Rights*, 3 Parts. ISBN 81-7141-607-3.

Vol. 6 *International Meetings on Human Rights*, 2 Parts. ISBN 81-7141-608-X.

Vol. 7 *Professional Training in Human Rights*. ISBN 81-7141-609-8.

Bhaskara Rao, Digumarti, Editor (2001). *Jomtein Decade of Education*. New Delhi: Discovery Publishing House. ISBN 81-7141-618-7.

Bhaskara Rao, Digumarti, Editor (2001). *Nuclear Materials: Issues and Concerns*, 2 Volumes. New Delhi: Discovery Publishing House. ISBN 81-7141-611-X.

Bhaskara Rao, Digumarti, Editor (2001). *World Conference on Education for All*. New Delhi: APH Publishing Corporation. ISBN 81-7141-274-9.

Bhaskara Rao, Digumarti, Editor (2001). *World Conference on Higher Education*, New Delhi: Discovery Publishing House. ISBN 81-7141-610-1.

Bhaskara Rao, Digumarti, Editor (2001). *World Conference on Science*. New Delhi: Discovery Publishing House. ISBN 81-7141-612-8.

Bhaskara Rao, Digumarti, Editor (2003). *Inspiring Experience in Teacher Education*. New Delhi: Discovery Publishing House. ISBN 81-7141-656-X.

Bhaskara Rao, Digumarti, Editor (2003). *International Studies in Education*, 3 Volumes, New Delhi: Discovery Publishing House. ISBN 81-7141-647-0.

Bhaskara Rao, Digumarti, Editor (2003). *Military Conversion: Impact on Science and Technology*, New Delhi: Discovery Publishing House. ISBN 81-7141-578-4.

Bhaskara Rao, Digumarti, Editor (2003). *United Nations Millennium Summit*. New Delhi: Discovery Publishing House. ISBN 81-7141-632-2.

Bhaskara Rao, Digumarti, Editor (2003). *World Assembly on Aging*. New Delhi: Discovery Publishing House. ISBN 81-7141-637-3.

Bhaskara Rao, Digumarti, Editor (2004). *World Conference on Human Rights*. New Delhi: Discovery Publishing House. ISBN 81-7141-661-6.

Bhaskara Rao, Digumarti, Editor (2003). *World Education Forum*. New Delhi: Discovery Publishing House. ISBN 81-7141-639-X.

Bhaskara Rao, Digumarti, Editor (2004). *Education Employment and Human Resource Development*. New Delhi: Discovery Publishing House. ISBN 81-7141-681-0.

Bhaskara Rao, Digumarti, Editor (2004). *Successfully Schooling*. New Delhi: Discovery Publishing House. ISBN 81-7141-677-2.

Bhaskara Rao, Digumarti, Editor (2004). *European Education and Teachers*. New Delhi: Discovery Publishing House. ISBN 81-7141-702-7.

Bhaskara Rao, Digumarti, Editor (2004). *Teachers in a Changing World*. New Delhi: Discovery Publishing House. ISBN 81-7141-694-2.

Bhaskara Rao, Digumarti, Editor (2004). *Learning to Live Together*, 4 Volumes. New Delhi: Discovery Publishing House.

Vol. 1 *International Conference on Learning to Live Together.*

Vol. 2 *Globalisation and Living Together.*

Vol. 3 *Curriculum for Learning to Live Together.*

Vol. 4 *Science Education for the Contemporary Society.*

Bhaskara Rao, Digumarti (2004). *International Guidelines on Open and Distance Education*, New Delhi: Discovery Publishing House.

Bhaskara Rao, Digumarti, Editor (2004). *Adult Learning in the 21st Century*. New Delhi: Discovery Publishing House.

Bhaskara Rao, Digumarti, Editor (2004). *Educational Practices: Research and Recommendations*. New Delhi: Discovery Publishing House.

Bhaskara Rao, Digumarti, Editor (2004). *Chernobyl: Never Again*. New Delhi: APH Publishing Corporation.

Bhaskara Rao, Digumarti, Editor (2004). *Virology and Immunology*. New Delhi: APH Publishing Corporation.

Bhaskara Rao, Digumarti, C.A.P. Swami and B.S.V. Dutt (1997). *Self-Evaluation in Student Teaching*. New Delhi: Discovery Publishing House. ISBN 81-7141-374-9.

Bhaskara Rao, Digumarti and B.S.V. Dutt, Editors (2003). *Education: Programmes and Policies*. New Delhi: APH Publishing Corporation. ISBN 81-7648-470-9.

Bhaskara Rao, Digumarti and D. Naresh Kumar (2004). *School Teacher Effectiveness*. New Delhi: Discovery Publishing House.

Bhaskara Rao, Digumarti and D. Sridhar (2002). *Job Satisfaction of School Teachers*. New Delhi: Discovery Publishing House. ISBN 81-7141-652-7.

Bhaskara Rao, Digumarti and Digumarti Pushpa Latha (1994). *Achievement in Biology*. New Delhi: Discovery Publishing House. ISBN 81-7141-264-5.

Bhaskara Rao, Digumarti, C. Sridevi and K. Vijaya (1995). *Achievement in Social Studies*. New Delhi: Discovery Publishing House. ISBN 81-7141-281-5.

Bhaskara Rao, Digumarti and Digumarti Pushpa Latha (1995). *Achievement in English*. New Delhi: Discovery Publishing House. ISBN 81-7141-283-1.

Bhaskara Rao, Digumarti and Digumarti Pushpa Latha (1994). *Achievement in Science*. New Delhi: Discovery Publishing House. ISBN 81-7141-280-70.

Bhaskara Rao, Digumarti and Digumarti Pushpa Latha (1995). *Achievement in Mathematics*. New Delhi: Discovery Publishing House. ISBN 81-7141-278-5.

Bhaskara Rao, Digumarti and Digumarti Pushpa Latha, Editors (1998). *International Encyclopaedia of Women*. 5 Volumes. New Delhi: Discovery Publishing House. ISBN 81-7141-410-9.

Vol. 1 *Status of World's Women*. ISBN 81-7141-494-X.

Vol. 2 *Women, Education and Empowerment*. ISBN 81-7141-498-1.

Vol. 3 *Women Challenges and Advancement*. ISBN 81-7141-497-4.

Vol. 4 *Women and Family Health*. ISBN 81-7141-497-4.

Vol. 5 *Women and International Action*. ISBN 81-7141-498-2.

Bhaskara Rao, Digumarti, Digumarti Pushpa Latha and Digumarti Harshitha, Editors (2001). *Biological Warfare*. New Delhi: Discovery Publishing House. ISBN 81-7141-597-0.

Bhaskara Rao, Digumarti, Digumarti Pushpa Latha and Digumarti Harshitha, Editors (2001). *Women as Educators*. New Delhi: Discovery Publishing House. ISBN 81-7141-602-0.

Bhaskara Rao, Digumarti and Digumarti Harshitha, Editors (2001). *Education in India*. New Delhi: APH Publishing Corporation. ISBN 81-7141-207-2.

Bhaskara Rao, Digumarti, Digumarti Pushpa Latha and Digumarti Harshitha, Editors (2001). *Assessing Learning Achievement*. New Delhi: Discovery Publishing House. ISBN 81-7141-601-2.

Bhaskara Rao, Digumarti, Digumarti Pushpa Latha and Digumarti Harshitha, Editors (2001). *Energy Security*. New Delhi: Discovery Publishing House. ISBN 81-7141-598-9.

Bhaskara Rao, Digumarti, Digumarti Harshitha and K.R.S.S. Rao, Editors (1999). *Advanced Biotechnology*. New Delhi: Discovery Publishing House. ISBN 81-7141-516-4.

Bhaskara Rao, Digumarti and K.R.S. Sambhasiva Rao, Editors (1996). *Current Trends in Indian Education*. New Delhi: Discovery Publishing House. ISBN 81-7141-311-0.

Bhaskara Rao, Digumarti and K. Vijaya (1995). *A Text Book of Evaluation*. Ambala Cantt: The Associated Publishers.